Putting
"Defense"
Back into
U.S. Defense Policy

Putting "Defense" Back into U.S. Defense Policy

Rethinking U.S. Security in the Post–Cold War World

IVAN ELAND

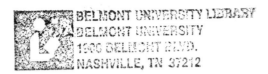

Westport, Connecticut
London

Library of Congress Cataloging-in-Publication Data

Eland, Ivan.
    Putting "defense" back into U.S. defense policy : rethinking U.S. security in the post-cold war world / Ivan Eland.
      p. cm.
    Includes bibliographical references and index.
    ISBN 0–275–97348–4 (alk. paper)
    1. United States—Military policy. 2. National security—United States. 3. World politics—21st century. I. Title.
    UA23.E398 2001
    355'.033073—dc21   2001016322

British Library Cataloguing in Publication Data is available.

Library of Congress Catalog Card Number: 2001016322
ISBN: 0–275–97348–4

First published in 2001

Praeger Publishers, 88 Post Road West, Westport, CT 06881
An imprint of Greenwood Publishing Group, Inc.
www.praeger.com

Printed in the United States of America

The paper used in this book complies with the
Permanent Paper Standard issued by the National
Information Standards Organization (Z39.48–1984).

10 9 8 7 6 5 4 3 2 1

Contents

Illustrations

Putting "Defense" Back into U.S. Defense Policy

1

U.S. National Security: Mismatch between Policy and Reality

People from across the political spectrum would probably agree that U.S. national security policy (that is, U.S. foreign and defense policies) should first protect U.S. citizens, territory, and society. They would also probably concur that the policy should protect American vital interests. Current U.S. national security policy fulfills none of those goals. U.S. policy endangers the American homeland, the people in it, and their way of life. In addition, the policy cannot safeguard U.S. vital interests, because the policy makers have never defined them.

The definition of any nation's vital interests—and therefore the country's national security policy—should depend on its geostrategic position. Yet U.S. national security policy has little relationship to the geostrategic environment facing the United States.

The United States has one of the most secure geostrategic positions of any great power in history. The nation's favorable location—away from the major centers of conflict—makes the possibility of a conventional attack by another nation unlikely. With two oceans as gigantic moats on the east and west, and friendly and weak neighbors on the north and south, the possibility of an invasion is even more remote. Furthermore, the U.S. nuclear force—the most potent force of its kind in the world—would make any enemy attack or invasion suicidal. Finally, no other great power competes with the United States in the Western Hemisphere.

NATIONAL SECURITY POLICY EVOLVES

As a result of this favorable geography, the founders of the republic realized that they had the luxury of staying out of other nations' wars (at the time, Europe's wars). They also realized that if the United States refrained from meddling in the business of other nations, those powers would have no excuse to intervene in its affairs.

George Washington, in his farewell address, noted that America's "distant and detached position" and "respectably defensive posture" allowed the nation to remain disengaged. The first president asked rhetorically: "Why forgo the advantages of so peculiar a situation? Why, by interweaving our destiny with that of any part of Europe, entangle our peace and our prosperity in the toils of European ambition, Rivalship, Interest, Humore, or Caprice?" He continued, "The Great Rule of Conduct for us, in regard to foreign nations is in extending our commercial relations, to have with them as little political connection as possible. . . . Tis our true policy to steer clear of permanent alliances."[1] Thomas Jefferson, in his first inaugural address, argued that America's policy should be "peace, commerce, and honest friendship with all nations—entangling alliances with none."[2]

In an early American warning, in effect, against the Clinton administration's policy of using military power to help enlarge the family of democratic nations, then-secretary of state John Quincy Adams cautioned in the early 1820s that the United States should avoid intervening in foreign conflicts even to export liberty abroad: "Wherever the standard of freedom and independence has been unfurled, there will America's heart, her benedictions, and her prayers be. But she goes not abroad in search of monsters to destroy." To intervene even under the "banners of foreign independence" would involve the United States in "wars of interest and intrigue, of individual avarice, envy, and ambition, which assume the color and usurp the standard of freedom. The fundamental maxims of her policy would insensibly change from liberty to force." The ideals of "freedom and independence" would be replaced by an "imperial diadem, flashing in false and tarnished luster, the murky radiance of dominance and power."[3]

In other words, one of the worst effects of profligate foreign interventions is the corruption of the American constitutional system at home. The founders of the nation realized that consequence when they declined to help republican France in its war with monarchical Britain in 1793. In fact, French policy demonstrated Adams' point: the ideals of the French revolution became corrupted, in part by the demands for patriotism in support of France's wars with other nations.

With the exception of World War I, the policy of military restraint overseas served the United States well for over a century and a half—until World War II and the Cold War ended it. The rare situation in World War II forever changed U.S. national security policy. During that war, the United

States and its allies confronted two hegemonic threats simultaneously. The first attack on U.S. territory since the War of 1812—the Japanese strike on Pearl Harbor in 1941—and the failure of Britain's appeasement policy toward Adolf Hitler at Munich in 1938 left an indelible mark on U.S. national security policy. The lesson drawn from those events was that aggression—no matter how trivial or where it occurs—must be checked immediately or the aggressor will interpret that inaction as a green light to make further conquests. The implication of this line of reasoning is that the United States should have resisted Japanese aggression against China during the 1930s and that Britain, France, and the United States should have resisted Hitler before he absorbed Czech lands rather than only later, after he made further conquests. In other words, the lessons that American leaders learned from World War II indicated that the U.S. defense perimeter should be extended as far forward as possible to stop aggression before it inevitably snowballed out of control.

As a result, during the Cold War, the United States extended its blanket of security to cover much of the world. Wherever communism threatened to make inroads—no matter how insignificant the country—the United States felt the need to respond in a tit-for-tat manner. This policy led to many U.S. interventions—large and small—including involvement directly or indirectly in wars in such backwater areas as Korea, Vietnam, Laos, Cambodia, Nicaragua, El Salvador, Cuba, the Dominican Republic, and Grenada. Discarded was the founders' premise that the relatively secure geostrategic position of the United States allowed U.S. vital interests to be construed narrowly.

Since the end of the Cold War and the demise of the Soviet superpower, the United States has retained and even expanded its already extended defense perimeter. The United States initiated expansion of the North Atlantic Treaty Organization (NATO) to provide security guarantees to three countries formerly in the sphere of influence of the Soviet Union. American influence is also being felt in many nations of the former Soviet Union, including Ukraine and Azerbaijan, as the United States attempts to wrench them away from the Russian orbit. The American military is busier than it was during the Cold War—conducting wars in Kosovo and Iraq, and peacekeeping and nation-building missions in such places as Bosnia, Somalia, and Haiti. After over fifty years of operation, an interventionist national security policy—an aberration in the history of U.S. foreign policy—now seems like the norm.

THE UNITED STATES IS OVEREXTENDED

Despite the end of the Cold War, military deployments are occurring at a record pace.[4] There were only twenty U.S. military deployments overseas during the last fifteen years of the Cold War, but there have been forty-eight in the 1990s.[5] As of late 1998, the army alone had thirty-four thousand troops on *temporary* duty in eighty-one countries.[6] President Clinton ordered more missions and commitments than any other president.[7] Many of those missions—for example, U.S. deployments to Bosnia and Kosovo—have little or nothing to do with U.S. vital interests.[8]

According to James Schlesinger, former secretary of defense,

The operations tempo of the U.S. Armed Forces is now at an all-time peak for peacetime. Force deployment in the post-Cold War years, driven by "military operations other than war," has been far more frequent, far larger, and of far longer duration than during the Cold War itself. That is a reflection of our willingness, in practice if not in theory, regularly to serve as the world's policeman. The myriad problems of ethnic unrest, internal conflict, and occasional external aggression have regularly, though not invariably, resulted in a U.S. response.[9]

Yet it is unlikely that even a superpower such as the United States can successfully police the entire world. No nation, no matter how wealthy, has the resources or national will to sustain such an effort. Thus, the policeman must pick and choose where to intervene.

In the United States, foreign military intervention is often justified on moral or humanitarian grounds (despite underlying motivations that are usually entirely different). So many "moral and humanitarian" crises crop up, however, that selective intervention often leads to policy that is inconsistent or hypocritical. For example, the United States pushed its NATO allies to attack Serbia for killing 2,000 to 3,000 Albanians after an Albanian uprising in the Serbian region of Kosovo. Yet the United States has not threatened Turkey—a NATO ally—to stop the killing of many more Kurds in its attempt to put down a Kurdish independence movement. Similarly, President Clinton did not intervene during the two occasions that Russia used brutal military tactics against civilians in its drive to tame the breakaway region of Chechnya; a U.S. intervention in Russia's internal affairs would have brought a confrontation with a nuclear-armed power. Nor did the United States intervene to stop the massacre in Rwanda by the then-ruling Hutu tribe of 500,000 to 800,000 members of the Tutsi tribe—one of the few recent instances of genuine genocide. Realizing that the United States had finite resources and a limited attention span, Secretary of State Madeleine Albright limited U.S. intervention in Rwanda so that the centerpiece of her Euro-centric foreign policy—U.S. involvement in the Balkans—could be preserved.

Nevertheless, the United States regularly intervenes haphazardly in foreign civil wars—for example, the conflicts in Lebanon in the early 1980s and in Somalia and Kosovo in the 1990s. Usually, U.S. interventions occur when the enemy is weak and television coverage of the conflict causes a groundswell from pressure groups or friendly nations for the United States to do something about the problem. Yet wars involving such internal ethnic or religious animosity have few adverse effects on U.S. security. In contrast, intervening in those conflicts can have several detrimental effects on U.S. security.

AN EXTENDED DEFENSE PERIMETER MAY UNDERMINE U.S. VITAL INTERESTS

Intervening anywhere and everywhere without a strategic rationale tends to obscure U.S. vital interests and, in some cases, undermine them. For example, the U.S.-led intervention in Bosnia, the war against the Serbs in Kosovo, and the expansion of NATO (which could lead to more interventions in Central and Eastern Europe) have strained the U.S. relationship with Russia. Stanching the proliferation of Russian nuclear, biological, chemical, and missile technology to Iran, Iraq, Syria, Libya, and other rogue nations should be one of the most important goals of U.S. national security policy. This goal is likely to be impeded by unnecessarily aggravating Russia.

In addition, one way to reduce the chances of proliferation is to reduce the size of the Russian arsenal of nuclear weapons. Yet strained U.S.-Russian relations and the extension of the NATO security perimeter contributed to the Russian Duma's slow, conditional ratification of nuclear arms reductions in the START II treaty. Russia is still the only nation that can obliterate U.S. society with nuclear weapons. Therefore, good U.S.-Russian relations should still be a top priority in U.S. security policy. Attempting to achieve questionable security gains by extending the U.S. security perimeter into the Russian backyard or conducting an unnecessary war against a Russian ally can actually undermine U.S. vital interests. Also, the war in Kosovo—especially NATO's bombing of the Chinese embassy—caused China to move closer to Russia to counter what the Chinese believe to be excessive U.S. global influence. Analysts in the Chinese military have become alarmed over the strengthening and expanding of American alliances and security partnerships worldwide after the end of the Cold War (the enhancement of the U.S.-Japanese alliance; the extension of Partnership for Peace to Central Asia; enhanced security relationships with Australia, Thailand, the Philippines, and Singapore; and even NATO expansion).[10] Because China is the only potential adversary other than Russia that can currently strike the U.S. homeland with nuclear weapons, good relations with that nation should be more important than achieving influence in far-flung areas of the world that do not affect U.S. vital interests (for example, the Taiwan Strait).

Profligate U.S. interventions around the world could also prompt rogue states to obtain nuclear, biological, chemical, or missile technologies to forestall U.S. meddling in their affairs. The Saddam Husseins and Kim Jong

Il's of the world have found that they cannot hope to defeat the powerful U.S. military in a conventional war. Thus, they have an incentive to obtain and threaten the American homeland with weapons of mass destruction (WMD), to give the United States pause before an intervention. Obtaining WMD is cheaper for relatively poor rogue nations than building large, high-tech conventional militaries that can take on that of the United States. Although the Clinton administration seemed to rank the proliferation of WMD as one of the most severe threats to U.S. security, its policy of profligate foreign interventions only exacerbated the problem.

Far-Flung Peacetime Interventions Can Undermine Recruitment and Retention of Soldiers

Conducting peacekeeping or peacemaking missions and fighting brushfire wars can impair the military's ability to attract and retain qualified personnel. According to Gen. Gordon Sullivan (Ret.), former chief of staff of the army, one of the "objections" to service in the armed forces that military recruiters need to overcome is "increasingly frequent family separation because of deployments to distant and desolate places." He noted that the air force and navy failed to achieve their recruiting quotas for fiscal year 1998. He maintained that the army was more successful only because its quota was lowered and because some recruits that contracted to enter the army in fiscal year 1999 were inducted early.[11] The services met their recruiting goals in 2000, but only because of a massive advertising campaign.

The services are also experiencing problems retaining skilled people in their ranks. Even William Perry, former secretary of defense, and Ashton Carter, former assistant secretary of defense, during the interventionist Clinton administration, admit that such interventions lead to a flight of personnel from the military.

Increased operational tempo ("op-tempo") of the U.S. military, as it responds to the many crises and peacekeeping missions of the post–Cold War world, has taken personnel away from their families more frequently and for longer periods than they had reason to expect when they chose military service. There are many signs that the trends in retention have become adverse.[12]

Actual survey data corroborate those impressions. After surveying almost ten thousand officers and enlisted personnel, a private research firm—hired by the army to discover why so many soldiers were leaving the service—found that the most cited reason was open-ended peacekeeping missions overseas.[13] A General Accounting Office report also noted the importance of nonpecuniary factors to recruitment and retention. According to the report, although military personnel care about pay and benefits, one of the top four reasons they cited for leaving the armed forces was frequent and extended deployments that separate them from their families.[14]

Retaining highly skilled air force pilots has been one of the biggest problems. Only one in four pilots accepts lucrative bonuses to remain in the military. The shortage of air force pilots is at least seven hundred and may climb to two thousand by 2002. According to the *San Diego Union-Tribune*, "Repeated overseas tours and the allure of high-paying jobs at commercial airlines are most often blamed for the shortage."[15] The extended military deployments away from home at irregular intervals contrast with the higher pay and regular schedules of employment with the airlines. For its part, the navy is 40 percent shy of its required totals for carrier-based aviators.[16] In 1998, only one in ten naval aviators accepted bonuses to remain in the service.[17]

It is not just family separation; the nature of peacekeeping missions and brushfire wars also drives pilots from the service. Pilots realize that such missions are not part of an overall vision for U.S. security that is designed to defend American vital interests. According to Bradley Graham of the *Washington Post*,

Many of the stresses and strains might be more acceptable, several airmen suggested, if the kinds of missions they were being asked to undertake in places such as the Persian Gulf and Bosnia did not seem so political or arbitrary.

"The problem comes down to a sense of mission," said Capt. Daniel L. Dorman, an A-10 pilot who joined the force six years ago. "There's a sense we're just being reactive. Is there really a plan for us?"

Added Master Sgt. Eric A. Harris: "You've got to stop using the Air Force for every little thing that comes down the road. We're running the wheels off the Air Force and running people out."[18]

Pilots, who joined the military to be highly trained warriors, are being asked to perform military social work. Also, the drudgery of conducting patrols to enforce the no-fly zones over Iraq has contributed to the exodus of pilots.[19]

According to James Crawley of the *San Diego Union-Tribune*, reporting on personnel shortages in the navy, "Officials acknowledge [that] most of the 18,022 unfilled positions throughout the Navy are aboard warships, a third of which are currently deployed to places like the Persian Gulf, the southern European waters near Bosnia, and the Far East." Deploying ships to those foreign theaters without full crews lowers the combat readiness from the highest rating, "C-1." A C-1 rating means that the ship has all the personnel and equipment required to carry out its wartime missions.[20]

The army also has had personnel shortages, particularly in infantry units.[21] According to Colin Clark of *Defense Week*, "The Army has had different readiness problems. Equipment has not been an issue. The problem has been too few soldiers, soldiers worked too hard and too often and not enough soldiers in the right places."[22]

Profligate Interventions Can Reduce the Readiness to Fight a Real War

Testifying before the Senate Armed Services Committee on the readiness of the U.S. military, Gen. Henry Shelton, chairman of the Joint Chiefs of Staff, said that the "forces are showing increasing signs of serious wear" and warned that "the long-term health of the total force is in jeopardy."[23] He blamed this decline on the proliferation of operations in Bosnia, the Persian Gulf, and elsewhere, operations that caused unpredicted wear on equipment and disruption in military family life.[24]

Four-star regional commanders around the world have also complained about the effect of day-to-day operations on their ability to fight major wars. According to a report to Congress, the commanders' top area of "strategic concern" is "ongoing operations," such as Bosnia and the Persian Gulf. The demand for troops and equipment has been so high that the Pentagon has used the Air Force Reserve almost as much as during the Persian Gulf War in 1991.[25]

Furthermore, fighting a major war requires skills that cannot be exercised when units are assigned to peacekeeping and other small-scale operations. When units participate in such operations, their skills needed for war erode. During peacekeeping operations, small units gain experience in restraining the use of force and in patrolling to carry out the functions of police. When training for war, in contrast, small units combine to form larger units and exercise combat skills by using force decisively. The decision to convert a substantial portion of a top-notch combat division—the First Cavalry Division—into a peacekeeping force for Bosnia raised howls of protest in Congress. According to one staff member of the House National Security Committee, "The Army is disassembling one of its most ready, most fearsome combat divisions. The action shows how the requirements to do Bosnia are detracting from the military's ability to do high intensity conflicts."[26] U.S. war plans had to be adjusted after part of the First Cavalry Division was diverted for use in Bosnia. In short, the mission in Bosnia undercut the cohesion of combat units and disrupted training cycles.

After returning home, army units that deployed to Bosnia needed about six months to restore combat skills that they could not exercise on the deployment. Similarly, monotonous patrols over Iraq to enforce the no-fly zone cause the combat skills of highly skilled pilots to erode. In addition, to cover the costs of overseas deployments, the army conducts fewer war games with large units, and the Air Force conducts fewer rigorous training exercises for its pilots.[27] As David Isenberg, author of a study on the *Misleading Military "Readiness Crisis,"* noted, "Questions about readiness stem in large part from U.S. participation in unexpected contingency operations such as those involving Rwanda, Haiti, Cuba, and Kuwait." He pointed out that "the cost of those operations, taken from O&M [operations and maintenance] accounts, caused various units to cancel training exercises and postpone maintenance of equipment, thus causing lowered readiness ratings."[28] Operations other than war cause combat skills to erode and also consume funding for the training and exercises needed to restore them.

The readiness problems in the U.S. military would quickly evaporate if the United States desisted from intervening in brushfire conflicts around the world. Easing the breakneck pace of deployment would dramatically decrease the wear on soldiers and equipment, and it would allow O&M funds to be used to buy spare parts and provide combat training.

In addition to fracturing large units and undermining combat training, peacekeeping and small contingencies may impede a response to a major emergency. Troops would need to be withdrawn from smaller operations— often over poor roads and rails, and through underdeveloped ports and airfields—loaded aboard scarce airlift and sealift, and redeployed to any major war. The two army divisions that had their readiness ratings lowered—and thus became infamous during the 2000 presidential election campaign—were unready because they were incapable of quickly extricating themselves from Balkan peacekeeping and redeploying to a larger conflict.

"Readiness Crisis" Indicates That Excessive Military Requirements Exceed Already Abundant Resources

The Joint Chiefs of Staff (JCS) went to President Clinton and informed him of their concerns about deteriorating military readiness. Since the signs of readiness problems had not appeared overnight, there is reason for suspicion that the timing of the JCS complaint was designed to get a share of the emerging budget surplus. The ploy worked; they received more money from the president and Congress. (Congress dipped into the surplus to give the Pentagon $8.3 billion in fiscal year 1999 emergency funding, but only $1.1 billion, or 13 percent, was allocated for improving the readiness of forces; the rest was for defense "pork" disguised as emergency requirements.) Even before the increase in funding for readiness, the money available for training and maintenance per soldier in the military was higher than during the Reagan military buildup.[29] In fact, the military spends about seventy thousand dollars a year per troop on operations and maintenance—30 percent higher in real terms than during the George H. W. Bush administration (when measured readiness was at its height).[30] Nevertheless, the record pace of worldwide military operations has strained even the abundant resources provided.

In other words, in some sense, the military is probably correct that the requirements exceed the funding available. James Schlesinger summarized the problem best:

The prevailing condition of American preponderance, in which few regions of the world are beyond our reach or influence, is not only exceptional but artificial. It was brought about by the sudden and unexpected collapse of the Soviet Union and the end of Cold War bipolarity. Inevitably, this exceptional period must fade, and to that we shall have to adjust. But beyond that inevitable adjustment, we shall have to make a fundamental choice among (1) spending far more on defense than we are spending, (2) retrenching on our present, ambitious foreign policy, and (3) accepting the higher levels of international risk involved in maintaining our existing commitments while allowing our defense capability to decline, which would tempt others to challenge us.[31]

To avoid the risk inherent in allowing the mismatch between requirements and resources to remain (Schlesinger's point 3), the United States must either reduce the requirements (2) or increase the resources allocated for national defense (1).

A report by the Congressional Budget Office quantified the discrepancy between requirements and resources. According to the report, if the United States expects its military to be able to win two wars in quick succession and perform frequent peacekeeping missions (the current national strategy) and also modernize each piece of equipment on a one-for-one basis, another fifty-one billion dollars would need to be added to the $289 billion spent on defense in fiscal year (FY) 2000.[32] (Other authors—for example, Dan Gouré and Jeffrey Ranney of the Center for Strategic and International Studies—have come up with higher numbers.[33]) Some of the press coverage of the study erroneously reported that CBO had concluded that the military was "woefully underfunded";[34] many hawks will trumpet the finding as an endorsement of whopping increases in defense spending.

The CBO made the questionable assumption that each piece of equipment would be modernized on a one-for-one basis; in fact, however, even the military does not plan to do so, because the new high-tech weapons have greater combat power than the old equipment. Relaxing that standard would reduce the disparity between the funding needed to sustain a modernized military and the current budget for national defense to less than fifty-one billion dollars.[35] But the report is probably correct that the military is overextended—that is, given the current national strategy, the current force cannot be modernized within the current defense budget.

But of course, increasing the defense budget is only one solution, and not the best one. Instead of "woefully underfunded," a better characterization is that U.S. armed forces are woefully overcommitted and overprogrammed (too many weapons are planned for the funds available). In the benign threat environment of the post–Cold War world, the United States should seriously reconsider the commitments of U.S. forces overseas, the current force structure, and even the modernization plans of the Department of Defense (DoD)—plans that are more modest than the one-for-one replacement assumption in the CBO report. In other words, reducing military requirements is a better alternative than increasing the defense budget.

THE AMOUNT SPENT ON THE MILITARY IS ALREADY HUGE

Advocates of higher military budgets bemoan the fact that U.S. spending on national defense has declined to about 3 percent of the nation's gross domestic product (GDP), its lowest point since 1940. As a result, they argue, U.S. security is being severely compromised. But although defense spending as a percentage of GDP is a good indicator of what proportion of the national wealth is siphoned off for defense, the measure is not an indicator of what amount *should* be spent on a nation's defense. If a nation's GDP quadruples, its defense budget does not necessarily need to quadruple. No nation ever fought another nation with a percentage of its GDP. Nations fight other nations with military forces that are purchased with finite quantities of resources.

In fact, if defense spending as a percentage of GDP is to be a meaningful statistic, the U.S. percentage should be compared with those of relatively wealthy allies in the G-7 group—the nation's chief economic competitors. Table 1.1 shows that each of those other nations spends a smaller portion of their GDPs on defense than does the United States (1999 is the last year for which data from all countries are comparable). U.S. allies realize the opportunity cost of defense spending—resources taken away from their private sectors—and prefer to remain under the U.S. protective shield rather than increase the percentage of their GDP being siphoned off to defense. The allies will continue to "free ride" as long as the United States continues to bail them out of security problems that they should take care of themselves—for example, the conflicts in Bosnia and Kosovo. Excessive U.S. defense spending is even worse than the statistics indicate, because the United States has a much more secure geostrategic position than any of the other countries (except perhaps Canada).

Actually, the absolute level of defense spending is probably the best single indicator of a nation's military strength. Other indicators of military power exist, such as numbers of military personnel and quantities of military equipment (tanks, aircraft, and ships), but the national budget for defense is the best overall measure.

Gregg Easterbrook, a senior editor at the *New Republic*, uses such non-budget indicators to argue that the American military is more potent relative to its enemies than any great power in world history—including the

Table 1.1
Percentage of Gross Domestic Product Spent on National Defense: The United States and Its Wealthiest Allies (G-7 Nations)

Country	Defense Spending in 1999 [a][b]	Gross Domestic Product [a]	Percentage of GDP Spent on Defense
United States	275.5	9,200	3.0
France	37.1	1,400	2.7
United Kingdom	36.9	1,400	2.6
Italy	22.0	1,100	2.0
Germany	31.1	1,900	1.6
Canada	7.8	644	1.2
Japan	40.8	4,300	0.9

Notes: a. In billions of 1999 dollars.

b. NATO's definition of defense spending was used for all nations. The year 1999 is the latest for which the calculation is available.

Source: International Institute of Strategic Studies, The Military Balance: *2000–2001* (London: Oxford University Press, 2000), pp. 25, 54, 58, 61, 66, 80, and 200.

Roman empire, nineteenth-century Britain, and Nazi Germany in 1940. He provides data that eloquently sum up the U.S. dominance in the military realm:

- Because of the dismal state of the Russian nuclear force and the robust nature of its U.S. counterpart, America's strategic nuclear deterrent is stronger relative to the rest of the world than at any time since the days of the U.S. nuclear monopoly in the late 1940s.

- The United States has larger numbers of heavy bombers, advanced tactical fighter aircraft, and aerial tankers than the rest of the world combined. The U.S. military services have three classes of stealth aircraft already deployed and three more in development; no other nation has even one on the drawing board.

- The U.S. Navy has more than twice the number of primary warships as the Chinese and Russian navies combined. The United States operates twelve supercarriers; the only other large carrier in the world is a decrepit ship in Russia. The U.S. Navy is the only fleet in the world that is designed to operate regularly outside its own region.

- The U.S. Army's nearly eight thousand M-1 Abrams tanks—the best armor in the world—total more than the combined number of modern Chinese and Russian tanks.

- The U.S. Marine Corps is the only standing heavy amphibious force in the world.[36]

Some defense analysts would argue that Easterbrook's indicators of military power are measures of output and are therefore superior to a nation's defense budget, a measure of input. Easterbrook's indicators are important because they address both the quantity and quality of military equipment and show one aspect of U.S. military dominance (superior hardware), but they are not a comprehensive measure of America's military supremacy.[37]

Modern war has shown that equipment is only one part of the equation. Smaller, highly trained volunteer militaries are more effective than larger conscript forces that have less training. The Persian Gulf War showed that large armies may not be effective if their equipment is of low quality or they lack the intangible "glue"—for example, intelligence, electronic sensors, and command and control systems, logistics, and training—to allow the troops and equipment to fight as integrated and effective forces. (The United States has the only truly integrated military in the world.) The national defense budget is the only indicator of military power that includes measures of the vital intangible items and the quality of weapons (both by their cost). Although the absolute defense budget of a particular nation measures inputs (resources expended), it does give—in one statistic—a crude indicator of the country's military power. In other words, most countries probably get the quality of military that they pay for.[38]

The amount a nation spends on defense should be based on its geostrategic situation and the threats to its vital interests. Since the Cold War, nearly all of the major nations have cut their armed forces.[39] After the Persian Gulf War, Gen. Colin Powell acknowledged that threats to U.S. vital interests were diminishing: "I'm running out of demons. I'm down to Kim Il Sung and Castro."[40] (One needs to be skeptical about whether even North Korea and Cuba are still a threat to U.S. vital interests. More will be said about that topic later.)

U.S. outlays for national defense during fiscal year 2001 were $303 billion (2002 dollars)—an average of more than a thousand dollars for each American citizen. Despite the demise of the Soviet Union, the U.S. defense budget, in real terms, is approximately what it was in 1981, during the Cold War. The decline of U.S. defense spending by roughly one-fourth after 1989—bemoaned by many conservatives—merely eliminated the largest U.S. peacetime military buildup in history during the Reagan administration and returned expenditures to about 90 percent of the Cold War average (see figure 1.1).

When total American spending on national defense is compared to that of other major nations, the true magnitude of U.S. expenditures becomes clear. The United States accounts for roughly one-third of worldwide defense spending, up from 28 percent in the mid-1980s, the height of the Reagan military buildup.[41] Although U.S. defense spending has declined since the mid-eighties, worldwide defense spending has declined faster. The United States and its allies now account for 72 percent of the world's spending for defense.[42]

As table 1.2 shows, U.S. spending roughly equals the combined spending

Figure 1.1
U.S. Military Spending (in billions of 2000 dollars)

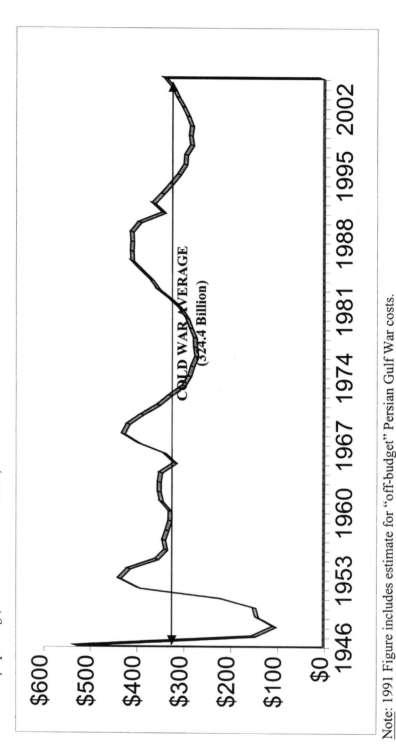

Note: 1991 Figure includes estimate for "off-budget" Persian Gulf War costs.
Sources: National Defense Budget Estimates for Fiscal Year 2000; Center for Defense Information. Data compiled by CDI.

Table 1.2
Spending on National Defense: The Top Eight Nations (in billions of 1999 dollars)

Country	Amount Spent in 1999 [a]	Rank
United States	275.5	1
Total of Countries 2–8	263.4	
Russia [b]	56.0	2
Japan	40.8	3
China [b c]	39.5	4
France	37.1	5
United Kingdom	36.9	6
Germany	31.1	7
Italy	22.0	8

Notes: a. NATO's definition of defense spending was used for all nations. The year 1999 is the latest for which the calculation is available.

b. The figure has been adjusted for purchasing power parity.

c. Official Chinese defense spending is roughly 12.6 billion dollars. If off-budget expenditures are included, total Chinese defense spending is about $39.5 billion.

Source: International Institute for Strategic Studies, The Military Balance: 2000-2001 (London: Oxford University Press, 2000), pp. 25, 58, 61, 66, 80, 120, 194, and 200

of the next seven nations, the vast majority of which are U.S. friends or allies. The United States spends almost as much as all of its wealthy major friends and allies combined, and almost one and a half times all of its rich NATO allies combined. More important, the United States spends about two and a half times the *combined* spending ($109 billion annually) of nations that are "potential threat states"—Russia, China, and the "rogue states" of Iraq, Iran, Syria, Libya, Sudan, Cuba, and North Korea (see table 1.3). Combined, the potential threat states account for 18 percent of the world's defense spending—compared with a U.S. share of about one-third.[43] The United States outspends the $13.8 billion in combined defense expenditures of the rogue states by a factor of about twenty. Iran, the rogue state that spends the most on defense, has an annual defense budget of only $5.7 billion and barely makes the list of top twenty nations. The rogue states that the United States seems most concerned about in its military planning—Iraq and North Korea—have combined defense spending that is only about 60 percent of Iran's military budget. A summary of U.S. defense spending compared to those of other nations appears in figure 1.2.

Furthermore, the gap between U.S. military capabilities and those of other nations is likely to widen in the future. The amount a nation spends on military research and development (R&D) is a good predictor of its

Table 1.3

Spending on National Defense in Potential Threat States (billions of 1999 dollars)

Country	Amount Spent on Defense in 1999 [a]
Russia [b]	56.0
China [bc]	39.5
Iran	5.7
North Korea	2.1
Syria	1.9
Libya [d]	1.5
Iraq	1.4
Cuba	.8
Sudan	.4
Total	109.3
United States	275.5

Notes: a. NATO's definition of defense spending was used for all nations. The year 1999 is the latest for which the calculation is available.

b. The figure has been adjusted for purchasing power parity.

c. Official Chinese defense spending is roughly 12.6 billion dollars. If off-budget expenditures are included, total Chinese defense spending is $39.5 billion.

d. A 1998 expenditure converted to 1999 dollars.

Source: International Institute for Strategic Studies, The Military Balance: 2000-2001 (London: Oxford University Press, 2000), pp. 120, 139, 140, 146, 153, 194, 202, 236, and 283.

future military power. According to the Stockholm International Peace Research Institute, in 1997 the United States accounted for $37 billion, or 64 percent of the $58 billion spent worldwide for military R&D.[44] The U.S. R&D budget vastly exceeds those of the next most capable militaries on the planet, the NATO allies. In 2000, the U.S. R&D budget was more than eight times greater than that of the United Kingdom, which was in second place in the alliance and approximately three and a half times those budgets of all NATO nations combined.[45] There is much worry among allies in NATO that overwhelming U.S. technological dominance in the future may make it difficult for their forces to operate with the Americans. When one calculates the cumulative effects of the disparity in annual R&D spending among the allies, U.S. dominance is bone crushing (see table 1.4) and confirms allied fears.

More important, the U.S. annual military R&D budget is roughly the same size as the entire yearly defense budget of China, France, or the United

Figure 1.2
Spending on National Defense in Key Nations

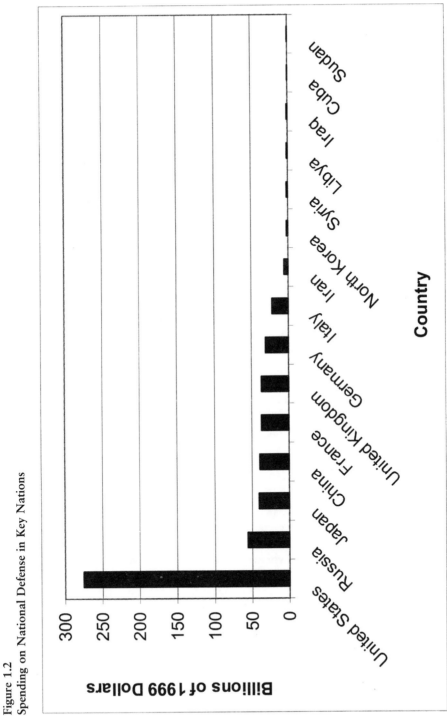

Source: International Institute for Strategic Studies, Military Balance 2000-2001.

Table 1.4
Cumulative Total of Government-Financed Military Research and Development
for Selected Allies (billions of constant 1999 dollars)

Country	Cumulative Military Research and Development Spending (1996–2000)
United States	183.2
United Kingdom	19.2
France	18.6
Germany	7.6
Italy	2.8
Spain	1.1
Canada	0.5
Netherlands	0.5

Source: International Institute for Strategic Studies, *The Military Balance 2000-2001* (Oxford: Oxford University Press, 2000), p. 41.

Kingdom. The United States still spends more in real terms on research and development than it did during most of the Cold War (See figure 1.3).[46]

In short, the formidable military forces of the United States and the huge amounts spent for R&D and procurement of complex and costly weapons have no relationship to the nation's security needs. The favorable geostrategic position of the United States should allow the maintenance of U.S. security with lower—not higher—absolute levels of defense spending than other major nations. A large portion of the approximately $300 billion spent per year on "national defense" has nothing to do with the actual defense of the United States or its security, but a great deal to do with the expensive, self-appointed role of "world leader."

A COMPLETE REVIEW OF U.S. SECURITY IS NEEDED

Since the John F. Kennedy administration, the United States has based its defense planning on the need to fight at least two conflicts at the same time. President Kennedy created the requirement to fight two major wars and one minor war at the same time (the two-and-a-half war strategy), but many analysts questioned whether enough resources were budgeted to carry out the policy. President Richard Nixon scaled back the requirement to one major war and one minor war (the one-and-a-half war strategy). After the Cold War ended in 1989, President George H. W. Bush's "Base Force" postulated fighting at least two minor (regional) wars at the same time. The Clinton administration's 1993 Bottom-Up Review (BUR) incrementally reduced forces from the Base Force, but it retained the requirement to fight two regional wars (using Iraq and North Korea as hypothetical adversaries) nearly simultaneously. In the 1997 Quadrennial Defense Review (QDR), the Clinton administration kept the force structure virtually the same as

Figure 1.3
U.S. Defense Research, Development, Test, and Evaluation Spending, 1945-2005 (billions of constant 2000 dollars)

Billions of constant 2000 Dollars

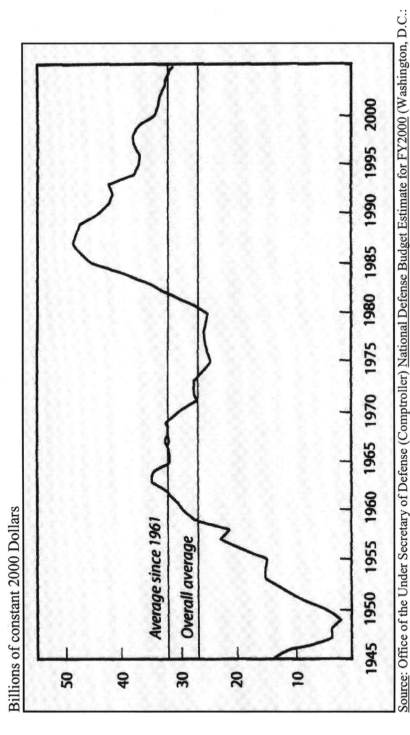

Source: Office of the Under Secretary of Defense (Comptroller) National Defense Budget Estimate for FY2000 (Washington, D.C.: Department of Defense, March 1999), pp. 106–11. Reprinted from Michael O'Hanlon, Technological Change and the Future of Warfare (Washington, D.C.: Brookings Institution, 2000), p. 183.

the BUR and reiterated its commitment to be able to fight two regional wars during the same time period. That commitment remains in effect today.

Defense planning based on fighting more than one war simultaneously is left over from the national trauma of World War II. In that conflict, the United States faced two powerful adversaries at the same time. Yet because World War II was a historical anomaly, planning for more than one war is somewhat anachronistic. During the Cold War, the Soviet Union did not attempt to take advantage of U.S. involvement in conflicts in Korea, Vietnam, or the Persian Gulf to perpetrate aggression in other theaters. Yet U.S. military planners are now assuming that a small regional power would opportunistically commit aggression at the same time that the United States was involved in a conflict with another small rogue state. The dual-war scenario involving two regional adversaries is much less likely than a rival superpower orchestrating two conflicts at once to tie down the United States.

Even in the unlikely event that wars with two regional adversaries occur at the same time, the absence of a rival superpower to take advantage of simultaneous wars would allow the United States the luxury of fighting the wars sequentially. (The second adversary would most likely be deterred by knowing that the full weight of U.S. military power would be used against it after the United States finished with the first small foe.) In the much more benign threat environment of the post–Cold War world, it is unlikely that even one regional conflict would involve U.S. vital interests (and thus justify U.S. intervention), much less that two would do so.

The National Defense Panel (NDP), a congressionally mandated independent panel created to evaluate the results of the QDR, realized the real purpose of planning for two wars at the same time:

A significant share of today's Defense Department's resources is focused on the unlikely contingency that two major wars will occur at almost the same time. The Panel views this two-military-theater-of-war construct as, in reality, a force-sizing function. We are concerned that, for some, this has become a means of justifying current forces.[47]

Yet the NDP did not propose an alternative criterion for sizing forces. That omission was necessary because the panel—made up of pillars of the national security establishment (ex-generals, former Pentagon officials, and representatives from the defense industry)—refused to question the assumptions underlying U.S. national security policy.[48] In fact, one particularly telling passage from the NDP report indicates that the panel was merely trying to find a better justification for maintaining excessively large military forces. The panel urged the abandonment of the two-war criterion because retaining it "could leave the services vulnerable[,] if one of the other major contingencies resolves itself before we have a transformation strategy in place, [to] a strong demand for immediate, deep, and unwise cuts in force structure and personnel."[49] (The oblique reference to a contingency resolving itself had to do with the Korean scenario. Many analysts predicted that the economically prostrate North Korean regime would eventually collapse. Alternatively, this weak nation might lessen its belligerent posture to obtain international assistance—as seems to be happening.) The NDP had it backwards; the panel wanted to maintain forces at their current levels but could not identify a threat that would justify that policy.

The national security establishment has realized that the Cold War is over but cannot shake the key assumptions on which U.S. security policy was based during that period. No major conventional threat to U.S. security now exists. Dire threats, such as those posed by the enemies of World War II and the Cold War, have occurred rarely in American history. Yet almost fifty years of battling those threats made that extremely hostile environment seem like the norm.

Because of its intrinsically secure geostrategic position and the demise of the worldwide threat from a rival communist superpower, the United States can retract the extended defense perimeter of the Cold War. When thinking about a post–Cold War world, policy makers must finally discard their Cold War lenses. In the Cold War, the superpowers watched each other carefully and checked each other's advances anywhere in the world, in a tit-for-tat manner. With no rival superpower to take advantage of instability around the world, most conflicts simply have no adverse effect on U.S. security. The world has always been an anarchic, unstable place, and it will probably always be that way.

The United States should intervene militarily only when its vital interests are at stake. Drastically reducing U.S. military presence overseas and adopting a "balancer of last resort" strategy—assisting friendly nations in key areas of the world only when the regional balance of power deteriorates because of severe hegemonic aggression—would maintain U.S. security and allow the United States to reduce its defense budget significantly.

To determine how large the U.S. defense budget should be, the analysis must proceed through five steps:

1. Define U.S. vital interests.
2. Determine threats to U.S. vital interests.
3. Formulate a security strategy to safeguard those interests.
4. Identify the military forces needed to carry out the strategy.
5. Propose a budget for national defense that will cover the costs of buying and supporting the forces.

Many analysts, when discussing the national security issue of the day, neglect to keep the big picture in mind. Concentrating on the five steps will keep the focus on designing a defense policy and budget that will ensure U.S. security without wasting public funds.

NOTES

1. Quoted in Eric Nordlinger, *Isolationism Reconfigured: American Foreign Policy for a New Century* (Princeton, N.J.: Princeton Univ. Press, 1995), pp. 50–51.

2. James D. Richardson, ed., *A Compilation of the Messages and Papers of the Presidents, 1789–1897* (Washington, D.C.: Government Printing Office, 1898), vol. 1, p. 323.

3. Quoted in Nordlinger, p. 186.

4. John Omicinski, "Downsized U.S. Military Poses Quandary for Policymakers," *Denver Post*, October 11, 1998, p. H4, and Adam Garfinkle, "Toward National Greatness? A July 4th Reflection," *Watch on the West* 1, no. 4 (July 1998), p. 2.

5. Rowan Scarborough, "Record Deployments Take Toll on Military," *Washington Times*, March 28, 2000, p. A6. Scarborough cites estimates by the Department of Defense for overseas deployments in the 1990s and also estimates by the Senate Armed Services Committee for deployments in the later years of the Cold War.

6. James Schlesinger, "Raise the Anchor or Lower the Ship: Defense Budgeting and Planning," *National Interest*, Fall 1998, p. 5. Emphasis added.

7. Comments by Senator John Warner at the hearings on military readiness before the Senate Armed Services Committee, September 29, 1998.

8. Ted Galen Carpenter, "Kosovo as an Omen: The Perils of the 'New NATO,' " in Ted Galen Carpenter, *NATO's Empty Victory: A Postmortem on the Balkan War* (Washington, D.C.: Cato Institute, 2000), pp. 178–181; and Barbara Conry, "U.S. Security Strategy," in *Cato Handbook for Congress* (Washington, D.C.: Cato Institute, 1999), pp. 459–464.

9. Schlesinger, p. 5.

10. David Shambaugh, "China's Military Views the World: Ambivalent Security," *International Security* 24, no. 3 (Winter 1999/2000), p. 66.

11. Gordon Sullivan, "Washington Tightwads Creating a Hollow Military," *Wall Street Journal*, September 22, 1998, p. A22.

12. William Perry and Ashton Carter, *Preventative Defense: A New Security Strategy for America* (Washington, D.C.: Brookings Institution, 1999), p. 214.

13. The *Washington Times* obtained a copy of the firm's report to the Army Research Institute. Bill Gertz, "Army Gripes," *Washington Times*, September 22, 2000, p. A10.

14. Dan Smith, "Running Out of a 'Few Good Men and Women,' " *Weekly Defense Monitor*, February 25, 1999, p. 2.

15. "Air Force Faces Pilot Shortage," *San Diego Union-Tribune*, October 1, 1998, p. A12. A pilot shortage is also noted in Jonathan Landay, "Signs of Erosion in U.S. Military Readiness," *Christian Science Monitor*, September 16, 1998, p. 2.

16. Elaine Grossman, "Navy Pilot Retention Improving, But Still Well Short of Requirements," *Inside the Pentagon*, September 3, 1998, p. 24.

17. Larry Korb, "Force Is the Issue: The United States Needs to Decide Just What Kind of Military Force It Wants in the Coming Years," *Government Executive*, January 2000, p. 31.

18. Bradley Graham, "Strains on Many Fronts Drive Pilots from the Skies, Airmen Say," *Washington Post*, August 13, 1998, p. A29.

19. Ibid.

20. James Crawley, "Shortage of Sailors Erodes Navy's Readiness for Combat," *San Diego Union-Tribune*, September 2, 1998, p. A1.

21. Editorial, "Military Readiness First, Let's Decide What We're Preparing For," *Dallas Morning News*, October 7, 1998, p. 16A; and Bradley Graham, "Army's Unready Divisions: Budget Feint or Fact?" *Washington Post*, November 15, 1999, p. A21.

22. Colin Clark, "Pentagon: We're Ready for Iraq," *Defense Week*, February 17, 1998, p. 3.

23. Quoted in Bradley Graham, "Senators Scold Military Chiefs: Top Officers Accused of Failing to Warn Soon Enough of Readiness Decline," *Washington Post*, September 30, 1998, p. A2.

24. Ibid.

25. Ernest Blazar, "Inside the Ring: Mixed Report," *Washington Times*, June 25, 1998, p. A7.

26. Bradley Graham, "Army to Shift Bosnia Duties: Critics Question Using 1st Cavalry to Relieve Europe-Based Units," *Washington Post*, April 17, 1998, p. A28.

27. Pat Towell, "Military's 'Can-Do' Budget Stance Heightens Hawks' Frustrations," *Congressional Quarterly*, March 14, 1998, p. 680.

28. David Isenberg, "The Misleading Military 'Readiness Crisis,' " Cato Institute Foreign Policy Briefing no. 35, July 25, 1995, p. 9.

29. Lawrence Korb, "Money to Burn at the Pentagon," *New York Times*, September 25, 1998, p. A27.

30. Greg Jaffe, "Military Could Face Modernization Problems: Aging Tanks, Planes May Eclipse Debate over U.S. Readiness," *Wall Street Journal*, September 5, 2000, p. A36.

31. Schlesinger, p. 3.

32. Congressional Budget Office, *Budgeting for Defense: Maintaining Today's Forces* (Washington, D.C.: CBO, September 2000), pp. vii–xiv.

33. Daniel Gouré and Jeffrey Ranney, *Averting the Defense Train Wreck in the New Millennium* (Washington, D.C.: Center for Strategic and International Studies, 1999), p. xiv.

34. Thomas Ricks, "Report: Pentagon Underfunded: $50 Billion Yearly Boost Is Needed to Keep Edge, CBO Says," *Washington Post*, September 15, 2000, p. A25.

35. CBO's assumption of one-for-one modernization is curious, because the agency usually estimates whether the budget is sufficient to fund the military's modernization plans, which do not make that assumption. So in a sense, CBO's report is irrelevant to whether the military has enough money to carry out its plans.

36. Gregg Easterbrook, "Apocryphal Now: The Myth of the Hollow Military," *New Republic*, September 11, 2000, p. 22.

37. Simply counting the numbers of personnel and equipment (tanks, ships, aircraft, etc.) in a nation's armed forces can give an erroneous image of the country's military strength. For example, during the Gulf War, Iraq had a military with large

numbers of personnel and equipment but was easily defeated because its hardware was obsolescent, its training and logistics were poor, and its command and control and generalship were atrocious.

38. It could be argued that the defense budgets of nations with conscript militaries (for example, China, Russia, or the rogue states) should be adjusted upward to reflect the real value of such artificially cheap labor (which nations with volunteer militaries—including the United States—have to pay fully for). But the Gulf War showed that the value of a conscript military (the Iraqi armed forces), when facing a volunteer force (the U.S. military), may not be very great. In the wake of that war, the trend of militaries worldwide changing from conscription to volunteer is quite telling. In any case, even if the defense budgets of Russia, China, or any of the rogue states were adjusted upward slightly to reflect any understated value from conscription, U.S. defense spending would remain many times that of any of them (see Tables 2 and 3).

39. National Defense University, *1997 Strategic Assessment: Flashpoints and Force Structure* (Washington, D.C.: National Defense University, 1997), p. 7.

40. Quoted in Carl Conetta and Charles Knight, "Inventing Threats," *Bulletin of Atomic Scientists*, March/April 1998, p. 32.

41. Ibid., p. 33.

42. Ibid.

43. Ibid., p. 39.

44. Rachel Stohl, "U.S. Leads World as Top Arms Exporter," *Weekly Defense Monitor*, June 18, 1998, p. 3.

45. International Institute of Strategic Studies, *The Military Balance 2000–2001* (London: Oxford University Press, 2000), p. 41.

46. Figure was reprinted in Michael O'Hanlon, *Technological Change and the Future of Warfare* (Washington, D.C.: Brookings Institution, 2000), p. 183.

47. National Defense Panel, *Transforming Defense: National Security in the 21st Century* (Arlington, Va.: NDP, December 1997), p. ii.

48. David Isenberg, "The Quadrennial Defense Review: Reiterating the Tired Status Quo," Cato Institute Policy Analysis No. 317, September 17, 1998, pp. 5–6, 23–25.

49. National Defense Panel, p. 23.

2

Defining U.S. Vital Interests

U.S. policy makers and pundits use the term "vital interests" promiscu-
ously. For example, a classified planning document from the Pentagon that
was leaked to the press in February 1992 indicated that the planners—
working under the vice chairman of the Joint Chiefs of Staff—had come
up with "illustrative" scenarios that they assumed affected U.S. vital interests. One of the scenarios postulated was a coup in the Philippines that
threatened American residents.[1] In addition, scholars Todd Sandler and
Keith Hartley suggest that NATO (and therefore the United States, which
dominates the alliance) may have a vital interest in taking military action
to rescue nations from the air and water pollution of their neighbors.[2]
Foreign policy analysts justify many of the frequent U.S. military interventions overseas by saying that vital interests are at stake. A definition of vital
interests, when provided at all, usually involves vague phrases such as "enhanced regional stability" or "the reassurance of allies." Goals of that nature hardly count as vital interests.

THE NATIONAL SECURITY STRATEGY

If the Clinton administration had stuck to the limited definition of vital
interests used in its publication *A National Security Strategy for a Global
Age* (December 2000) and used military forces to defend only those interests, its national security policy might have been somewhat more coherent.
The document defines U.S. vital interests as follows:

Those directly connected to the survival, safety and vitality of our nation. Among these are the physical security of our territory and that of our allies, the safety of our citizens both at home and abroad, protection against WMD [Weapons of Mass Destruction] proliferation, the economic well-being of our society, and the protection of our critical infrastructures.[3]

Of course, even that passage has some glaring problems. The use of the word "among" implies that other vital interests exist that are not listed. That loophole allows the list of vital interests to be expanded when the circumstances dictate (usually when the United States is engaged in one of its many military actions overseas).

The passage specifically defines U.S. vital interests as including the physical security of our territory and that of our allies. The document takes for granted that those alliances, formed during the Cold War, are still essential to U.S. security. But the rival superpower and its empire, which those alliances were designed to counter, have dissolved. In U.S. history until the advent of the Cold War, permanent military alliances were eschewed to avoid entanglement in the wars of other nations. In world history, military alliances during peacetime are a rarity, because they unnecessarily inhibit the flexibility of the foreign policies of the participating nations.

The other most prominent example of peacetime military alliances—those formal and informal arrangements formed between the major powers in Europe prior to World War I—ended in disaster. The arrangements, formed in the late 1800s and early 1900s, created the impression that Europe was safe from conflict, but they ultimately dragged the great powers reluctantly into World War I. For example, Germany formed an alliance with the Austro-Hungarian Empire to restrain the Austro-Hungarians from causing a war in the Balkans. Circumstances changed, and Austria-Hungary ended up dragging Germany into the Great War. A formal alliance with Russia pulled in France, and the informal entente between France and Britain then dragged in Britain. Today, U.S. foreign-policy makers constantly worry about "uncertainty" but fail to take the one action that would increase their flexibility to deal with a more uncertain (but in many ways less dangerous) post–Cold War world—withdrawal from outdated Cold War alliances.

But the official "National Security Strategy" also indicates that military action will be used to safeguard interests that go beyond its already excessively broad definition of "vital interests." The document notes that "important national interests"—that is, interests that "affect our national well-being or that of the world in which we live"—drove the U.S. intervention in Kosovo.[4] Safeguarding that additional open-ended category of interests with military action makes the possibilities for U.S. military intervention virtually limitless.

Similarly, the U.S. government attempts to stretch its role in safeguarding the economic well-being of its citizens. One of the justifications for U.S. military presence and intervention in various regions of the world is that they provide stability that fosters U.S. commerce and investment. Yet trade and investment occur naturally, because of the mutual interest of the private parties involved; trade and investment flows usually route themselves around wars. For example, when war with Iran made Iraqi ports on the Persian Gulf inoperable, Iraq had to develop alternative land routes for oil exports through Jordan, Turkey, Saudi Arabia, Kuwait, and even Syria (a nation friendly to Iran) by settling border disputes and making payments to some of those nations.[5] During World War I, the battling European nations—which had had their trade disrupted—saw a loss of export markets and a rise of industrial production in areas remote from the war—that is, Asia and Latin America.[6] In other words, staying out of wars can be profitable.

Wars can impede the commerce of nonbelligerents, but that effect may be less than is believed. According to an analysis by academics Eugene Gholz and Daryl G. Press, if a major war occurred in the world, trade and investment patterns might change, but the economic losses to neutral nations from disrupted trade and increased interest rates would probably be small. (The authors reported that A.F.K. Organski and Jacek Kugler reached a consistent finding—that is, the Gross National Product of neutral countries was not substantially affected in the medium- or long-term by the two World Wars.) Press and Gholz concluded that the global economy is flexible and resilient, able to adapt to even large wars. In fact, if neutrals took over the markets abandoned by the belligerents, increased trade with them in war materiel and other goods, lent money at higher interest rates, and acted as a safe haven for capital, they might actually be better off than before the war. (As a "neutral" nation for most of World War I, the United States profited from trade and capital flows with other neutrals and the belligerents. Japan and Sweden also prospered by remaining neutral in that conflict.) Even using worst case assumptions about the amount of fighting that would occur in the absence of U.S. overseas military presence and about the vulnerability of the U.S. economy to wartime disruption, Gholz and Press show the cost of the current overextended U.S. defense perimeter would far exceed the purely economic cost of a conflagration to a United States that remained neutral.[7]

The Clinton administration defined vital interests too broadly and was too willing to use military action to defend interests that fell outside even that expansive definition. The National Security Strategy appeared to create a hierarchy of national interests, but the reality was that its expansive definitions allowed the U.S. government to use military power anywhere and everywhere. The George W. Bush administration should undertake a more rigorous analysis of U.S. vital interests that would construe them much more narrowly. U.S. military intervention should be restricted to action only when the stakes are high.

A CONCRETE AND NARROW DEFINITION OF U.S. VITAL INTERESTS

Most interests that are regarded as vital in government circles, in the media, and in academic discourse are not vital at all. U.S. vital interests can be boiled down to four goals (in order of importance):

1. Protect U.S. citizens, territory, and institutions. This goal should be the highest priority of the nation's national security policy. For the most part, throughout U.S. history, achieving that goal has been an easy task. As noted earlier, the United States may enjoy the most secure geographical position of any great power ever. The founders of the nation realized that geographical advantages allowed them to stay out of foreign wars that did not concern America. Protecting U.S. citizens and territory includes protecting U.S. diplomats and embassies abroad. U.S. embassies are recognized as American territory, and U.S. diplomats must represent American interests even in times of crisis with a host nation. The U.S. government should not, however, come to the rescue of its nationals, tourists, and business people who ignore government warnings and travel to, or remain in, dangerous countries.

2. Prevent either of the two regions with preeminent economic and technological power—that is, Europe and East Asia—from falling to a hegemonic aggressor. If one or both of those regions fell to an aggressor, the new hegemon might be able to use its newly acquired economic power and technology to threaten, directly or indirectly, the United States or its way of life. The unusual situations during the Cold War (with the Soviet Union as the potential aggressor) and World War II (with Japan and Germany as the aggressors) fit that description. Most other wars in Europe, including World War I, do not. For most of its history, the United States stayed out of major European wars with few adverse consequences to its security. In fact, U.S. security improved during those wars, because European nations were distracted and had no cause to meddle in U.S. affairs. In East Asia, a substantial portion of the economic power is centered on offshore islands that are more easily defended than is continental Europe. Thus, the chance of a catastrophic failure of the regional balance of power is less likely. Only in the rare case where danger exists of a complete breakdown in the power balance in Europe or East Asia should the United States intervene militarily, as a "balancer of last resort," to shore it up.

3. Ensure that no country or group can interdict U.S. trade on the high seas. That goal should be narrowly construed. Nations or groups (terrorists or pirates) cannot be allowed to stop or seize U.S. ships or cargoes in international waters. Therefore, a strong navy is needed, but the permanent or near-permanent presence of U.S. ground, air, and naval forces overseas is not needed to ensure regional stability or prevent regional wars in the name of protecting U.S. trade

and investment. As noted earlier, trade usually reroutes itself around regional wars, and the United States—provided that it is not a belligerent—is unlikely to lose much money (and may even make money) during such circumstances. The U.S. Navy needs to take action only when the neutrality rights of American ships are violated by belligerents or other parties.

4. Ensure that no nation can interfere with the U.S. use of space for commercial and military purposes. The United States, more than any other nation, relies on space for intelligence gathering, communications, navigation, early warning, and a multitude of commercial activities. This vital interest is relatively new, and assuring U.S. freedom of action is a complex undertaking. Some key questions need to be asked. What, if anything, should be done to ensure that vital satellite networks cannot be put out of commission? Should the United States "harden" its satellites against attacks or simply rely on redundancy to ensure that vital functions cannot be knocked out during a war? Does the United States need antisatellite weapons to deter other nations from using such weapons, or will obtaining such weapons merely cause an arms race in space? This book will not answer those difficult questions; suffice it to say that U.S. freedom of action in space is a vital national interest.

WHAT IS NOT VITAL

What is left out of the narrow set of vital interests is as significant as what is included. The conventional wisdom in the American national security community is that the United States should be prepared to fight to keep South Korea free of communism and to ensure the security of Persian Gulf oil. In fact, the U.S. military justifies the size of its current forces on the unlikely contingency of fighting those major theater wars nearly simultaneously.

A key question that needs to be asked is *why* the United States should defend South Korea or Persian Gulf oil. U.S. foreign policy remains on autopilot almost a decade after the end of the Cold War. During the Cold War, the United States believed that it had to respond to Soviet meddling around the world in a tit-for-tat manner. Washington had the misplaced fear that if global communism took over one country, other countries would go down like dominoes. U.S. leaders also held the questionable belief that if they failed to respond to a communist insurgency in one part of the world—no matter how strategically insignificant (for example, Vietnam)—the communists would be emboldened in other parts of the world. Yet the United States lost Nicaragua, Vietnam, Laos, and Cambodia, but not all of Southeast Asia or Central America.

Regardless of the dubious rationale for entering brushfire conflicts during the Cold War, in a post–Cold War world most conflicts are clearly no longer strategic to the United States. Contrary to conventional wisdom, even in the unlikely event that North Korea overran the Korean Peninsula and Iraq simultaneously attacked Kuwait and Saudi Arabia, U.S. vital interests would not be harmed. A careful analysis shows that neither the Korean Peninsula nor the Persian Gulf is a vital area of interest for the United States. In addition, the United States should not conduct wars in vain attempts to "defend" (really promote) its values.

Korea

Before 1950, top U.S. policy makers did not believe that Korea was strategic. According to Doug Bandow of the Cato Institute,

Indeed, were it not for the existence of the Soviet Union in 1950, policymakers then would probably have written off the Korean conflict. In September 1947, for instance, the Joint Chiefs of Staff declared the Korean peninsula strategically unimportant. In the view of the Joint Chiefs, U.S. airpower based in Japan would be sufficient to neutralize the impact of a communist takeover of the peninsula. And while Secretary [of State Dean] Acheson's speech treating South Korea as outside the U.S. defense perimeter is quite famous, less well known is the fact that before the war General [Douglas] MacArthur also didn't believe that the ROK [Republic of (South) Korea] warranted defense by the United States. Indeed, the Pentagon supported the withdrawal of U.S. forces from South Korea in 1949 because it considered the country of "little strategic interest," even though it recognized that Soviet domination of the ROK thereafter would "have to be accepted as a probability." Similarly, Washington later refused to carry the war into China and accepted a negotiated settlement, both pragmatic decisions that suggested that policymakers understood that the conflict affected no vital U.S. interests.[8]

If the preservation of South Korea was not regarded as strategic before 1950, it should not be so regarded in a much more benign post–Cold War international environment. The National Defense University's *1997 Strategic Assessment* concedes that the rationale for U.S. defense of South Korea has had to be changed since 1950 to justify a continued U.S. military presence.

Since 1950, the U.S. has supported South Korea against the threat of aggression from the North. The original rationale was the geostrategic importance of the Korean Peninsula during the Cold War, including the importance of forward defense of Japan from Soviet or Chinese aggression. That no longer remains valid. The North, devoid of external backing, remains the only direct threat to the South. At the same time, however, U.S. interests on the peninsula have grown from their original, Cold War security aspects. The South's economic growth and its increasingly democratic political institutions have transformed it from solely a bulwark against communism to a dynamic international player with whom the U.S. desires to maintain a close, multifaceted relationship.[9]

The very economic growth that makes a relationship with South Korea attractive should enable that nation to defend itself without U.S. assistance. Even absent American forces and reinforcement, South Korea need not fall to an invasion from the North. In 1950, South Korea was a poor nation with weak armed forces, confronted by a much stronger North Korea subsidized with arms and other assistance from China and the Soviet Union. Now, South Korea's gross domestic product (GDP) is almost thirty times that of North Korea's prostrate economy.

The Persian Gulf

Similarly, the conventional wisdom here is that the United States must defend Saudi Arabia and Kuwait to ensure the flow of cheap oil from the Persian Gulf to the West. But as Lawrence Korb, former assistant secretary of defense, argues, "Why does the U.S. spend $50 billion a year to safeguard access to $10 billion a year worth of oil from the Persian Gulf while the Europeans, who use $30 billion a year, spend next to nothing?"[10] Western Europe gets 24 percent of its oil from the Persian Gulf, and Japan gets 70 percent; in contrast, the United States gets only 19 percent.[11] The United States is spending vast sums to ensure that its wealthy economic competitors in Europe and East Asia have cheap supplies of oil. (In a global oil market, any production cutback by Persian Gulf states will raise the price of oil for all consumers. The greatest transaction costs, however, will probably be incurred by the Europeans and Japanese, because they must sacrifice the most efficiency by switching more of their purchases to other suppliers.) Japan and most of the Western European nations spend far smaller portions of their GDPs on defense than does the United States. By lowering the percentage of their societies' resources that must be allocated for defense, those nations give their companies a competitive edge over U.S. firms, which are burdened by a higher societal defense bill.

The *1997 Strategic Assessment* acknowledged that the unequal burden of defending the Persian Gulf region should be rectified: "Europe and Japan rely more heavily on Gulf oil and conduct high levels of commercial trade with the GCC [Gulf Cooperation Council], but the United States and the GCC will increasingly bear the defense burden for the region. This growing imbalance in roles will give the United States and GCC a strong interest in having Europe and Japan share in the defense burden."[12]

In fact, it is likely that no one needs to defend Persian Gulf oil. The world oil market has changed substantially since the oil embargo of 1973. Even then, petroleum shortages of the 1970s reduced the U.S. GDP by only 0.35 percent, according to economist Douglas Bohi. Many economists now concur that the wage and price controls, inflationary monetary policy, and economic mismanagement by the Nixon, Ford, and Carter administrations caused the economic recessions of the 1970s.[13] Despite Washington's misguided energy policies, the higher worldwide prices resulting from the embargo have caused new non-OPEC (Organization of Petroleum Exporting Countries) sources of oil to be developed. Development of new sources is accelerating; new deposits in China, Colombia, and Central Asia are being exploited. As a result, the share of world oil production originating from the Persian Gulf has declined from 37 percent in 1973 to 28 percent today. In addition, significant new technology is enabling oil from normally expensive deposits to be extracted economically even when world prices are low. Finally, significant gains in energy efficiency lower the amount of oil needed to produce a dollar's worth of goods and services. The U.S. economy is now less dependent on oil than it was in 1973 (only three percent of the GDP is spent on oil today, versus nine percent in the 1970s) and can switch among fuels more easily.[14]

In short, OPEC, like most cartels, has failed to have much effect on the long-term price of its commodity. Even when the OPEC cartel tries to raise the oil price by withholding production, member nations can make increased profits by pumping more than their production quotas and selling it at the new higher price. Such cheating brings the price back down.

In the very worst case imaginable—an Iraqi invasion and occupation of Kuwait, the United Arab Emirates (UAE), and Saudi Arabia—the effects on the U.S. economy would be modest. Because Saudi Arabia has such large oil supplies in the ground (about one-quarter of the world's proved reserves), it prices oil conservatively compared with other oil producers. If the price goes above a certain level, the long-term demand for Saudi oil still in the ground will likely decrease, because of the conservation of petroleum and the substitution of alternative fuels. A higher world price would also cause an increase in oil production from other sources.[15] Thus, if Iraq conquered Kuwait, the UAE, and Saudi Arabia, Baghdad's increased market power (it would then control about 20 percent of the world's oil production) would allow for only a slight increase in the oil price.[16] Iraq might withhold some oil from the market to get a higher price but would be unlikely to halt shipments of its major foreign-currency-earning export.

According to an economic study done before the Persian Gulf War by David R. Henderson, an economist for the Reagan administration's Council of Economic Advisers, the small price increase from such an invasion would amount to only one-half of 1 percent of U.S. GDP.[17] Economists from across the political spectrum—including James Tobin, Milton Friedman, and William Niskanen—agreed with Henderson's analysis and concluded that such small economic effects did not justify a war.[18]

Ironically, the amount of oil that Saddam Hussein probably could have economically withheld from the world market after conquering Kuwait, the UAE, and Saudi Arabia was less than the amount of oil actually lost from the international boycott of Iraqi oil exports.[19] The destruction of Kuwait oil wells during the Gulf War took even more production off-line. Ultimately, Western intervention to keep oil flowing most likely had the effect of reducing supplies from what they would have been even in the worst case of Iraqi aggression. Moreover, no evidence indicates that Saddam planned to overrun Saudi Arabia and the UAE after he conquered Kuwait.

Iraq regarded Kuwait as an artificial creation of the West, one that ignored the region's culture and politics, and it had claimed the territory of that nation as early as June 1961 (the date when Kuwait became independent from Britain).[20]

Some argue that if Saddam invaded Saudi Arabia today, he might disregard economic considerations and withhold large amounts of oil to punitively price oil higher than the market would normally allow (an unlikely scenario after his economy has already been devastated by economic sanctions and the Gulf War). As noted earlier, in the long term, oil conservation, development of alternative fuel sources, and increased oil production elsewhere would render such a policy suicidal—especially for the new "owner" of the world's largest oil reserves. Even in that extremely unlikely case, the United States would still retain the option of privately threatening massive air strikes to compel Baghdad to return to an economically rational policy. If needed, forces based in the United States, aircraft carriers and U.S.-based bombers, could still deploy to the gulf region. One must question spending fifty billion dollars per year on forces to fight a second major theater conflict—and keeping some of those forces or their equipment regularly deployed to the Persian Gulf region—in anticipation of an improbable threat to the oil supply.[21]

Commentators who fear that Iran could close the Strait of Hormuz, a strategic choke point in the Persian Gulf through which a high volume of oil passes, fail to consider that the Iranians use the strait to ship their own commerce, especially their major export, oil. As in Iraq, the life's blood of the Iranian economy is the hard currency earned from oil exports (Iran gets 80 percent of such earnings from oil).[22] In short, the economies of Iraq, Iran, and other Middle Eastern oil exporters depend more on exporting oil (oil exports as a percentage of total exports) than the economics of the West depend on importing it (imports of oil as a percentage of total imports). Thus, Iran and Iraq have no incentive to stop the flow of oil.

Contrary to conventional wisdom, in the post–Cold War world neither the Korean Peninsula nor the Persian Gulf is of vital strategic interest to the United States. The potential adversaries of North Korea and Iraq or Iran—South Korea and the GCC states together, respectively—now have economies that are much larger than those of the rogue states. Those rich states should defend themselves instead of relying on U.S. power. North Korea, Iraq, and Iran all are destitute and have economies that are less than 1 percent of U.S. GDP. Those nations are half a world away from the United States. In most instances, they pose no threat to America's vital interests. The one threat that they might pose—obtaining proliferated weapons of mass destruction (proliferation is hard to prevent) and attacking U.S. territory with them—is likely to be exacerbated by an interventionist U.S. foreign policy.

Defending Values

Some commentators believe that the United States also has an interest in "defending" its "values."[23] Of course, that line of argument really means using military force to enshrine U.S. values overseas. Commentators who use such reasoning would employ armed force to defend other democracies or allies, refashion failed states in the U.S. image, promote a more peaceful international system, and prevent "genocide."

The need for the United States to defend other democracies is questionable. In Europe, East Asia, and the Middle East, U.S. allies (many of them democracies) are much wealthier than their potential rivals. Like South Korea and the Persian Gulf states, they are very capable of financing their own defense against weaker opponents.

Using armed force to "nation build" in failed states has a history of failure (for example, the poor results in Haiti, Somalia, Bosnia, and Kosovo). Americans, usually coming from half a world away, have little familiarity with long-standing and often intractable local problems causing conflict. In addition, the American military and civilian relief agencies have limited resources and attention spans to deal with such deep-seated problems. Civilian relief agencies have enough to do in relatively peaceful areas of the world without expecting the U.S. military to facilitate humanitarian aid in war zones by fighting its way in and strong-arming uncooperative belligerents to stop fighting. More important, the American public has limited patience for U.S. military involvement in "social work" missions.

It is difficult to see how the United States is promoting a more peaceful international system by constantly waging brushfire wars around the globe. In Kosovo, U.S.-led NATO attacked a sovereign nation without provocation and without a U.N. Security Council resolution declaring a threat to peace. Constantly making war to achieve peace is a dubious undertaking; if a peaceful international order is desired, the United States, as the most powerful nation, should set a good example. Instead of conducting a military crusade to remold the world in the U.S. image, the nation should set an example as a beacon of liberty and peaceful conduct.

But some would say that the United States is morally obligated to use force to stop ethnic cleansing or genocide around the world. First, the term "genocide" can be manipulated by any interest group or nation that wants to pressure the United States into taking military action. The term is often used when it is not warranted by the severity of the situation. Second, military action can actually exacerbate the killing. A despot has nothing to lose once the threat of military action is actually implemented. For example, when NATO began bombing Serbia and Kosovo, Slobodan Milosevic accelerated his ethnic cleansing (the numbers killed were not sufficient to call his human-rights violation "genocide"). Third, if the United States believes that genocide is actually being committed, the U.S. government could sell or give weapons quickly to the victims so that they could fight back—rather than commit American forces to the conflict.

Instead of being defended by intervention in brushfire wars overseas, American values are undermined by involvement in such conflicts. Threatening or attacking other nations that have not threatened or attacked the United States undermines the rule of law, American principles, and the Constitution. Furthermore, before conducting non-defensive military actions overseas, recent presidents have maintained that they did not need to ask Congress for a declaration of war or some other form of authorization. The Constitution clearly requires such an authorization, but the constitutional order has been so undermined that U.S. presidents openly flaunt the requirement.[24] Wars also undermine the constitutional system by eroding civil liberties as new laws are passed and existing laws are more strictly enforced to ensure domestic security. In some cases, wars have caused dissent to be curtailed and citizens to be incarcerated for no valid reason (for instance, the interment of Japanese-Americans in camps during World War II).

To safeguard American values and the Constitution, the United States should intervene only as a last resort, when its vital interests are at stake. In this way, the nation can preserve a constitutional order that is the envy of the world and at the same time be a beacon of liberty. Allowing other countries to accept the successful U.S. model voluntarily is more effective and comports more with American values than launching military crusades to foist those values on unwilling recipients.

CONCLUSION

A list of specific U.S. vital interests has been offered here. Such a list has not been developed by any U.S. administration during the decade following the Cold War (or prior to that time, for that matter). An assessment of truly vital U.S. interests is long overdue. Those vital interests entail protecting U.S. citizens, territory, and institutions; preventing a hegemonic great power from dominating regions of high economic or technological output (Europe and East Asia); and ensuring that no country or group can interdict U.S. trade on the high seas or prevent U.S. use of space for commercial and military purposes. The principal threats to those vital interests will now be identified.

NOTES

1. Ted Galen Carpenter, *A Search for Enemies* (Washington, D.C.: Cato Institute, 1992), p. 168.

2. Todd Sandler and Keith Hartley, *The Political Economy of NATO* (Cambridge: Cambridge Univ. Press, 1999), p. 4.

3. The White House, *A National Security Strategy for a Global Age* (Washington, D.C.: The White House, 2000), p. 4 [hereafter referred to as National Security Strategy].

4. Ibid.

5. Dilip Hiro, *The Longest War: The Iran-Iraq Military Conflict* (New York: Routledge, 1991), p. 57.

6. Jeremy Black, *War and the World: Military Power and the Fate of Continents, 1450–2000* (New Haven, Conn.: Yale Univ. Press, 1998), p. 245.

7. Eugene Gholz and Daryl G. Press, "The Effects of Wars on Neutral Countries: Why It Doesn't Pay to Preserve the Peace," *Security Studies* 10, no. 4 (forthcoming).

8. Doug Bandow, *Tripwire: Korea and U.S. Foreign Policy in a Changed World* (Washington, D.C.: Cato Institute, 1996), pp. 10–11.

9. National Defense University, *1997 Strategic Assessment* (Washington, D.C.: N.D.U., 1997), p. 104.

10. Lawrence Korb, "Start with Logic to Put the Pentagon on a Businesslike Footing; Defense: The Highly Touted Cost-Cutting Approach, Such as Base Closures, Skips the Essential Management Mission," *Los Angeles Times*, November 25, 1997, p. B-7.

11. National Defense University, *1997 Strategic Assessment*, p. 94.

12. Ibid.

13. Jerry Taylor, "Oil: Not Worth the Fight," *Journal of Commerce*, September 1, 1998, p. 4A.

14. Jerry Taylor, "No Need to Panic over Oil Prices," *National Review*, September 14, 2000, p. 1.

15. David R. Henderson, "The Myth of Saddam's Oil Stranglehold," in *America Entangled: The Persian Gulf Crisis and Its Consequences*, ed. Ted Galen Carpenter (Washington, D.C.: Cato Institute, 1991), pp. 42–43.

16. William A. Niskanen, "Oil, War, and the Economy," in *America Entangled*, ed. Carpenter, p. 54.

17. Henderson, p. 41.

18. Ibid., p. 44; and Niskanen, p. 54.

19. See Henderson, p. 43; and Michael E. Canes, "How Oil Markets Respond to Supply Disruptions," in *America Entangled*, ed. Carpenter, p. 47.

20. Bruce Watson, Bruce George, Peter Tsouras, and B. L. Cyr, *Military Lessons of the Gulf War* (London: Green Hills Books, 1991), pp. 15–16.

21. Korb, p. B-7.

22. Gawat Bahgat, "Oil Security in the New Millennium: Geo-Economy vs. Geo-Strategy," *Strategic Review* 26, no. 4 (Fall 1998), p. 25.

23. A prominent example of that line of reasoning is contained in Stanley Hoffman, *World Disorders: Troubled Peace in the Post–Cold War Era* (Lanham, Md.: Rowan and Littlefield, 1998), p. 147.

24. Stanley Kober, "Reclaiming the War Power," in *Cato Handbook for Congress, 106th Congress* (Washington, D.C.: Cato Institute, 1999), pp. 511–518.

3

Threats to U.S. Vital Interests

Serious military threats to U.S. vital interests have diminished dramatically since the end of the Cold War. A good summary statement of the threat environment currently facing the United States comes from an unlikely source—the National Defense University's *1998 Strategic Assessment: Engaging Power for Peace*:

The United States now enjoys a secure and promising position in the world, because of its economic, technological, and military strengths. The other most successful nations are its closest friends; its few enemies are comparatively weak, isolated, and swimming against the current of the information age.[1]

A similar assessment comes from President Bill Clinton's *A National Security Strategy for a Global Age*:

As we enter the new millennium, we are blessed to be citizens of a country enjoying record prosperity, with no deep divisions at home, no overriding external threats abroad, and history's most powerful military ready to defend our interests around the world.[2]

A more detailed assessment of the current threat to the three categories of U.S. vital interests will now be provided.

THE THREAT TO U.S. CITIZENS, TERRITORY, AND INSTITUTIONS

Because the United States has vast oceans as moats on the east and west and friendly, weak neighbors on the north and south, it is virtually immune from invasion. Even when conducted over a small body of water, an amphibious assault is one of the most risky and complex military actions—consider, for example, the allied assault on Normandy across the English Channel in 1944. Any aggressor force would have vastly greater difficulty conducting an amphibious assault with its supply lines extended over thousands of miles of ocean, especially if the defender has a reasonably capable navy to intercept the amphibious task force before it can launch an assault.

Of course, an attack from the air—either by missile or aircraft—is possible. The Japanese bombed the U.S. Pacific outpost of Hawaii in 1941. Yet very few nations have the long-range aircraft or missiles needed to strike the United States. In the nuclear age, those nations would be committing suicide to launch such an attack against the United States. The United States has the most capable nuclear force in the world and would be likely to use it if its territory were attacked. The U.S. nuclear force should be sufficient to deter any such attack. Thus, a corollary of the first goal should be to maintain a safe, reliable, and adequate, nuclear deterrent. The United States should also maintain the advanced air defense system provided by the North American Aerospace Defense (NORAD) command.

Russian Nuclear Attack

Even during the Cold War, the major threat was not from invasion but from a long-range nuclear attack by the Soviet Union using aircraft or missiles. With 6,000 to 7,500 warheads, the Russians still have approximate strategic nuclear parity with the United States. In addition, they have 22,000 tactical nuclear warheads—almost double the number in the U.S. arsenal.[3]

However, even if the Strategic Arms Reduction Talks II (START II) treaty never enters into force, the danger of an intentional Russian nuclear attack on the United States has greatly diminished in the post–Cold War era. Whether or not START II is implemented (reducing each side's nuclear warheads to 3,000 to 3,500) or whether or not even lower warhead totals are enshrined in a START III agreement (2,000 to 2,500 warheads), many analysts believe the Russians will be forced by extreme financial pressures to reduce their nuclear arsenal to a relatively small number of warheads (1,000 or less). Such pressures would also allow Russia to modernize its nuclear arsenal only slowly. In late 1997 the Russian military began deploying the Topol M-2 (SS-27) mobile intercontinental ballistic missile

(ICBM).[4] But Russia will probably be able to afford to produce the missile only in small numbers.

In fact, after the Cold War, the more likely threat is from an accidental or unauthorized launch caused by a deterioration of the Russian command and control system. With the breakup of the Soviet Union, the Russian early-warning system has unraveled significantly. An accidental launch almost occurred in 1995, when the Russians mistook a scientific rocket launched from Norway for an incoming nuclear attack. For the first time, the briefcase housing Russia's nuclear codes was activated.[5] Fortunately, the low level of tension between Russia and the United States in the early post–Cold War era contributed to a restrained response by Boris Yeltsin. A 1997 agreement between Russia and the United States to share early-warning data should help reduce the chances of an accidental launch. Given the potential for computer glitches at the turn of the millennium, the United States shared early-warning data to avoid a repeat of the incident in 1995. Such sharing of data is to be made permanent by establishing a joint early-warning center in Moscow. Nevertheless, the United States might want to do more. The United States may want to provide a limited amount of assistance to help the Russians repair their early-warning system. In addition, a limited, ground-based national missile defense could provide the United States with some insurance against any small Russian accidental launch.

An unauthorized launch against the United States from a rogue military commander or regional leader in Russia is possible but less probable. More than likely, such a rogue leader would use the missiles to extort the Russian central government (for example, into approving the secession of the region) rather than to intimidate the United States.

Chinese Nuclear Attack

The threat of a Chinese nuclear attack—either intentional or accidental or unauthorized—is also remote. China has about twenty intercontinental ballistic missiles and one ballistic missile submarine with twelve shorter intermediate-range submarine-launched ballistic missiles (SLBMs).[6] (The Chinese are planning to add eight more ICBMs to this force.) The Chinese air force has no long-range strategic bombers. In total, the Chinese could deliver about twenty warheads onto U.S. soil, compared to the 6,000 to 7,500 that the United States could deliver onto Chinese territory. That small Chinese force is a minimal deterrent, designed to strike enemy cities (instead of hardened military targets). By threatening nuclear retaliation, China aims to dissuade other nations from threatening to use, or using, nuclear weapons.

Compared with U.S. and Russian nuclear forces, China's nuclear deterrent is tiny, vulnerable, and primitive; it is much less sophisticated even than the French and British nuclear arsenals.[7] China has avoided competing in the arms race in long-range missiles between Russia and the United States.[8] Also, China has never shown an interest in developing a preemptive first-strike capability—that is, large numbers of missiles armed with multiple warheads. China's ICBMs are liquid fueled and are not yet deployed with multiple warheads (the Chinese have, however, tested missiles with multiple warheads). According to sources in the intelligence community and the Department of Defense, China's forces—unlike American and Russian nuclear forces—are not on ready alert. The warheads and propellant are stored separately from the missiles, making the missiles difficult to fire rapidly on warning of attack. About forty-eight hours would be needed to assemble and fuel the missiles before launching them. (An accidental launch, therefore, is also very unlikely.) Therefore, a large portion of China's land-based nuclear deterrent is vulnerable to a first strike.

Even China's lone ballistic missile submarine (another is under construction) is vulnerable to a first strike, because most of its time is spent at the dock dealing with technical problems. Currently, when the submarine is in port, its intermediate-range missiles cannot reach the United States. Even when the submarine is out to sea, it may be somewhat vulnerable, because the limited range of its missiles requires patrol stations that are closer to the United States than if missiles of intercontinental range were used. Those longer-range missiles—as well as new types of submarines—are under development, but whether they will be any more successful is a question. The Chinese have never really mastered the technical challenges of launching missiles from a submerged submarine.[9]

In short, China's small nuclear deterrent is a defensive force that does not present the American homeland with a substantial threat of an intentional offensive first strike or an accidental launch. Moreover, an unauthorized launch of Chinese missiles is unlikely, for the same reason that an unauthorized launch of Russian missiles is improbable.

A furor was generated by Congressman Christopher Cox and his committee over the possibility that China had been able to obtain data on the small, accurate W88 nuclear warhead through espionage. Yet just because China has data on the small warhead—which can be used to kill hardened military targets and to build mobile missiles—does not mean that the Chinese will be successful in manufacturing it.[10] Even if the Chinese can duplicate it, they would need to change their nuclear doctrine (from attacking cities to attacking military targets) and drastically increase numbers of warheads to take full advantage of the technology. If the United States continues to meddle regularly in East Asia, China may have more temptation to do just that, to deter U.S. intervention. But the Chinese learned a lesson from the collapse of the Soviet Union—in part caused by its excessive military spending—and therefore will probably wish to avoid an expensive nuclear arms race with the United States (see the subsequent section on the conventional threat to East Asia for evidence of China's reluctance to enter an arms race).

The fielding by China of a road-mobile ICBM may not be a totally negative development. Although giving nuclear technology to a potential rival is not usually a good idea, there may be a silver lining here. During the Cold War, an invulnerable nuclear force was regarded as a factor enhancing stability. During a crisis, a vulnerable force was thought to increase the likelihood that a nation would feel it had to use its nuclear weapons or lose them. The small Chinese ICBM force is currently very vulnerable to an enemy first strike. A road-mobile ICBM would make the Chinese force more survivable and could enhance nuclear stability during a crisis.

Some improvements to the Chinese nuclear force are likely, especially if the United States builds a missile defense that erodes the effectiveness of the small Chinese nuclear force. But road-mobile ICBMs that make China's nuclear arsenal more survivable and multiple warheads that make China's weapons more effective against U.S. defenses are only improvements to a long-range nuclear force that can already strike the United States.

Threats from Rogue States

Policy makers take for granted that the United States should attempt to prevent the proliferation of weapons of mass terror (nuclear, biological, chemical, and missile technologies) to additional countries. In particular, a nuclear or biological weapon—if deployed effectively—could cause hundreds of thousands of casualties. Yet the spread of those weapons to some nations is more of a threat to U.S. security than is proliferation to others. In addition, despite all efforts to stem such proliferation, countries that are willing to invest time and resources are likely to obtain such capabilities if they truly want them.

Some Proliferation Is Worse than Others

The United States should try to manage proliferation rather than try in vain to prevent it. The furor in U.S. foreign policy circles caused by India's and Pakistan's conducting nuclear tests and becoming declared nuclear powers was an overreaction. The U.S. foreign policy community seemed shocked that Washington had failed to prevent the unpreventable. Prior to the tests, those two nations had had well-known nuclear aspirations; India had already conducted a nuclear test in the 1970s. Although the increased threat of nuclear war on the Asian subcontinent was not a welcome development, it did not directly threaten U.S. security. Unlike the rogue states that want or have weapons of mass destruction (Iran, Iraq, Syria, Libya, and North Korea), neither India nor Pakistan is hostile to the United States. Pakistan is developing nuclear weapons to respond to India's nuclear program, and India is developing them to respond to its regional rivalry with Pakistan and to China's nuclear weapons. In the absolute worst case, the nuclear fallout from a limited nuclear war between India and either Pakistan or China would cover South Asia and Southeast Asia. To reduce the chances of such a conflict, the United States should focus its efforts on mediating disputes between India and Pakistan or India and China, and helping them to develop or refine secure nuclear command and control procedures, confidence-building measures (such as a hotline), and nuclear doctrine.

One reason that the United States retains a military presence in, and an extended nuclear deterrent over, Europe and East Asia is so that other nations (particularly Germany, Japan, South Korea, and Taiwan) will not feel threatened enough to produce their own nuclear weapons. Yet all of those nations would most likely be responsible nuclear powers. Initially, the neighbors of Japan and Germany might be worried about them becoming nuclear powers, but that fear would fade over time. Other nations in those regions would eventually realize that other great powers would probably pose a bigger threat than Japan or Germany (China and Russia, respectively). Those two former axis powers have learned their lessons from the devastation they experienced in World War II. Over fifty years after World War II ended, they still have pacifistic tendencies and are reluctant to commit troops overseas even under the auspices of international action. Because Japan is the only nation ever to be attacked by nuclear weapons, it might be reluctant to develop them even if the U.S. military presence and extended deterrent were removed.

With the much lower threat environment in a post–Cold War world, it no longer makes sense for the United States to extend its nuclear umbrella over those countries. In a world with no superpower rival, why should the United States hold its own society at risk to protect those wealthy nations? For example, is it really worth putting Los Angeles at risk to defend Taiwan from China? Conservatives may pound their chests and insist that the United States must not appease China, but they must answer that fundamental question. The smart answer is "no." The same conclusion can be reached for the defense of other affluent nations.

Proliferation to Rogue States

Proliferation of nuclear, biological, chemical, missile, and information-warfare technology to rogue states is more serious but may not be preventable. Despite international treaties, suppliers groups, inspections, and military action designed to retard such proliferation, the diffusion of technology can only be slowed. About twenty-five nations—some of which have been regarded as outlaw states (for example, Iran, Iraq, Syria, Libya, and North Korea)—have programs to develop nuclear, biological, or chemical weapons. More than twenty countries are developing ballistic missile programs that could carry such weapons. In particular, Iran and North Korea have the greatest potential to develop missiles that can strike the continental United States. The computer technology needed to disrupt key infrastructure in the United States—for example, the stock market, electric power grids, water treatment plants, air traffic—is available worldwide.

International regimes such as the Nuclear Nonproliferation Treaty (NPT), Nuclear Suppliers Group, the Chemical Weapons Convention (CWC), Biological and Toxin Weapons Convention (BWC), and the Australia Group have been created to control the spread of weapons of mass destruction (WMD) and the materials, equipment, and technologies used in making them.[11] But enforcing the provisions of such agreements has proved difficult; nations and companies have flouted the provisions. According to William Perry, a former secretary of defense, and Ashton Carter, a former assistant secretary of defense for International Security Policy, "Chemical, biological, and ballistic missile programs have proliferated widely despite efforts to establish global regimes of restraint through the Chemical Weapons Convention, the Biological Weapons Convention, and the Missile Technology Control Regime."[12] Carter further notes that "export controls alone cannot prevent proliferation," because determined leaders like Saddam Hussein can "home grow their weapons of mass destruction or get them from other countries."[13] Historically, enforcement of the economic embargoes has been difficult, because exporters that covertly evade such measures can earn high profits. That maxim is especially true when the materials, equipment, and technologies are widely available—as is the case for the production of chemical or biological weapons. According to the Senate Governmental Affairs Committee, such export control regimes "can only slow the spread of WMD . . . technology."[14]

Significant proliferation of WMD technologies, especially for biological and chemical technologies, will occur despite the best efforts to prevent it. Biological and chemical weapons can be easily and inexpensively produced, using readily obtainable raw materials and technologies. There are so many commercial facilities capable of making chemical and biological weapons in the world that such production would be easy to hide. Thus, intrusive inspections of commercial businesses under the auspices of the international agreements provide a false sense of security, while at the same time forcing innocent businesses to expose their industrial secrets to competing nations.[15] The loss of industrial information could be especially devastating for biotechnology and pharmaceutical companies.[16]

A Case Study in Failure: Preventing Proliferation to Iraq

The intense interest of the international community and the most relentless inspections in history have been focused on Iraq's WMD programs. The spotlight has been much greater than that arising from the normal enforcement of the international agreements. Even if the suspended inspections are resumed, the international community will never be assured that all of Saddam Hussein's weapons and the facilities needed to make them have been uncovered and destroyed. (In fact, the only reason the international community knew about Saddam's biological-weapons program was that his son-in-law defected and revealed its existence.)[17] Despite the extensive efforts to determine the location of Iraqi weapon stockpiles and production facilities, information is far from complete. "Put bluntly, we don't really know what Iraq has. And that's the heart of the problem," said Charles Duelfer, once deputy chief of the UN Special Commission in charge of inspecting suspected Iraqi sites.[18] (For example, biological weapons can be manufactured quickly and hidden, and they can be destroyed quickly if in danger of being found by inspectors.) Even military action—that is, bombing—is unlikely to wipe out Iraq's chemical and biological weapons labs, which are small, mobile, and easily hidden (for example, in hospitals and fertilizer plants).[19]

In the unlikely event that the international community did succeed in destroying all existing stockpiles and facilities, Saddam could produce more agents, using readily available commercial technologies, after the inspectors left.[20] Gen. Henry Shelton, chairman of the Joint Chiefs of Staff, has admitted how easy it would be for Iraqi technicians to transform a hospital, a veterans clinic, or a fertilizer plant into a facility for making anthrax or mustard gas weapons: "You can convert one of them quickly and resume making chemical or biological weapons. One day he's making fertilizer, the next day chemical [weapons] and the next day fertilizer."[21]

If Saddam can still conduct those weapons programs under such close scrutiny, other rogue nations, and terrorist groups, are likely to be even more successful in doing so. Even if inspectors became permanent fixtures in Iraq, the international community does not have the energy or resources to conduct such inspections in every nation that it suspects of developing, or of harboring terrorists that are developing, chemical or biological weapons.

Although the United States is obsessed with its ill-fated attempt—through ineffective economic sanctions, weapons inspections, and military attacks—to compel Iraq to give up its quest for weapons of mass terror, other rogue states have many of the same capabilities. The United States does not have the time, resources, or will to use the same coercive techniques to corral the other rogue states. The U.S. government claims more urgency in the case of Iraq because Saddam Hussein has actually used such weapons. But Libya used chemical weapons during its intervention in Chad's civil war during the 1980s, the Soviet Union employed them in Afghanistan during the same period, and Egypt did so in Yemen in the 1960s.[22] Certainly the other despotic rogue states might have as little compunction about using weapons of mass terror against their neighbors. It is difficult to see how Iraq is unique among the rogue states in this regard. The United States seems to focus on Iraq because of an emotional animus that arose from the Persian Gulf War.

The Demise of the Soviet Union: Proliferation Made Easier

Because of the relatively tight controls on nuclear material (enriched uranium or plutonium), a rogue state or terrorist group would have more difficulty acquiring fissionable materials to build a nuclear device than obtaining the more readily available materials and equipment for chemical and biological weapons. With the breakup of the Soviet Union, however, it has become easier to obtain both fissile material and nuclear technology. According to William Potter, director of the Center for Non-Proliferation Studies at the Monterey Institute of International Studies, "The former Soviet Union's nuclear weapons and material stockpile is at risk, and America is extraordinarily vulnerable to terrorists employing weapons of mass destruction."[23]

Poor economic conditions in the former republics of the USSR, lax security at dozens of facilities with nuclear material, poor accounting and control of fissionable material, and efforts by organized crime to profit from the smuggling of such material all make it more likely that terrorists could get nuclear-related items. Russian nuclear scientists, engineers, and technicians, facing drastic drops in income, could profit from the sale of nuclear materials and know-how. Experts have warned that gangs in Russia have tried to steal enriched uranium and smuggle it out of the country.[24] According to a letter from the Russian ambassador to the United Nations, Sergey Lavrov, to Secretary General Kofi Annan, the world community has more than once encountered cases of "leakage" of nuclear components.[25] Customs officers in Uzbekistan confiscated ten lead-lined containers with enough radioactive material to make dozens of crude radiological weapons (conventional weapons used to spread radioactive material), which could have contaminated large areas. The smuggled material was destined for Pakistan, and U.S. government officials were afraid that it may have been headed for anti-American terrorist groups funded and trained by Osama bin Laden. In 1995, Chechens planted a radiological bomb in a Moscow park.[26]

Proliferation of Information-Warfare Technology

According to Senator Jon Kyl, lawmakers have learned in classified briefings that foreign groups are increasingly capable of conducting information warfare against the United States.[27] Arnaud de Borchgrave, of the Center for Strategic and International Studies, has noted, "Things like logic bombs and worms are the new arsenal in a new geopolitical calculus that enables the non-states, and even individuals, to take on a superpower."[28]

The Defense Science Board's Task Force on Information Warfare maintains that "information warfare is also relatively cheap to wage, offering a return on investment for resource-poor adversaries. The technology required to mount attacks is relatively simple and ubiquitous."[29] Adm. Mike McConnell, former director of the National Security Agency, agrees that all of the attack tools needed can be downloaded from the Internet. He asserts that there is a "tremendous, richly robust hacker group that shares all these techniques" used for penetrating computer systems. In addition, he notes that commonly available Silicon Graphics work stations make very capable platforms for cyber attacks.[30] A recent attack by hackers on eleven defense computers is believed to have been the most organized assault on such military systems ever. Although authorities believe that the attack was initiated by vandals, not terrorists, they noted that the hackers used software that was widely available.[31]

Unlike other terrorist attacks, information warfare could be carried out safely from the other side of the world. The U.S. intelligence community believes that attacks from other parts of the world have already victimized U.S. banking and financial information systems. Some electronic transactions have embedded attack codes designed to cause havoc in the markets.[32] The London *Times* reported that several London financial institutions had paid up to $400 million to extortionists, who had used logic bombs (software programs that cause systematic errors) to demonstrate that they could destroy the global operations of those institutions.[33]

A Changed Strategic Environment for a Superpower

In sum, rogue states either possess or can obtain weapons of mass terror (as can many other nations). Such weapons are the great equalizer in the post–Cold War era. No longer will the world's only superpower be able to intervene in many parts of the world without fear of retaliation. States such as Iran, Iraq, North Korea, Libya, and Syria could deter U.S. intervention in their parts of the world by threatening American forces with attacks by weapons of mass terror. Although it is unlikely that any of the rogue nations yet have long-range ballistic missiles that can deliver such powerful weapons to U.S. territory, they will probably obtain them in the future. (The Department of Defense has admitted that North Korea is closer to that end than U.S. intelligence agencies had originally forecast.) Even now, those countries might attack U.S. territory with those weapons, using shorter-range missiles launched from an aircraft or ship, or by sponsoring a terrorist strike. (Terrorists could bomb a U.S. nuclear reactor or detonate a crude nuclear bomb carried in a truck or ship; they could use a crop-dusting aircraft or a rooftop sprayer to spread deadly chemical or biological agents; or they could hack into vital computer systems that control the U.S. stock market or power or telecommunications grids.) Even a superpower might find it hard to deter such nearer-term threats. Those attacks—unlike long-range missile launches that can be traced to the territory of their country of origin by U.S. infrared satellites—may not be readily attributable to a particular country. Thus, retaliation against, and therefore deterrence of, a perpetrator is rendered more difficult than in the case of a long-range missile launch.

With rogue states and even terrorist groups possessing or attempting to obtain weapons of mass terror, the strategic environment of the United States has changed dramatically. Now, even the weakest members of the international system might bring a superpower to its knees. Yet, the United States continues an interventionist foreign policy developed during the Cold War, when it responded worldwide in a tit-for-tat manner to the moves of a rival superpower. Intervention in many conflicts overseas—which no longer even remotely affect U.S. vital interests (if they ever did)—actually harms U.S. security, by creating hostility toward the United States among states and groups that are most likely to launch an attack on U.S. forces or territory with weapons of mass terror. Instead of trying to prevent the inevitable diffusion of technologies of mass terror, the United States should concentrate on managing such proliferation by restraining its own military policy to remove many of the motivations for rogue nations to obtain such weapons and use them in attacks against the United States. Although not always the primary factor spurring developing nations to attempt to obtain weapons of mass destruction and long-range missiles to deliver them, the threat of U.S. intervention in their region is an important contributing factor. Even a former army chief of staff of India, a nation that has no real quarrel with the United States, noted that the Gulf War showed that the lack of Iraqi nuclear weapons allowed U.S. intervention.[34] After the U.S.-led air campaign in Kosovo and Serbia, the North Koreans—fearful of U.S. military intervention against them—expressed a reluctance to give up their long-range missile program.

Thus, an interventionist foreign policy—through which the U.S. foreign policy community derives prestige from the nation's status as a superpower—actually undermines the security of U.S. citizens (both at home and abroad), territory, and institutions. Safeguarding those interests should be the first priority of any nation's foreign and national security policies.

In short, the threat to U.S. citizens, territory, and institutions from an invasion using conventional military means is virtually nil. The danger of an intentional launch of nuclear weapons by China is low, unless the United States augments security guarantees to Taiwan (an emotional hot button for China). The way Chinese nuclear forces are configured, an accidental launch of China's nuclear weapons is unlikely. An intentional Russian nuclear attack is unlikely, unless continued NATO expansion and U.S. military exercises around the Russian periphery cause a substantial rise in U.S.-Russian tensions. The possibility of a Russian accidental launch, once a real threat, is being reduced somewhat by American sharing of early-warning data to compensate for the abysmal state of the Russian early-warning system. The United States could further reduce the chances of a mishap by providing limited assistance to the Russians to fix their early-warning capabilities; the consequences of such a launch could be reduced by building a limited, ground-based national missile defense. The likelihood of an unauthorized launch by China or Russia against the United States is low.

The use of proliferated weapons of mass terror by rogue states and terrorist groups is one of the few potential threats to U.S. citizens, territory, and institutions in the post–Cold War world. Terrorist attacks (using means of delivery other than missiles) are the greatest threat, followed by attacks (from terrorists or rogue states) with short-range ballistic and cruise missiles fired from a ship off the U.S. coast, followed in turn by long-range missile attacks from rogue states.

In the future, as rogue nations obtain nuclear weapons and the long-range missiles needed to deliver them to U.S. territory, the threat of an accidental launch from those nations will increase. Their missiles may be aimed at the United States and they may not have well developed command and control systems, security systems, or nuclear doctrine. That situation may be the single best reason for the United States to develop a limited national missile defense.

THREATS TO MAJOR REGIONS OF U.S. INTEREST

Care must be taken when moving out from the core of U.S. security policy—protecting U.S. citizens, territory, and institutions—to an extended defense perimeter. As noted, the hyperextended defense perimeter that the United States has pursued, during the Cold War and now after it, could actually reduce U.S. security by providing few gains and much danger—by potentially motivating rogue states and terrorist groups to attack the United States with weapons of mass terror. Now that the Cold War has ended, conflicts in most regions do not affect U.S. vital interests and do not warrant U.S. intervention.

There are overseas regions that matter to U.S. security. If an aggressive great power threatened to overrun an entire region of high economic output and great technological sophistication—that is, East Asia or Western Europe—it might use those added resources to intimidate, coerce, or attack the United States. Although the scenario is rare in history, it happened during World War II and the ensuing Cold War. The scenario is far less likely now.

Yet many analysts believe that the United States needs to keep military forces in Europe and East Asia to prevent the "renationalization" of defense policies by Germany and Japan and the possible reignition of strategic rivalries leading to another major conflagration in one or both of those regions. But the implication that the Germans and the Japanese are intrinsically aggressive peoples is unfair and borders on bigotry.

Germany was justifiably blamed for the start of the Second World War but may have been unfairly blamed for the First World War simply because it lost. The rise of Hitler found its roots, in part, from the harsh treatment of the Germans by Britain and France after World War I. In any event, it is possible for nations to learn from catastrophe, and Germany and Japan have done so. Those nations exhibit pacifistic tendencies that have arisen from the ashes of the total destruction they experienced in World War II. Germany has become integrated in the European Union, and both nations are well integrated into the world economy. Both are wealthy nations, with every incentive to support the status quo in their respective regions. As noted earlier, even if both nations acquired nuclear weapons, they would be more responsible nuclear powers than nations that are worth more worry—for example, such rogue states as North Korea, Iraq, and Iran.

Japan and Germany are not, and probably will not be, threats to U.S. vital interests in East Asia and Europe, respectively. U.S. micromanagement of affairs, as well as the continuing presence of U.S. forces, in those theaters is unnecessary to "keep down" those nations. Instead, those nations should be used by the United States to balance two more plausible future adversaries—China and a resurgent Russia. As the following analysis shows, however, even those more plausible threats are currently fairly weak and may not materialize.

The Threat to East Asia

In the media and academic circles, China is cited as the nation most likely to challenge the United States in Asia. But although China is a rising power, twenty to thirty years would be required to transform its bloated and obsolete military into a major threat to U.S. vital interests. That long warning time would allow the United States sufficient time to make any needed adjustments in its own defense posture.

Yet even if the Chinese economy grows by more than a whopping 8 percent per year until 2015, China's economic output would still be only $2.2 to $2.9 trillion per year. China must use that output to support a large population. In comparison, U.S. economic output in 2015 is projected to be $13.3 trillion, which must support a much smaller population.[35] China's rapid growth could eventually provide the resources to expand its military power. But analysts in Beijing have learned from the fate of the Soviet Union that excessive military spending can be dangerous for economic growth and a regime's survival.[36] A study published for the Pentagon's Office of Net Assessment, which contains translations of writings on strategic matters by Chinese military and party leaders, notes that Chinese generals even believe that the United States is plotting to cause China's collapse by forcing them into an arms race![37] Perhaps the United States should encourage that belief.

Chinese military writers state that China's greatest strategic objective is economic modernization and the realization of "comprehensive national strength."[38] Since Deng Xiaoping opened China to the outside world in the late 1970s, military modernization has been the lowest priority of the Chinese government's "four modernizations." Seth Faison of the *New York Times* summed it up best in an article on the release of China's white paper on defense: "China's military forces are still rudimentary by international standards."[39]

China's Conventional Military Capabilities

After the Gulf War, the Chinese were apparently shocked by the devastating victory of an American-led force—equipped with sophisticated electronics and weapons and using the U.S. Army's decentralized Air-Land Battle doctrine—over an Iraqi force using Soviet equipment and heavily centralized battle doctrine. During the war in Kosovo they were further impressed by U.S. "over-the-horizon" attacks that required no troops to be engaged on the ground.[40]

China is still trying to convert a bloated, Maoist "army of the people," oriented toward defending against ground attack from the Soviet Union, into a smaller, more mobile force possessing high-technology weapons (especially modern ships and aircraft).[41] For example, the People's Liberation Army (PLA) plans to reduce military personnel by a hundred thousand or more troops every year for the next ten years and to cut the number of fighter aircraft from 4,500 to 1,000.[42] But cutting personnel is much easier than funding and developing high-technology weaponry and the doctrine to use it. Most of the PLA leadership is made up of ground force field commanders with no experience in modern warfare, especially the high tech air, naval, nuclear, and precision weapons needed for power projection.[43]

Some analysts point to rapid increases in China's defense expenditures, but that rapid rise is largely an illusion. Until recently, China's growing economy produced substantial inflation as a by-product. Although official defense spending rose 159 percent from 1986 to 1994, that huge nominal increase resulted in a real increase of a mere 4 percent per year when inflation was factored out, according to the General Accounting Office.[44] Even that figure is misleading, because it compensates for an earlier period of dramatically declining purchasing power for the Chinese military. From 1980 to 1989, although defense spending increased about 30 percent, inflation rose almost 100 percent. That disparity resulted in a substantial decline in real operating funds for the military.[45]

Furthermore, the recent increases in defense spending have been quickly absorbed in operating and maintaining the enormous, antiquated, and ill-trained armed forces. Much has been spent on housing, feeding, training, and paying it. Huge additional sums will be needed to buy new weapons and equipment to convert the outdated military into a modern fighting force. The Chinese government's top priority of fostering economic growth will constrain increases in funding for defense. Although much of Chinese defense spending is "off the books"—the official Chinese defense budget is around fifteen billion dollars per year—a midrange estimate of true Chinese defense spending is still only $28 billion to $36 billion per year.[46] (Recently, official defense spending has increased to offset declines in "off-the-books" military expenditures caused by the Chinese leadership's insistence that the military divest itself of its profitable commercial businesses and devote more emphasis to national security.)[47]

China's total spending on defense is roughly equivalent to what each of the medium-sized powers—Japan, France, Germany, and the United Kingdom—spend per year (but much less than the $300 billion per year that the United States spends). That amount of funding may adequately support the high-technology forces of the medium-sized powers but will not be sufficient to finance the huge task of rapidly transforming the vast and antiquated Chinese military into a modern force.

China Will Modernize Its Military Slowly

According to Lt. Col. Dennis Blasko, a former intelligence officer with the U.S. Army and the Defense Intelligence Agency,

Even though Beijing has accumulated vast foreign exchange reserves, the senior leadership has yet to divert sufficient resources from economic development to large-scale military purchases. For example, expenditures on culture, health, education, and civilian science and technology have outpaced official figures for defense spending over the past decade. It would take huge sums to buy the modern systems necessary to transform the Chinese military, which is primarily equipped with materiel based on the technology of the 1950s and 1960s, to a force based on that of the 1980s.[48]

Blasko also notes, "Over the next few years PLA forces are likely to be reduced in size while their budget is modestly increased. Such a trend will advance the modernization of selected units." He concludes that the pace of Beijing's military modernization might make its neighbors wary but that it "will not pose a significant threat to [the] major powers for some time."[49]

Indeed, China's military modernization will most likely be slow. Russell Travers, an analyst for the Defense Intelligence Agency, concludes that China "is still decades away from being able to project sufficient power to constitute a significant challenge to the U.S. military." According to Travers,

China's military is benefiting from impressive economic growth, but many Western observers have an exaggerated view of how rapidly it is developing because of inadequate appreciation of the very low starting point of the People's Liberation Army (PLA). Overall, this military is too big and too old to pose a threat to the

U.S. military any time soon; in its training and doctrine, it is decades behind its Western counterparts. Other than its potential to play missile diplomacy against its neighbors, the PLA has very limited ability to project force from its shores. Nor is China improving this force at a breakneck pace: high profile purchases of SA-10 surface-to-air missiles, SU-27 fighters, and Kilo submarines from Russia have given a misleading sense of the overall modernization rate of the Chinese military.[50]

NDU's *1997 Strategic Assessment* concurs that China's military modernization is slow and that it is decades away from being a major threat:

The PLA can inflict damage in limited campaigns against any of its immediate neighbors but is years away from being able to project sustained military force at any distance from China's borders. China lacks the capability either to produce or to purchase new systems in the quantities necessary, and the PLA in 1996 was probably two decades away from challenging or holding its own against a modern military force. . . . The effort to procure and field modern weapons is proceeding relatively slowly. The PLA is also slowly developing the doctrinal concepts required for high-technology warfare.[51]

John Schulz, a former Voice of America correspondent in East Asia and professor at the National War College, expresses similar sentiments about China's ability to project power:

Nuclear-armed China will not even be a regional conventional threat for decades to come. The PLA's long list of systemic problems, coupled with those facing China as a whole, constrain military modernization efforts in ways that may ultimately be insurmountable. "Strategic planners"—whose views are "long term"—should thus be aware that China will not be able to project and sustain offshore military operations for at least thirty years. "Strategists" who think instead in global or regional (geographic) terms can also rest easy; the PLA will be restricted to limited "quick skirmish" capability over limited ranges offshore during that time, and is already being outstripped by other regional military modernization programs.[52]

Paul Godwin, formerly of the National War College, and one of the nation's foremost experts on the Chinese military, agrees that other nations in Asia are modernizing their militaries faster than is China: "Beijing looks out on an Asia undergoing major military renovation that in many areas exceeds the PLA's current capabilities and will continue to outmatch China's programs for at least a decade."[53] Michael Richardson of the *International Herald Tribune* suggests that China is falling behind Japan, South Korea, Singapore, and Taiwan in harnessing sophisticated technology (combining computers, communications, and sensors with precision-guided weapons) to enhance its military strength, in integrating the technology into its armed forces, and in operating it effectively.[54]

A prime example of the mismatch is in tactical fighter aircraft. Anti-quated MiG-19s and MiG-21s, which make up the bulk of the Chinese air force, would most likely be blown out of the sky by the F-15s and F-16s flown by the regional powers in East Asia.[55]

China is only slowly taking steps to modernize its air force. China has purchased 74 Su-27 fighters from Russia and has a license to produce two hundred more planes locally within the next five years.[56] In 1999, China signed a contract to buy thirty to sixty Su-30 MK fighters (a more modern version of the Su-27).[57] Taiwan is already taking deliveries of more than two-hundred American F-16s and French-made Mirage 2000 aircraft. The Taiwanese also have a new indigenously produced fighter. Taiwan has one of the best-equipped militaries in East Asia.

According to a senior Western diplomat, the systems that Russia has sold China have been inferior. For example, the Su-27 fighters are not as capable as Taiwan's F-16s and Mirage 2000 aircraft. Also, unlike some of the new diesel subs being produced by Western nations, the four Russian Kilo sub-marines purchased by China do not have air-independent propulsion, which allows submarines to enhance their survivability by staying under-water for much longer periods. Also, questions arise about whether China can absorb Russian technology.[58]

As China enters the next century, only small pockets of its military will have advanced far enough to incorporate 1980s technology. Most of China's present air, ground, and sea weapons were designed in the 1940s and 1950s. Sometime after 2000, China will produce and field a fighter aircraft that has technology equivalent to that of an early-model F-16 of the 1970s. The Chinese are currently working on a tank that is equivalent to the Soviet-built T-72 of the 1970s. Although China has purchased fifty T-72 tanks from Russia, obsolete Soviet-built T-54 tanks, incorporating 1950s technology, are the backbone of the armored force. China will prob-ably not have an aircraft carrier until well into the twenty-first century.[59]

China Will Be Limited in Its Ability to Project Power

The Chinese navy cannot mount survivable, long-range, sustained op-erations. As noted earlier, for the next thirty years the Chinese will have the ability to inflict only limited damage on their neighbors, through quick skirmishes at a modest distance from China's shores. The surface ships (frigates and destroyers) that China is now building contain 1970s tech-nology. The Chinese navy possesses more than fifty surface combatants, making it the third-largest navy in the world. But China's ships have severe deficiencies in electronics, air defense, and surface-to-surface missiles. Fur-ther, the newest surface ships in the Chinese fleet are vulnerable to the modern European-built submarines purchased by South Korea and the Southeast Asian nations. Only a few boats in the large fleet of Chinese submarines are adequately maintained. The small numbers of *Sovremenny*-class destroyers and Kilo submarines that China is purchasing from Russia change the aforementioned realities only at the margins.

China has huge ground forces but few enemies on land. Tensions with past enemies—Russia, India, and Vietnam—have been reduced. Thus, the Chinese army has been given a lower priority for modernization than the navy or air force.[60] The army is essentially an excessively large infantry force that lacks adequate firepower, mobility, communications, logistical support, training, and educated recruits. It has a limited capability to conduct combined arms operations with naval and air forces. A few units of the army can take advantage of transport aircraft to strike over long distances, but most units are weak in both transport and logistical supply. Deficiencies in air refueling limit the projection of power by the air force.[61]

Despite the persistent fear that China will launch an amphibious assault on Taiwan, China lacks sufficient transportation assets to get a large invasion force across the strait to the island. (Both the strait and beaches are unsuitable for an amphibious assault.) According to Vice Adm. Thomas Wilson, director of the Defense Intelligence Agency, even by 2015 China probably will not have the large amphibious capability necessary for an invasion. Wilson stated, "When you are the attacker versus the defender in the traditional warfighting sense, you need to have a significant numerical advantage. Taiwan has got a reasonably strong military . . . and so the issue for China is how they would be able to mount the lift."[62] In addition, most rapid deployment forces (including airborne forces) are currently focused on internal security missions, and only a small contingent is adequately trained to conduct amphibious operations.[63]

The Federation of American Scientists has noted that the Chinese do not have the overwhelming odds needed to succeed in an amphibious assault on Taiwan; it concludes that they would be badly mauled. In 1944, during the invasion of Normandy, the Allied force—with 176,000 troops in three thousand landing aircraft, covered by 136 warships and superior airpower (ten thousand aircraft), and possessing better intelligence—barely made it ashore against fifty thousand Germans, who had only four hundred aircraft and no naval support. In contrast, China would have fifteen thousand troops in three hundred landing craft, sixty warships and 3,300 largely obsolete aircraft (flying far from home) against a defending army of 220,000 soldiers covered by forty warships and 490 modern fighters, flying near home.[64]

Moreover, Chinese ships have inadequate air defenses, and Taiwan has a modern air force that is being further improved. Taiwan's capable air force could probably deter a Chinese air attack spearheaded by the limited number of modern Su-27s. According to the Center for Defense Information and the Federation of American Scientists, China's air bases are poorly located for any attack on Taiwan; so only one-third of the 3,300 Chinese aircraft could participate.[65] Most of those are antiquated. In short, the PLA air force would probably be unable to wrest control of the skies over Taiwan or the Taiwan Strait from the Taiwanese air force—much less carry out a sustained bombing campaign.[66] The 150 F-16s, sixty Mirage 2000s, and new Taiwanese fighters in Taiwan's air force—as well as Patriot air defenses and sophisticated radars—could probably defeat China's force of Su-27s.[67] Without air superiority, Chinese amphibious ships or surface vessels would be "sitting ducks" in the strait.

John Roos of *Jane's Defence Weekly* notes that Taiwan's defense forces are designed to kill a Chinese amphibious force before it lands:

Taiwan's highly skilled military forces and the modern equipment they possess would exact a heavy toll—some contend an unacceptable toll—from an invading PRC force. Designed almost exclusively to thwart a trans-strait invasion, Taiwan's military might is tailored to prevent an invading force from ever reaching shore. The ROC's [Republic of China's] attack aircraft, backed by long-range army missile batteries would augment naval activities designed to keep the conflict well out to sea.[68]

According to Adm. Dennis Blair, commander of the U.S. Pacific Command, the biggest problem facing a Chinese amphibious assault across the strait "has to do with the 70 to 100 miles of open water between Taiwan and the mainland, as well as Taiwan's defenses and the slow pace of China's military modernization. . . . I think that . . . should China undertake military action to try to invade Taiwan, they would not be successful in taking it and holding it."[69] In testimony before Congress, Blair was more definite: "The PLA still lacks the capability to invade and control Taiwan. It maintains a quantitative edge in all branches of services, but does not have an adequate power-projection capability to quickly overcome Taiwan's more modern air force and inherent geographical advantages."[70]

Some analysts, desperate to see a threat, are now postulating a Chinese airborne assault on Taiwan rather than an amphibious one. In this scenario, China would begin with preemptive missile strikes that would be followed by an airborne landing in the central part of the island. After disabling major airfields with missile strikes, Chinese airborne forces would capture an airport or harbor that could be used for the delivery of supplies and reinforcements.[71]

The Chinese cannot count on their relatively inaccurate missiles to take out airfields or the Taiwanese air force on the ground. Furthermore, even if Chinese airborne forces had adequate training and transport to conduct such a daring assault, the risks of failure are high. Airborne assaults are risky enough as ancillary parts of military operations (for example, to block a retreating enemy), let alone as a key part of an invasion plan. Lightly armed airborne troops would more than likely run into stiff opposition from heavier Taiwanese reinforcements when they tried to capture an airport or harbor. In addition, the capable Taiwanese air force could interdict the shipping of forces and supplies from the mainland. Without reinforcement and resupply, the Chinese airborne forces would probably perish on Taiwan.

As noted earlier, China, aside from its ability to intimidate its neighbors with missile diplomacy, has only a limited ability to project force from the mainland and sustain it. Most Western military experts say that it will be years, if not decades, before China is a credible military threat to Taiwan.

The most likely scenario, then, is a Chinese missile attack to devastate the Taiwanese economy, terrorize the population, or disrupt the shipping lanes. China's two hundred medium-range missiles—each carrying a five-hundred-pound warhead—could inflict damage equivalent to an earthquake.[72] The attack, however, could only be sustained for a few days, and the Chinese missiles are too inaccurate to hurt significantly the Taiwanese military. Besides, the U.S. sale of the Pave Paws long-range radar to monitor ballistic missiles should provide Taiwan with an early warning of missile launches. China would probably be reluctant in any case to undertake such a missile attack, because most foreign trade and investment (including thirty billion dollars from Taiwan) would dry up and leave the Chinese economy in shambles. Besides, strategic bombardment of the civilian population and economy (for example, the Allied bombing of Japan and Germany during World War II) usually leads to increased defiance by the opponent. In the wake of any such missile strikes, Taiwan might declare independence and receive international support in doing so. The failure of China's aggressive gambit might lead to the fall of the regime in Beijing.

A Chinese naval blockade would be difficult to coordinate given the limited command, control, and communications that the Chinese navy possesses. More important, a blockade is an act of war that would put vulnerable Chinese ships at the mercy of the Taiwanese air force.[73] According to Richard Halloran, writing in the *Washington Times*, "Many naval observers believe the Chinese do not have the staying power or the logistics to sustain a blockade against a Taiwanese navy equipped with 110 frigates and fast attack missile craft and an air force flying U.S.-built F-16s, some French-made Mirage 2000s and Taiwan's own new defense fighters."[74] Despite the addition of a few Russian Kilo diesel submarines, the decrepit Chinese submarine force is probably incapable of carrying out a naval quarantine of Taiwan.

Neither missile strikes nor a blockade would achieve China's primary objective—reunification with Taiwan—but either would engender international hostility that could threaten the mainland's vital economic links with the West.[75] With such limited ability to project power, the Chinese military is best suited to defensive warfare on the mainland or in coastal regions.

China's Defense Industry Lacks Sophistication

China remains decades behind the United States (and the West generally) in key military technologies. The gap is likely to continue to grow, as U.S. yearly funding for military research and development vastly outstrips that of China. Yearly U.S. spending on military research and development is roughly equivalent to the total amount spent annually by the Chinese on defense.

China's current defense industry is incapable of designing or producing modern military equipment. Most Chinese defense production consists of upgrading foreign systems, using pre-1970s technology, and manufacturing techniques. That situation is not likely to change without enormous foreign assistance. The Chinese have a history of failure in fielding indigenous weapons—for example, the F-8 fighter and its follow-on, the F-8II.[76] Manufacturing processes that incorporate high technology are still twenty years away. According to John Frankenstein, an expert on the Chinese defense industry, "The Chinese defense industries represent a worst-case example of the problems of the Chinese state-owned enterprises—under capitalized, lagging technology, overstaffed and poorly managed."[77]

China's purchase of Russian weapons shows that the Chinese are not satisfied with their own weapons production. Yet fears of Russian arms and technology sales to China have been overblown. The Chinese have failed even to reverse-engineer Russian weapons—for example, the Su-27. Sales have been modest, because of China's budget constraints and Russia's suspicions that those weapons might eventually be used against it.[78] The Chinese have been unable to take full advantage of even those limited weapons purchases, because of poor maintenance and restricted training (meant to avoid losses).[79]

The Chinese military has been much more successful in commercial enterprises, such as international hotels, nightclubs, airlines, telecommunications, and prostitution rings. The Chinese civilian leadership has realized that such business activities impede the Chinese military's ability to fight wars and that they add to the corruption in society. In 1998, the leadership ordered the military to get out of many commercial businesses (the exceptions were "strategic" industries, such as railroads, civilian aviation, postal services, and telecommunications). Military units have used the divestiture to dump many money-losing enterprises. Retaining ownership of ten thousand profitable businesses, the Chinese military's influence over the Chinese economy still remains great. Revenue from civilian businesses was supposed to be replaced by increased military budgets, but China's growing fiscal debt precludes funding the military from the defense budget alone.[80] In short, the Chinese military will continue to be distracted by commercial ventures.

Chinese Intentions

Because of China's population, abundant resources, and rapid economic growth, it is the country most capable of aggressively challenging the United States in the twenty-first century. Whether it will do so is another matter. The United States should adopt a wait-and-see attitude (using sophisticated intelligence collection systems to monitor military developments) and refrain from creating a self-fulfilling prophecy.

Traditionally, China has not been an expansionist power. In fact, China, like the United States, was a victim of European colonialism and exploitation. The American experience under colonialism conditioned the United States to restrain its own colonial expansion. China's history of being carved up by the West might also act to restrain its territorial ambitions.

In 1995 Charles William Maynes, then editor of *Foreign Policy*, characterized China's relationship with its neighbors in the following way: "China has minor border disputes with its neighbors, but none of them seem non-negotiable."[81] In the 1960s and 1970s, China settled most of its territorial disputes peacefully (the exceptions were the war with India in 1962 and the war with the Soviet Union along the Ussuri River in 1969). Although China has not resolved its territorial disputes with India, the threat of conflict is minor, and the two countries have widened their political and economic relations. In 1996 the Chinese resolved border and territorial disputes with Russia and the Central Asian states.[82]

China's conciliatory attitude may not extend to the status of Taiwan, which China regards as an internal matter. China test-fired missiles in the Taiwan Strait in 1996 to deter Taiwan from consolidating its de facto independence and seeking greater international recognition. In 1999, China blustered when Taiwan demanded to be treated as an equal. In 2000, China threatened to invade Taiwan if reuniting the island with the mainland takes too long. As noted earlier, China would have difficulty—given the Chinese military's limited ability to project power—launching a successful amphibious invasion of Taiwan. The vulnerability of Chinese ships and the inability of the Chinese navy to coordinate air, surface, and subsurface facets of a naval blockade of the island probably rule out that option, too.

Yet Taiwan is such an emotional issue that an irrational act is possible. China's major military lever against Taiwan is its force of inaccurate surface-to-surface missiles.[83] Should it attack, defending Taiwan is not required to safeguard American vital interests. Instead, the United States should sell Taiwan a theater missile defense system, not operate a U.S. system to protect Taiwan.

In general, the United States should sell Taiwan sophisticated weapon systems to defend itself—including ships with Aegis air defense and antisubmarine warfare systems, P-3 antisubmarine warfare aircraft, and diesel submarines for coastal defense against Chinese submarines—rather than implicitly or explicitly committing itself to defend that nation.

As for the dispute over islands in the South China Sea, China probably will not readily solve it by force. The Chinese forces cannot yet attack and occupy those islands. Even if they could, they would be vulnerable to counterattack by the capable forces of other claimants to the islands. Again, U.S. vital interests are not affected by who owns the Spratlys and other small island chains in the South China Sea.

Nevertheless, China aspires to be a great power, and it will probably achieve that goal in twenty or thirty years. Even that would not necessarily be a threat to the United States. China is surrounded by other regional powers—India on the south and west, Russia on the north, and Japan and South Korea to the east. (In contrast, in the 1930s no Asian great powers existed to resist Japanese aggression. Russia was preoccupied with Germany in Europe, and the European colonial powers were overextended in Asia.) If China became more aggressive, those powers, either acting alone or in a regional alliance, could easily respond as a counterbalancing force.

The United States would need to respond as a "balancer of last resort" only if the balance of power eroded significantly in a hegemonic China's favor. Moreover, Asia is much harder to overrun than Europe, because key economic centers (Japan and Taiwan) and resources (Indonesian oil)—likely targets—are on islands. Islands are easier to defend than large tracts of land (for example, Europe). Amphibious assaults are among the most difficult military operations to conduct. But the current U.S. policy of implicitly or explicitly protecting Japan, Taiwan, and South Korea discourages those nations from developing the military capabilities needed to balance the potential capabilities of China. Also, the current overextended American security perimeter in the Western Pacific is bound to threaten China's legitimate interests at some point in the future, creating the possibility of unnecessary conflict between the two nations. The United States has no vital interest in maintaining a forward military presence in that area.

An aggressive China is not a given. As noted earlier, China's main goal appears to be rapid economic development, and achieving that objective depends heavily on foreign trade and investment to fuel growth. China will continue to have many incentives to pursue stability in East Asia as a status quo power and so preserve its international economic relationships. For example, China's increasing prosperity is based on foreign trade, and the United States alone takes one-third of its exports.[84] Some Chinese leaders already suspect that the United States is trying to contain their country; Washington should refrain from actions that intensify such suspicions. Indeed, the United States should recognize China as a great power and attempt to improve political, military, and economic relations. To do otherwise would be to create an enemy unnecessarily.

The Threat to Europe

With the end of the Cold War and the breakup of the Soviet Union, the threat to Western Europe declined dramatically. The threat to that region from conventional Russian military forces has disintegrated and would take many years to reconstitute. The now-decrepit Russian military is no longer in Central Europe, threatening the economic centers of Western Europe, but has retreated far to the east within the drastically shrunken borders of Russia.

Resources for the Russian Military Are Scarce

Much has been written about the decline of the Russian military. The defeat at the hands of ragtag Chechen fighters in 1993 and 1994 confirmed that the Russian military had sunk to a dismal state. Although performing better in the second war in Chechnya that began in 1999, the Russian military has used crude and brutal tactics and will be preoccupied with pacifying that region for years to come. The Russians were afraid to match their forces with Chechen guerrillas in close combat and relied on over-whelming, indiscriminate firepower from aircraft and artillery so that their ground forces could advance without opposition. Although the Russians may face a protracted guerrilla war, they have never developed a doctrine to fight one (despite their involvement in Afghanistan). The war in Chechnya is likely to strain the cash-starved Russian ground forces for some time; for example, all-important military training may have to be reduced.[85] In fact, spending to pacify the Chechens will likely put pressure on funding for all of Russia's armed forces.

The Russians are conducting some research and development on new weapons, but their moribund economy provides little money to buy the latest systems or to operate and maintain existing ones. Even when small quantities of relatively modern systems are fielded, they are likely to fail because of poor training, lack of operational expertise, or poor mainte-nance of equipment—as shown by the sinking of the guided missile sub-marine *Kursk*. The Russian economy, with its official GDP and industrial production cut in half, is undergoing a shrinkage comparable to that of the United States in the Great Depression.[86] The official Russian GDP is now only the size of New Jersey's and Pennsylvania's combined.[87]

Shortages of resources, personnel, and fuel permit only scant military training. For example, Russian pilots fly some twenty to forty hours per year, compared with the 150 to two hundred flown by NATO pilots. Draft evasion and low morale are rampant.[88] Officers are unpaid, desertion is common, and conscripts are without food.[89] According to then–Defense Minister Marshall Sergeyev, other than the elite Strategic Nuclear Forces and some airborne army forces, virtually no units were ready to fight in 1997; half of the aircraft in the air force could not fly.[90] Even the strategic nuclear bombers receive only 6 percent of the resources they require for training and could conduct only about 40 percent of their scheduled training missions.[91] The Russian navy can keep only one ballistic missile submarine (Russia's ultimate nuclear deterrent) each deployed in the Pacific and Arctic theaters. Because the main threats facing Russia are perceived to be from internal instability rather than from external aggression, Interior Ministry forces have been better financed (until recently) than the military.

The end of the Cold War and the breakup of the Soviet Union led to a dramatic decline in defense resources available to Moscow. Of all the regions of the world, Russia has seen the biggest decline in defense spending. In 1998, Russian defense spending was only 20 percent of the Soviet defense budget in 1989.[92] Official defense spending shrank from 30 percent of the Soviet economy to only 5 percent of the much smaller Russian economy.[93]

The breakup of the Soviet Union threw the still large Russian armed forces into chaos. Because Soviet armed forces were positioned west toward NATO during the Cold War, the best fighting units were absorbed into Ukrainian and Belarussian militaries when the Soviet Union collapsed or were dissolved as they returned from Eastern Europe. For example, only about half of the Soviet Union's combat aircraft were retained by Russia. Similarly, the best military facilities are now in Ukraine and Belarus or were abandoned in Eastern Europe.[94]

The Russians, like the Chinese, are trying to turn their obsolescent, bloated military from the bygone communist era into a smaller, more mobile force. The Russians have reduced their armed forces from 1.7 million in 1997 to about one million in 2000.[95] (According to John Steinbruner and Clifford Gaddy, even a force of that size is far larger than Russia can afford. Realistically, Russia can probably afford a military force of no more than 400,000. Such a force could not carry out traditional missions against any major military adversary.)[96] However, efforts at reforming and restructuring the Russian military, which has been based on Soviet organization and doctrine (inflexible, centrally driven command), have foundered on the generals' vested interest in keeping the status quo.

The Russian Defense Industry

The breakup of the Soviet Union fractured the defense industrial base. Armaments factories in Russia have had their supply shipments disrupted because the suppliers are in non-Russian parts of the former Soviet Union.

Most Russian defense spending is allocated to shoring up an oversized, sagging force rather than to developing and buying new equipment. Russian defense production has declined to 13 percent of its 1991 level.[97] Most military equipment produced continues to be exported. In 1998, Russia added only fifteen tanks and thirty-five ground-attack aircraft to its arsenal; it added no major surface ships. In 1999, only 30 tanks were added.[98] That situation should be compared with the Soviet Union's robust military production during the 1970s and 1980s.

Meager defense production in the post–Cold War years is contributing to a rapid aging and shrinking of the Russian military force. Obsolete weapons that are decommissioned are often not replaced. For example, roughly 70 to 75 percent of Russian tanks need to be replaced. Only 2 to 5 percent of the tank force consists of modern vehicles, and the percentage is expected to increase to only 30 percent by 2005. Of all the aircraft in the Air Force, only twenty percent are modern and only half the total are fully operational.[99] Even new systems that have a high priority can be produced only in very small quantities—for example, submarines and intercontinental ballistic missiles. Between 1990 and 1995, the number of navy ships was cut in half, and the number of naval aircraft fell by 66 percent.[100]

The Decline of the Russian Military Is Unlikely to Be Reversed Soon

According to Dmitry Trenin, a military analyst at the Carnegie Endowment in Moscow, "You simply cannot talk of the Russian armed forces as a coherent defense force."[101] Russia's conventional military capabilities will continue to erode through 2002, according to the State Department's Bureau of Intelligence and Research. State's report concluded that "offensive operation, particularly ground operations, against most neighboring countries will be difficult to impossible, depending on the adversary."[102]

Russia's declining military will take years to recover. According to Travers, "The problems confronting the Russian military are so deep and so all-encompassing that it could be decades before it could again be considered healthy." He concludes that "the future for the Russian general-purpose forces will continue to be bleak well into the next century."[103]

In short, even if its political system becomes more autocratic, Russia will take many years to become once more a military threat to Europe. Even if it does, the Europeans are fully capable of assuming the first line of defense. Unlike the early years of the Cold War, the countries of Western Europe are now wealthy. Combined, their GDP exceeds Russia's many times over; the combined economies of the nations of the European Union exceed even that of the United States. Germany, France, and the United Kingdom each has a GDP larger than that of Russia. It is questionable why the United States should be so involved in providing security for wealthy nations—particularly in the more benign post–Cold War threat environment. U.S. intervention in Bosnia after the Europeans failed to address the problem is an indicator that the United States often cares more about European security than the Europeans do.

Despite renewed rhetoric about creating a viable all-Europe military force after the war in Kosovo demonstrated the deficiencies in European militaries, most European defense budgets are declining. Wealthy Germany's budget has declined to a meager 1.6 percent of GDP. Yet Germany, with its large GDP and military, is a key country in the effort to build an all-Europe force.

The United States does have vital interests in Europe, but it can act as a balancer of last resort rather than as the first line of defense. The United States should not let rich European nations have a free ride.

Even the Threats to Nonstrategic Regions Have Declined

Earlier, I argued that the conventional wisdom about the strategic importance of the Persian Gulf and Korean Peninsula was flawed. The U.S. government tends to overstate regional threats (for example, Iraq and North Korea), because it still sees them through Cold War lenses. A rival superpower no longer exists to back surrogates or to exploit potential regional conflicts. There is no longer any danger that Middle East oil or the Korean Peninsula will be controlled by the Soviet Union. Before the Persian Gulf War, prominent economists from across the political spectrum noted that the small costs (in higher oil prices) to the U.S. economy of Saudi Arabia's potential fall did not warrant American military action. Saudi Arabia and the other oil-rich Persian Gulf states have economies that combined greatly exceed those of Iran or the weakened Iraq. (Saudi Arabia alone has a larger economy than Iran and a much larger economy than Iraq.) Likewise, South Korea's economy surpasses that of North Korea by many times. Those wealthy nations can afford to defend themselves.

Even if those two regions were strategic to the United States, there would still not be much of a threat from North Korea, Iraq, or Iran—or for that matter, any other of the so-called rogue states. The expanded list of rogue states that are hostile to the United States usually includes North Korea, Iraq, Iran, Syria, Sudan, Libya, and Cuba. Before assessing the overrated military capabilities of each of those nations, one must ask why the United States should be concerned with a threat from any of them.

Those nations are all unfriendly to the United States, but none has, or is likely to have, a large enough economy or a sufficiently capable military to challenge American vital interests in the post–Cold War international environment. In contrast to the $9.2 trillion American economy, the *combined* gross domestic product of those seven nations is only $240 billion, or about 2.6 percent of the U.S. GDP. In contrast to the approximately 275.5 billion per year that the United States spends on defense, those nations *together* spend less than $13.8 billion per year, roughly 5 percent of the U.S. total.[104] Further, a few of those nations possess some capable weapons, but none has a fully integrated military like that of the United States. A fully integrated military requires superior personnel, training, maintenance, and doctrine—which such nations usually lack. In short, if the United States cannot trounce any two of those nations nearly simultaneously (the unlikely scenario for which the Pentagon is planning), the taxpayers have a right to ask what the Pentagon has been buying with their hard-earned money.

The Department of Defense Bottom-Up Review (BUR) that was completed in 1993 stated a requirement for enough U.S. forces to fight two major regional wars nearly simultaneously. The department's Quadrennial Defense Review, published in 1997, essentially reaffirmed that requirement. Although the BUR claimed that the two scenarios it used—a North Korean invasion of South Korea and an Iraqi invasion of Kuwait and Saudi Arabia—were only illustrative, the worldwide defense community quickly realized that the Clinton administration believed that conflicts in the Persian Gulf region and on the Korean Peninsula would be the greatest threats to U.S. security.

At the time the BUR was completed, only a very slim chance existed that two major regional wars would break out nearly simultaneously. After all, the Soviet Union, a hostile superpower, had never orchestrated a second conflict by one of its rogue client states when the United States had been involved in the Korean, Vietnam, or Persian Gulf Wars. After the demise of the Soviet Union, it seems even less likely that one rogue state would take advantage of a U.S. conflict with another rogue state. Even if that improbable event occurred, it would be much less relevant to U.S. security than it would have been during the Cold War.

Although it can be debated whether Soviet conquest of the Korean Peninsula or oil fields in Saudi Arabia during the Cold War would have threatened U.S. vital interests, the previous analysis shows that aggression by rogue states against those regions would not do so in a post–Cold War world. Besides, the National Defense University's *1997 Strategic Assessment* admits that "the prospect[s] of near-simultaneous conflicts in both theater[s] are declining." The assessment also noted that "in both cases, the threat is diminishing. It is even possible that the Korean threat will collapse."[105] In their February 6, 1998, testimony before the Senate Armed Services Committee, George Tenet (then acting director of the Central Intelligence Agency) and Lt. Gen. Patrick Hughes (director of the Defense Intelligence Agency) downplayed any immediate threats to U.S. security. They stated that the war on drugs, humanitarian missions, and responses to terrorist attacks were more likely to require the services of the U.S. military in the next decade than was any major conflict.[106]

Even if simultaneous acts of aggression occurred and the United States chose to respond, the U.S. military, having no superpower rival, would have the luxury of fighting the aggressors sequentially and on its own timetable. There is no longer a danger that the Korean Peninsula and the oil fields in the Middle East will simultaneously fall into the hands of a totalitarian rival superpower.

In fact, even without U.S. protection, it is questionable whether either

South Korea or the Gulf Cooperation Council states would be in danger from regional powers. North Korea, Iraq, and Iran are all beset by problems and are much poorer than their wealthy adversaries.

North Korea

In 1950, South Korea was a poor nation with weak armed forces (mainly infantry forces, with few tanks and aircraft) confronted by a much stronger North Korea, subsidized with arms and other assistance from China and the Soviet Union. The North Koreans had the best Soviet armor and airpower available. Now, even with its current problems, South Korea's GDP is thirty times that of North Korea's prostrate economy. Seoul has outspent Pyongyang on defense since the mid-1970s.[107] North Korea's defense budget has remained static since the early 1980s; South Korea's defense budget has tripled.[108] North Korea has a large military, but it is obsolete and poorly equipped. The modernization of the South's forces has made them qualitatively superior in almost every category. For example, South Korea has been buying F-16 C/D fighter aircraft and is buying new helicopters and obtaining a satellite reconnaissance program. In contrast, North Korea, with its economy deteriorating to the point of starvation and collapse, cannot afford to replace its obsolete weapons and has no fuel for an invasion of the South. In addition, South Korea now has important diplomatic and trade relations with Russia and China, both of which are opposed to war on the Korean Peninsula.

Larry Niksch, a specialist in Asian Affairs at the Congressional Research Service, notes:

The substantial decline in North Korean conventional military capabilities facing South Korea: obsolete offensive weaponry, declining big unit military exercises, marginal supplies of fuel and food, poor morale, and the deteriorating physical and mental state of North Korean draftees owing to a decade of malnutrition.

North Korea appears no longer capable of launching a massive invasion across the Demilitarized Zone. There is evidence North Korean political and military leaders are well aware of this situation. The loss of the invasion option greatly limits Pyongyang's options for using missiles and nuclear weapons against the United States and its allies.[109]

Militarily, any North Korean attack would need to be a frontal assault against prepared defenses (the narrow peninsula does not allow a safer flanking attack). The terrain would channel the attack through several well-fortified routes. Historically, even with air superiority and numerical advantage, frontal assaults on prepared defenses have been difficult—recall the slow Allied progress against the Germans around the Siegfried Line during World War II. But the North Koreans would not have air superiority and instead would be subjected to relentless air attacks in their channels.[110]

Yet the United States continues to subsidize the defense of a wealthy nation. Although South Korea has a hostile neighbor to its north, the U.S. military presence and defense commitment have led South Korea to decrease its defense spending to less than 3 percent of its GDP and to build some of its weapons to counter peaceful, democratic Japan instead of North Korea. According to the NDU's *1997 Strategic Assessment,*

The South's spectacular economic growth finances a steady qualitative improvement in South Korean forces, narrowing the gap with the KPA [Korean People's Army] in terms of combat power. However, the remaining gap would be even smaller or non-existent had South Korea in the late 1980s not begun to cut its defense budget as a percent of GNP and not devoted significant defense funds to the purchase of equipment and capabilities designed for hypothetical, non-peninsula threats rather than the extant threat from the North. Apparently acting on the assumption that North Korea will not attack as long as the U.S. remains committed to defending the South, South Korea has devoted considerable resources to more mobile forces that could make it a regional power. South Korea pays close attention to its military might relative to Japan.[111]

The forces being built for "non-peninsular threats" include new German-built Type 209 submarines, Aegis destroyers, long-range aircraft, and airborne early-warning aircraft to control fighter aircraft.[112]

Thus, NDU's *1997 Strategic Assessment* acknowledges that the U.S. military commitment enables South Korea to avoid the expenses of providing adequately for its own defense, as well as to buy weapons that could undermine stability in the region. A gradual withdrawal of U.S. forces would give South Korea time to increase the percentage of GDP spent on defense and would probably induce that nation to buy weapons solely for its own defense. Any additional weapons purchased with an eye toward Japan would require a large increase in South Korea's defense budget.

Iraq

As a result of the pounding Iraq took during the Gulf War, the Iraqi military is about half as strong as it was before that conflict. Almost ten years of grinding economic sanctions have also taken their toll on the force. The Iraqi military is probably incapable of launching a ground invasion over an extended territory of the kind that would be needed to attack and occupy Saudi Arabia.

Any ground attack Iraq could muster might be stopped by the strong Saudi Arabian air force. The Gulf War showed that an air force could decimate ground forces on an open desert.

Even if a military imbalance exists between Iraq and its neighbors, little is stopping the GCC states from rectifying it. The combined economies of the six states are over thirteen times that of Iraq. (Saudi Arabia alone has an economic output that is more than seven times that of Iraq.) The combined population of the GCC exceeds that of Iraq.[113] The United States should gradually wean those states away from U.S. protection by strengthening the security aspects of the GCC, selling its nations arms, and helping to train their militaries. No reason exists for the United States to station forces or equipment permanently in the region or to defend those countries against an attack by a relatively poor neighbor.

If Iraq invaded a GCC nation, another non-GCC regional power (or powers)—for example, Turkey, Syria, or Iran—could become alarmed that the balance of power in the region was shifting against it and attack Iraq from another direction, especially if it was known that the United States would no longer intervene. In Desert Storm, Syrian forces participated in the ground war, and Turkey allowed coalition aircraft to fly from its air bases. At minimum, Iraq would need to consider the reaction of those powers when contemplating any adventures.

Iran

If there is any threat to the flow of Persian Gulf oil, it is more likely to come from Iran rather than from Iraq. Iran has three times the territory and population of Iraq. Even that threat, however, is remote. Iran's military and economic power was eroded by the Islamic revolution and the long war with Iraq.[114] Iran's ability to afford enhancements to its military has been diminished in recent years by economic stagnation, a growing population, outdated infrastructure for producing oil and gas, and shortages of hard currency.[115] Whenever the oil market experiences slack demand, Iran has a tough time improving its military. The Iranians spent only about $5.7 billion on defense in 1999.[116]

In particular, the media have highlighted Iran's purchase of naval weapons—for example, several Russian Kilo submarines. The Iranians have also been buying fast patrol boats and antiship cruise missiles and improving their capabilities to lay mines. Some analysts fear that those items could be integrated to block oil shipments that transit the narrow Strait of Hormuz.

In the unlikely event that Iran attempted to close the strait (Iran depends on the strait for exports of its own oil), the GCC states are wealthy enough to buy a small fleet to keep the narrow passage open. Their combined annual military spending ($31.6 billion) is five and a half times that of Iran. Their combined economies are almost two and a half times the size of Iran's.[117] The GCC states have improved their militaries, and they have the economic capacity to do much more. Once again, further strengthening the militaries of the GCC states would enable an improved regional balance of power to substitute for the narcotic of U.S. protection.

If the reformers in Iran can wrest power from the Islamic hard-liners, any threat that Iran poses to the strait might be reduced.

Syria

Although Syria is unfriendly toward the United States and is still a threat to Israel, albeit a declining one, it poses little threat to U.S. security. When the Soviet Union disintegrated, Syria lost its main source of economic and military aid. Thus, unlike Israel—which already has a military that is qualitatively superior to those of its Arab neighbors—the isolated and debt-ridden Syria has been able to modernize its military only incrementally.[118] Severe financial constraints will probably inhibit future Syrian modernization. Israel's annual defense spending ($8.9 billion) exceeds that of Syria ($1.9 billion) by four and a half times, and Israel's GDP ($99 billion) is greater than that of Syria ($39 billion) by two and a half times.[119]

Further, Israel's security has never been better. After making peace with Egypt (the most populous and powerful Arab state) and with Jordan, Israel no longer faces a multiple-front war. The Israelis can direct their military efforts against an already weakened Syria. But Israel has been negotiating peace even with Syria. The recent low-level Palestinian violence is not a direct threat to the existence of Israel.

Also, Israel has higher economic growth than its neighbors and has become a regional center of technology. Because Israel is now a rich nation, U.S. aid will be cut from three billion dollars per year to $2.4 billion. (Under those circumstances, an important question is why the United States continues to provide aid at all.)

If peace talks break down, the presence of thirty-five thousand Syrian troops in Lebanon, and Syrian support for anti-Israel terrorists based there, could still cause an Israeli-Syrian conflict. If the unlikely happens, Israel and Syria would probably try to limit any conflict to Lebanon—as they did in 1982—to avoid a spillover into the Golan Heights. If Syria attempted to retake the Heights, Israel would probably win any conflict easily, even without the help of the United States.

Although Syria has chemical weapons and short-range missiles to deliver them, the Syrians should be wary of attacking a state that undoubtedly has chemical, biological, and nuclear weapons.[120] Because in the 1980s Syria abandoned its goal of achieving conventional military parity with Israel, its chemical weapons are probably designed mainly to be a deterrent to Israeli attack.[121]

If Israel and Syria go to war, the conflict would be far less serious for the United States than it would have been during the Cold War. During that tense period, any Arab-Israeli war had the potential to draw in the superpowers, with their nuclear weapons. In contrast, an Arab-Israeli conflict today has no such potential and, therefore, is little threat to U.S. vital interests.

The only way Syria could adversely affect American security is by sponsoring a terrorist attack on U.S. soil using a weapon of mass destruction.

Syria is a sponsor of international terrorism, has chemical weapons, and is probably seeking biological weapons. Yet without U.S. meddling in the Middle East, Syria would have little or no incentive to attack American targets.

Libya

Other than the important exception of sponsoring a terrorist attack on U.S. soil with chemical weapons, Libya cannot substantially affect American security. Libya's small economy is the victim of years of socialist planning. Its army and air force are antiquated and suffer from the demise of Libya's Soviet patron. The country's radical leader, Muammar Qaddafi, may cause problems in the north African region, but that is an area of no strategic value to the United States. Egypt—a nation with a much larger population, economy, and defense budget than Libya and a bigger, more modern military—can act as a counterweight in the region to Qaddafi.

If Libya improved its missile technology, it might become able to strike Europe. Therefore, the European nations might want to invest in missile defense. But Libya poses no comparable threat to the United States. Qaddafi's extradition of two suspected terrorists in the Pan Am 103 bombing may eventually lead to a warming of relations between Libya and the United States.

Sudan

Sudan is a destitute nation, with a GDP of only nine billion dollars. The nation has an antiquated military, which is fighting a civil war that has killed two million people. Sudan is a sponsor of terrorism and could sponsor terrorist attacks on U.S. soil. Other than that, however, it is hardly a threat to U.S. security.

Cuba

Cuba, ninety miles off the U.S. coast in the Caribbean, is in a more strategic location than the other rogue states. However, a congressionally mandated intelligence community assessment of the threat from Cuba bluntly concluded that "at present, Cuba does not pose a significant military threat to the U.S. or to other countries in the region. Cuba has little motivation to engage in military activity beyond the defense of its territory and political system."[122] The report continued,

The disintegration of the Soviet bloc in 1989 triggered a profound deterioration of the Cuban Revolutionary Armed Forces (FAR), transforming the institution from one of the most active militaries in the Third World into a stay-at-home force that has minimal conventional fighting ability. The end of the Soviet economic and military subsidies forced Havana to cut the military's size and budget by about 50 percent after 1989.[123]

Retired marine general John Sheehan, former commander of the U.S. Atlantic Command, met regularly with senior Cuban military officers during his tenure and noted that "it became very clear to those of us on the U.S. side that Cuba was changing and that this was not the Cuba of the '60s and '70s." He agreed with the intelligence community assessment by noting that "the Cuban military has become a home defense force."[124]

The intelligence community's assessment notes that a substantial portion of Cuba's heavy military equipment is in storage. Shortages of spare parts require the "cannibalization" of that equipment to provide parts for equipment still used by the forces. Scarce resources have forced training to be severely curtailed. Thus, Cuba's forces are not ready to fight. The army is unable to conduct large-scale operations, the navy cannot sustain operations outside of its territorial waters, and the air force is incapable of defending Cuban airspace from attacks by large numbers of high-performance military aircraft. The Cuban air force has fewer than twenty-four operational MiG fighters. As a result of Cuba's military and economic weakness, Fidel Castro recently has been trying to improve relations with nearby countries.[125]

Despite all the fanfare about post–Cold War threats from rogue states, those states have changed little since the Cold War, except in one important respect: most of them have lost the support of their Soviet sponsor. Iran and Iraq have also been ravaged by war, low oil prices for long periods of time, economic sanctions, and systemic economic problems. North Korea has endured the latter two maladies. The U.S. economy dwarfs the combined economies of the rogue states, and the U.S. military has bone-crushing superiority over any of their forces. In short, in most instances, rogue states pose very little threat to the United States.

THREATS TO U.S. TRADE

The United States no longer needs to protect ships carrying war materiel and troops to resupply and reinforce NATO forces in Europe against an invading Warsaw Pact army. But the United States has a vital interest in protecting its commercial trade on the high seas against any hostile nations or modern-day pirates. Today, the mission of protecting trade against a much more limited threat should be narrowly defined. A U.S. forward naval presence (U.S. Navy ships and marines) worldwide is no longer needed to carry out this mission. Naval forces based in the United States and "surged" to meet any threat should suffice. The large U.S. fleet—even at home in port—should deter any hostile power from stopping or interfering with U.S. commercial shipping.

In the unlikely event that a hostile nation closed a strategic chokepoint, such as the Strait of Hormuz, the United States would first rely on regional navies to open it. If they could not do so and the United States chose to intervene, U.S.-based naval forces could be dispatched to handle the crisis. However, even this scenario should be defined narrowly. In most cases, if a chokepoint—such as the Panama Canal, the Suez Canal, or the Straits of Malacca—was closed by a regional war, trade would probably just find an alternative route. From the time of the Middle East war in 1967 to the mid-1970s, the Suez Canal was closed; trade simply rerouted itself around the blocked waterway.

If the United States has the best army in the world and a world-dominant air force, it has overwhelming superiority in the naval sphere. Most nations cannot afford to buy capable navies. The Russian navy is still large but has essentially collapsed. A shortage of funds keeps almost all of its ships and most of its submarines deteriorating at the dock.

The U.S. Navy has the only super carriers, twelve in all, in the world. It also has twelve medium-sized amphibious carriers with aircraft that take off and land vertically. In comparison, Russia has only one moderately large aircraft carrier equipped with conventional aircraft, France has one medium-sized carrier equipped with conventional aircraft, and other navies with carriers have either one or two small flat decks equipped only with aircraft that take off and land vertically. The United States also has superiority under the sea, with its fleet of *Seawolf* and *Los Angeles*-class submarines. No rational trading nation that uses the seas has an incentive to block their use, but U.S. naval dominance ensures that any closed sea lanes could be reopened.

THE CHIMERA OF INSTABILITY

Given the lack of a credible threat from any specific country, people who desperately search for enemies—that is, advocates of foreign intervention or large defense budgets—must settle on the vague notion of "instability." But instability has always existed in the anarchic international system and probably always will. Instability in most parts of the world is rarely a threat to the United States.

In the years of its superpower rivalry with the Soviet Union, the United States regarded any instability in the world as a potential opportunity for communist inroads. Thus, in the abnormal global strategic environment of the Cold War, the United States intervened anywhere and everywhere to promote stability—that is, to protect the status quo.

The strategic realities have been altered dramatically by the demise of the Soviet Union, but U.S. foreign policy is still on autopilot. Although no rival superpower now exists to exploit the venues of instability, the United States seems compelled to intervene almost anywhere in the world that a conflict arises, even in regions that are not strategic. For example, the United States has undertaken an indeterminate commitment to provide stability to Bosnia and Kosovo in a region that had no relationship to U.S.

vital interests even during the Cold War. In addition, the United States attempted to conduct "nation building" in Somalia, which is also in a region that is nonstrategic. This overextended U.S. defense perimeter is expensive and unnecessary.

Not only has the main beneficiary of instability, the Soviet Union, dissolved, but evidence exists that the end of the Cold War has brought more stability to the world, not less. Contrary to the conventional wisdom of the proponents of military intervention, the end of the Cold War has not unleashed a host of repressed conflicts. According to the Conflict Data Project at the University of Uppsala, Sweden, the number of armed conflicts actually declined by more than half, from fifty-five in 1992 (the year after the demise of the Soviet Union) to twenty-four in 1997. The Unit for the Study of Wars, Armaments and Development at the University of Hamburg, Germany came up with similar numbers, noting that the number of conflicts in the world declined from 51 in 1992 to 25 in 1997.[126] The Stockholm International Peace Research Institute (SIPRI) listed twenty-seven major conflicts in 1999. But SIPRI noted that only fourteen of those conflicts were large enough to kill more than a thousand people during the year.[127]

In addition, most conflicts occurred within states, not between them. Of the 101 conflicts occurring from 1989 to 1996, ninety-five were between combatants within states, and only six were between belligerent states.[128] Of the twenty-seven conflicts that SIPRI listed in 1999, all but two were internal.[129] Aggression across borders has been declining for decades, and that trend is unlikely to be reversed.[130] Any threats to U.S. security from conflicts are more apt to arise from interstate aggression (especially those very rare wars involving an aggressive great power in a key region) than from feuding among groups within a state. In short, the end of the Cold War actually increased stability in the world: there was no longer a superpower sponsoring client groups and states to challenge those supported by a rival superpower.

Another indicator of increased international stability in the post–Cold War world is the substantial reduction in worldwide military expenditures since during that period. The Stockholm International Peace Research Institute estimates that such expenditures totaled $780 million in 1999—dropping almost a third since 1990. (The institute also notes that U.S. spending on defense represents 36 percent of the current world total.)[131]

The international arms market has also been drastically reduced. From 1986 to 1995, world arms sales plummeted 55 percent.[132] (The level of global arms transfers has remained stable since 1995.)[133] In addition, during the same period, the United States and its allies increased their share of the worldwide arms market. The U.S. share of the market increased from 22 percent to 49 percent, and NATO's share increased from 44 to 78 percent.[134] In fact, from 1995 to 1999, U.S. arms sales totaled almost as

Table 3.1
Global Arms Trade (from 1995 to 1999 in billions of dollars in constant 1990 prices)

Top Dealers

United States	$53.4
Russia	14.6
France	11.7
United Kingdom	7.3
Germany	6.1
Netherlands	2.2
China	2.2
Ukraine	2.0
Italy	2.0
Canada	1.1

Biggest Buyers

Taiwan	$13.9
Saudi Arabia	9.2
Turkey	6.5
South Korea	6.0
Egypt	4.7
India	4.6
Japan	4.3
Greece	4.1
China	4.0
United Arab Emirates	3.3

Source: Stockholm International Peace Research Institute.

much as the rest of the world combined. Russia was in second place, with less than 30 percent of the U.S. total.[135]

The U.S. and NATO shares increased as a result of greatly diminished subsidized sales of Soviet and Russian weapons to third-world outlaw states such as Iraq, Syria, Libya, and Cuba. (After the Cold War, sales from the United States and other arms exporters to developing countries also slowed down.) Table 3.1, which lists the top exporters and importers of arms worldwide for the recent past, shows that China and the rogue states are not among the top importing nations. China is ninth and the rogue states did not even make the list of the top 10. (China is on the list of top arms dealers because it produces and exports low-quality weapons to the third world.) In fact, some of the largest arms importers are nations friendly to the United States that are rivals of nations that are potential threats—that is, Taiwan, Saudi Arabia, South Korea, Japan, and the United Arab Emirates.

Much of the instability that remains in the international system—and there will always be some instability—is not very amenable to military solutions. Patrick Hughes, the director of Defense Intelligence Agency, identified the nine most important conditions causing instability in the post–Cold War world—only three of them connected to military matters. Uneven economic and demographic development; disparities in wealth and resource distribution; ethnic, religious, and cultural strife; transnational crime; reaction to Western cultural expansion; and natural disasters and environmental issues are best solved by nonmilitary means. Only uncertain regional and global security structures, the proliferation of high-technology weapons, and rogue groups and states have any military connection.[136]

CONCLUSION: A RANKING OF THREATS

Since the first responsibility of any government is to protect its nation's territory, citizens, and way of life, threats to the homeland need to be ranked at the top. (That priority was lost as the United States policed an extended defense perimeter during the Cold War, but it is now getting renewed attention.) With weak and friendly neighbors on its northern and southern borders and vast oceans to the east and west, the United States faces only a negligible threat from a conventional attack. Further, when the Cold War ended, the threat from an intentional Russian nuclear first strike declined dramatically. The recent sharing of U.S. early-warning data with Russia, to compensate for the decrepit state of the Russian early-warning system, has reduced somewhat the chance of an accidental Russian nuclear launch. The fact that China's nuclear force is defensive and not maintained on high alert, renders a rapid Chinese intentional first strike or accidental launch very unlikely. In the future, when rogue states develop nuclear weapons and long-range missiles, the risk of an accidental launch will increase, because of their underdeveloped command and control, security, and nuclear doctrines.

Thus, the threat of a terrorist attacking the U.S. homeland with a weapon of mass destruction is now probably the greatest single threat to U.S. security. The second-greatest threat is a rogue state or terrorist group using a weapon of mass destruction carried on a cruise or ballistic missile launched from a ship offshore. Long-range ballistic missiles launched from a rogue state's territory are only the third-greatest threat to U.S. security. The United States can detect the origin of ballistic missile launches and has a powerful nuclear deterrent to dissuade such strikes by rogue states.

Next are threats to U.S. vital interests worldwide. Such threats are currently very minor. No conventional threat to either of the major economic centers—Western Europe and East Asia—from a regional hegemon is likely to arise for the next twenty or thirty years. As noted earlier, Russia, with its military and economy in shambles, is not likely to menace Europe for a long while, if ever. China, with its rapid economic growth, has been much slower in modernizing its military, which started from a very low point. Paul Godwin, a noted expert on the Chinese military at the National War College, commenting on China's potential to be a significant military threat, estimates "the window for China's becoming one of the world's major military powers . . . at somewhere between 2020 and 2050."[137] Of course, China may never travel that road. China will have the economic resources to modernize its military, but that modernization is likely to be gradual.

If the balance of power in either Europe or East Asia erodes and a threat arises, the United States will have ample time to build up its armed forces and to *help* like-minded nations. (The economies of like-minded nations in Europe and East Asia are larger than those of their potential adversaries, Russia and China.) It takes much longer to develop and field modern high-technology weapon systems than it took to develop and field systems in the 1930s during the rise of Hitler. Instead of starting late and racing to catch up, as America did during the years immediately preceding World War II, the United States now begins with an overwhelming lead in military power and technology.[138] In fact, in the future the United States will probably widen its already commanding technological lead. According to the Stockholm International Peace Research Institute, the United States accounts for 64 percent of the world's military research and development expenditures and spends many times more than what the second-place nation spends.[139]

Most of the Pentagon's military planning covers areas of the world that are not very critical to U.S. vital interests, which indicates how few real threats to U.S. security currently exist. As argued earlier, prominent economists argued that going to war in 1991 for Persian Gulf oil was unnecessary. Without an adversary superpower to benefit, even a North Korean invasion of South Korea would be far less important to U.S. security than during the Cold War.

All of the military threats from three of the remaining rogue states—Syria, Libya, and Cuba—have declined dramatically after the demise of their Soviet patron. However, proliferation of weapons of mass destruction to some of those nations, as well as to Iraq, Iran, and North Korea, may be an increasing problem. International efforts to curb proliferation will, at best, only slow it down. Unnecessary U.S. military interventions against those nations or in their regions might actually spur proliferation and bring catastrophic retaliation against U.S. forces or the American homeland through missile attacks or terrorism. In this changed strategic environment, the United States should rely on a policy of military restraint overseas.

It is difficult to believe that a nation with such a secure geostrategic position spends almost $300 billion per year on national defense—roughly the combined defense spending of the next seven nations (most of which are friendly states). In the past decade or so, the U.S. share of world defense spending has increased from 27.5 percent to 32 percent. The potential adversaries—Russia, China, and the rogue states—now have a combined share of only 18 percent.[140]

The time has come to adopt a policy of military restraint overseas and reduce U.S. defense spending to match the more benign threat environment in the world today. Lower defense spending will give the American taxpayers the break they deserve. Military developments in China bear watching, but hysteria is unnecessary.

NOTES

1. National Defense University, *1998 Strategic Assessment: Engaging Power for Peace* (Washington, D.C.: National Defense University, 1998), p. 1.

2. The White House, *A National Security Strategy for a Global Age* (Washington, D.C.: The White House, 2000), p. iii.

3. Center for Defense Information, *1997 CDI Military Almanac* (Washington, D.C.: CDI, 1997), p. 7.

4. Richard Staar, "Russia's New Blueprint for National Security," *Strategic Review* 27, no. 2 (Spring 1998), pp. 34, 37.

5. Judith Graham, "Some Think It's Time to Slow Our Nuclear Response," *Chicago Tribune*, January 30, 2000, p. 1.

6. International Institute of Strategic Studies, *The Military Balance 2000/2001* (London: Oxford University Press, 2000), p. 194.

7. John Schulz "China as a Strategic Threat: Myths and Verities," *Strategic Review* 26, no. 1 (Winter 1998), pp. 11–12.

8. Walter Pincus, "U.S. Gains Intelligence Data in China Launches," *Washington Post*, June 13, 1998, p. A18.

9. Kevin Sullivan, "Indian Nuclear Sub Plan Reported," *Washington Post*, June 27, 1998, p. A20.

10. William Broad, "Spies vs. Sweat: The Debate over China's Nuclear Advance," *New York Times*, September 7, 1999, p. A1.

11. U.S. Department of Defense, *Proliferation: Threat and Response* (Washington, D.C.: Government Printing Office, 1997), p. 60.

12. William Perry and Ashton Carter, *Preventative Defense: A New Security Strategy for America* (Washington, D.C.: Brookings Institution, 1999), p. 139.

13. Committee on Governmental Affairs, U.S. Senate, *Proliferation Primer: A Majority Report of the Subcommittee on International Security, Proliferation, and Federal Services*, January 1998, summary and p. 69.

14. Ibid., p. 69.

15. Bradley Graham, "Clinton Proposes Inspections for Germ War Ban," *Washington Post*, January 28, 1998, p. A12.

16. Zachary Selden, *Biological Weapons: Defense Improves, but the Threat Remains* (Washington, D.C.: Business Executives for National Security, December 1997), p. 3.

17. Richard Perle, "No More Halfway Measures," *Washington Post*, February 8, 1998, p. C1.

18. Neil King Jr., "Iraq's Weapons Supply Remains a Mystery to U.S." *Wall Street Journal*, February 9, 1998.

19. Bradley Graham and Barton Gellman, "Cohen Says U.S. Would Not Seek to Topple Iraqi," *Washington Post*, February 1, 1998, p. A22; Joseph Cyrulik, "So We Control the Air," *Washington Post*, February 3, 1998, p. A17; and Andrew Koch, "Can Bombing Remove Saddam's Chemical and Biological Weapons?" *Weekly Defense Monitor*, February 19, 1998, p. 11.

20. Perle, p. C1; and *Proliferation Primer*, p. 69.

21. John Mintz, "Air War on Iraq Would Be Similar to Desert Storm," *Washington Post*, February 15, 1998, p. A1.

22. Robert W. Chandler, *New Face of War: Weapons of Mass Destruction and the Revitalization of America's Transoceanic Military Strategy* (McLean, Va.: Amcoda Press, 1998), p. 82.

23. Thalif Deen, "UN Prepares to Counter Nuclear Terrorist Threat," *Jane's Defence Weekly*, February 11, 1998, p. 5.

24. James Ford and Richard Schuller, *Controlling Threats to Nuclear Security a Holistic Model*, as cited in Raymond Zilinskas, "The Other Biological-Weapons Worry," *New York Times*, November 28, 1997, p. A39; and Charles Horner, "Military Force Has Its Limits," *New York Times*, February 7, 1998, p. 17.

25. Deen, p. 5.

26. Julian West, "Atomic Haul Raises Fears of Bin Laden Terror Bomb," *London Sunday Telegraph*, April 23, 2000, p. 1.

27. Cited in Chuck McCutcheon, "Computer-Reliant U.S. Society Faces Growing Risk of 'Information War,' " *Congressional Quarterly*, March 14, 1998, p. 675.

28. "Cyberterrorism," *American Banker*, September 8, 1997, p. 15.

29. Defense Science Board, *Report of the Task Force on Information Warfare—Defense* (Washington, D.C.: Department of Defense, November 1996).

30. "Cyberterrorism," p. 15.

31. Bradley Graham, "11 Military Computer Systems Breached by Hackers This Month," *Washington Post*, February 26, 1998, p. A1.

32. Gordon Platt, "New from the Navy: Wall Street War Games," *Journal of Commerce*, December 22, 1997, p. 1A.

33. "Cyberterrorism."

34. Cited in Heritage Foundation, *Defending America: Ending America's Vulnerability to Ballistic Missiles* (Washington, D.C.: Heritage Foundation, 1996), pp. 16–17. Unfortunately, the Heritage Foundation does not seem to realize that profligate U.S. interventions overseas lead to the proliferation of weapons of mass terror and missiles.

35. Oscar Lurie, "Overkill for the Likely Mission," *Weekly Defense Monitor*, March 30, 2000, p. 3.

36. Dennis Blasko, "Evaluating Chinese Military Procurement from Russia," *Joint Forces Quarterly*, no. 14 (Autumn–Winter 1997–98): 94.

37. Michael Pillsbury, *China Debates the Future Security Environment* (Washington, D.C.: Department of Defense, 2000), cited in Bill Gertz, "Pentagon Study Finds China Preparing for War with U.S.," *Washington Times*, February 2000, p. A4.

38. Bates Gill, "Modernization of the People's Liberation Army," *Joint Forces Quarterly*, no. 14 (Autumn–Winter 1997–98), pp. 137–139. The article is a review of Michael Pillsbury, ed., *Chinese Views of Future Warfare* (Washington, D.C.:

National Defense University Press, 1997), a compilation of writings from the Chinese PLA Academy of Military Science.

39. Seth Faison, "Still a Puny Military Force by the World's Standards," *New York Times*, July 28, 1998, p. A6.

40. David Shambaugh, "China's Military Views the World: Ambivalent Security," *International Security* 24, no. 3 (Winter 1999/2000), p. 58.

41. Andy Sywak, "Chinese Defense Spending: A Great Increase, but to Where?" *Weekly Defense Monitor*, April 30, 1997, pp. 6–7; and You Ji, *The Armed Forces of China* (Australia: Allen and Unwin, 1999) pp. 2–12.

42. "More Cuts Planned for Lean, Mean PLA," *South China Morning Post*, June 25, 1998, p. A1; and "New-Look PLA Plans More Cuts," *South China Morning Post*, June 30, 1998, p. A1.

43. Shambaugh, p. 55.

44. General Accounting Office, *National Security: Impact of China's Military Modernization on the Pacific Region* (Washington, D.C.: Government Printing Office, 1995), p. 6, cited in Schulz, p. 6.

45. A September 1990 article in *Jingji yanjiu* (Economic Research), cited in Schulz, p. 6.

46. Schulz, p. 6.

47. Robert Karniol, "China Boosts Its Budget Yet Again," *Jane's Defence Weekly*, March 15, 2000, p. 12.

48. Blasko, p. 92.

49. Ibid., pp. 95–96.

50. Russell Travers, "A New Millennium and a Strategic Breathing Space," *Washington Quarterly* 20, no. 2 (Spring 1997), p. 104.

51. National Defense University, *1997 Strategic Assessment: Flashpoints and Force Structure* (Washington, D.C.: National Defense University, 1997), p. 50.

52. Schulz, p. 5.

53. Quoted in Schulz, p. 6.

54. Michael Richardson, "Imbalances of Power: Gaps Show as Asian Nations Retool Forces," *International Herald Tribune*, January 7, 2000, p. 1.

55. Schulz, p. 7.

56. Olga Kryazheva, "Russia-China Arms Trade Growing," *Weekly Defense Monitor*, 4, February 3, 2000, p. 10.

57. John Pomfret, "Russians Help China Modernize Its Arsenal: New Military Ties Raise U.S. Concerns," *Washington Post*, February 10, 2000, p. A17.

58. Ibid.

59. Travers, p. 104; and Chinese naval sources quoted in Paul Beaver, "China Will Delay Aircraft Carrier," *Jane's Defence Weekly*, June 3, 1998, p. 1.

60. Robert Karniol, "Power to the People," *Jane's Defence Weekly*, July 12, 2000, p. 26.

61. Schulz, pp. 9–11.

62. Quoted in Richard Lardner, "DoD Intelligence Chief Downplays China's Threat against Taiwan, U.S.," *Inside the Pentagon*, March 2, 2000, p. 2.

63. "Regional Rapid Deployment: Reaching Out," *Jane's Defence Weekly*, April 15, 1998, pp. 29–32.

64. Cited in Richard Halloran, "Analysts Downplay Threat Beijing Poses to Taiwan," *Washington Times*, May 15, 2000, p. A1.

65. Vernon Loeb, "China vs. Taiwan," *Washington Post*, May 17, 2000, p. A25.

66. Shambaugh, p. 60.

67. Craig Smith, "Behind China's Threats," *New York Times*, March 7, 2000, p. A1.

68. John Roos, "The Cutting Edge: A Beijing-Taipei Showdown Would Pit Quantity vs. Quality," *Armed Forces Journal International*, May 2000, p. 13.

69. Thomas Crampton, "High-Tech China Upsets Power Balance," *International Herald Tribune*, February 26, 2000, p. 1.

70. Halloran, p. A1.

71. Ibid.

72. Ibid.

73. Smith, p. A1.

74. Halloran, p. A1.

75. Comments by Rear Adm. Eugene Carroll at the Cato Institute's policy forum, "Trouble in the Taiwan Straits?" March 30, 2000.

76. Schulz, p. 7.

77. Pomfret, p. A17.

78. Blasko, pp. 91, 94.

79. Jonathan Brodie, "China Moves to Buy More Russian Aircraft, Warships, and Submarines," *Jane's Defence Weekly*, December 22, 1999, p. 13.

80. Mark Magnier, "Chinese Military Still Embedded in the Economy," *Los Angeles Times*, January 9, 2000, p. A1.

81. Charles Maynes, "Relearning Intervention," *Foreign Policy*, no. 98 (Spring 1995), p. 99.

82. Schulz, pp. 13–14.

83. John Pomfret, "China Aims More Missiles at Taiwan," *Washington Post*, February 11, 1999, p. A1.

84. Lurie, p. 6.

85. Michael Orr, "Second Time Lucky?" *Jane's Defence Weekly*, March 8, 2000, pp. 35–36.

86. Daniel Williams, "Russia, Allies at Odds," *Washington Post*, April 29, 1998, p. A23.

87. Charles Maynes of the Eurasia Foundation, remarks at the Cato Institute's policy forum on Russia, May 28, 1998.

88. Christopher Foss, "Russia's Forces Out of Shape," *Jane's Defence Weekly*, April 2, 1994, p. 15.

89. Steve Liesman, "Moscow Seems to Finally Get Serious about Paring, Reorganizing Military," *Wall Street Journal*, March 3, 1998, p. A17.

90. Quoted in Martin Nesirky, "Russia's Armed Forces Seem Close to Collapse: Nuclear Weapons Are Well Cared for, but Not Much Else; Planes Don't Fly, Sailors Don't Eat," *St. Louis Post-Dispatch*, April 22, 1998, p. 1.

91. Olga Kryazheva, "Russia's Strategic Bomber Force Growing," *Weekly Defense Monitor*, March 30, 2000, p. 8.

92. Stockholm International Peace Research Institute website, http://www.sipri.org

93. Jim Hoagland, "Hammering Russia," *Washington Post*, January 8, 1998, p. A21; and *Military Balance 2000–2001*, p. 120.

94. For more on this point, see Ivan Eland, *The Costs of Expanding the NATO Alliance* (Washington, D.C.: Congressional Budget Office, March 1996), p. 14.

95. "Yeltsin Moves for Reductions in Armed Forces," *USA Today*, November 26, 1997, p. 17 and *Military Balance 2000/2001*, p. 120.

96. John Steinbruner and Clifford Gaddy, "The Bear Has Lost Its Roar," *Los Angeles Times*, May 3, 1998, p. M5.

97. David Ruppe, "Russian Nuke Force Gains as Conventional Force Wanes," *Defense Week*, December 8, 1997, p. 5.

98. *Military Balance 2000–2001*, p. 117.

99. Ibid., p. 117.

100. National Defense University, *1997 Strategic Assessment*, pp. 18–19.

101. Quoted in Nesirky, p. A1.

102. Quoted in ibid.

103. Travers, pp. 103–104.

104. *The Military Balance 2000–2001*, pp. 25, 139, 140, 146, 153, 202, 236, and 283.

105. National Defense University, *1997 Strategic Assessment*, p. 236.

106. Rick Maze, "Security Officials Downplay U.S. Threat," *Defense News*, February 9–15, 1998, p. 14.

107. Doug Bandow, *Tripwire: Korea and U.S. Foreign Policy in a Changed World* (Washington, D.C.: Cato Institute, 1996), p. 7.

108. Lonnie Henley, "A War Scenario: Korean Cataclysm," *Washington Post*, May 4, 1997, p. C1.

109. Larry Niksch, "Ignored Issue in the Taiwan Debate," *Washington Times*, May 25, 2000, p. A19.

110. Michael O'Hanlon, *How to Be a Cheap Hawk* (Washington, D.C.: Brookings Institution, 1998), p. 65.

111. National Defense University, *1997 Strategic Assessment*, p. 101.

112. Corwin Vandermark, "South Korea Is Ready to Defend Itself," *Weekly Defense Monitor*, March 30, 2000, p. 7.

113. *Military Balance 2000–2001*, pp. 136, 140, 144, 149, 151, 152, and 155.

114. Ibid.

115. Travers, p. 103.

116. *Military Balance 2000–2001*, p. 139.

117. Ibid., pp. 136, 139, 144, 149, 151, 152, and 155.

118. Steve Rodan, "Debt Issue Fails to Derail Russia-Syria Talks on S-300," *Defense News*, June 1–7, 1998, p. 54.

119. *Military Balance 2000–2001*, pp. 142, 153.

120. Dana Priest, "U.S. Goes Easy on Allies in Arms Control Crusade," *Washington Post*, April 14, 1998, p. A11. Table on the proliferation of chemical, biological, nuclear, and ballistic missile technologies compiled from the Congressional Research Service and government intelligence sources.

121. Office of the Secretary of Defense, *Proliferation: Threat and Response* (Washington, D.C.: Government Printing Office, November 1997), p. 37.

122. Defense Intelligence Agency, *The Cuban Threat to U.S. National Security*, May 6, 1998, p. 4.

123. Ibid.

124. Jack Sheehan, "Across the U.S.-Cuban Divide: A Retired General Takes a Step," *Washington Post*, May 3, 1998, p. C2.

125. Defense Intelligence Agency, pp. 1–4.

126. Figures from The Conflict Data Project at the University of Uppsala, Sweden, and Unit for the Study of Wars, Armaments and Development at the University of Hamburg, Germany cited in Michael Renner, "Sun Journal: Military Budgets, Warfare Waning," *Baltimore Sun*, May 13, 1998, p. A1.

127. Stockholm International Peace Research Institute, *SIPRI Yearbook 2000: Armaments, Disarmament and International Security* (Oxford: Oxford University Press, 2000), www.sipri.org. Different organizations compiling data on the number of conflicts in the world use slightly different methodologies but arrive at similar numbers.

128. Renner, p. A1.

129. SIPRI.

130. Yahya Sadowski, *The Myth of Global Chaos* (Washington, D.C.: Brookings Institution, 1998), pp. 87–88.

131. SIPRI.

132. Carl Conetta and Charles Knight, "Inventing Threats," *Bulletin of Atomic Scientists*, March–April 1998, p. 33.

133. SIPRI.

134. Conetta and Knight, p. 33.

135. SIPRI.

136. Daniel Smith, "The 21st Century Intelligence Forecast," *Weekly Defense Monitor*, February 19, 1998, pp. 2–7.

137. Quoted in Conetta and Knight, p. 38.

138. Ibid., p. 37.

139. Stockholm International Peace Research Institute as cited in Rachel Stohl, "U.S. Leads World as Top Arms Exporter," *Weekly Defense Monitor*, June 18, 1998.

140. Cited in Conetta and Knight, p. 33.

4

U.S. Security Strategy

As noted earlier, the first priority of any country's national security policy is to protect its citizens, territory, and institutions. The Clinton administration's security strategy of "engagement and enlargement," which meant intervening overseas to enhance stability and enlarge the community of democratic nations, should really have been called "entanglement and endangerment." The extended defense perimeter required by the strategy not only endangered the lives of American soldiers in foreign entanglements and conflicts that were not vital to U.S. security, but also put at risk U.S. civilians at home and abroad. Many of those conflicts involved volatile ethnic disputes (for example, Somalia, Bosnia, or Kosovo) that could have spawned terrorist groups—state sponsored or independent—that might have attacked U.S. troops stationed abroad or U.S. citizens at home. Thus, "engagement and enlargement" might have been called a foreign policy (albeit a poor one), but it was certainly not a national security policy.

Both President Clinton and the Defense Science Board acknowledged that terrorism against U.S. targets has increased because of U.S. intervention overseas.[1] Also, the National Commission on Terrorism has noted that "religiously motivated terrorist groups, such as Usama bin Ladin's group, al-Qaida, which is believed to have bombed the U.S. Embassies in Africa, represent a growing trend toward hatred of the United States" and that "if al-Qaida and Usama bin Ladin were to disappear tomorrow, the United States would still face potential terrorist threats from a growing number of groups opposed to perceived American hegemony."[2]

In the past, terrorism has been a mere pinprick to great powers. Terrorists might take a few hostages or kill a few people and make governments squirm until the much-publicized incident had passed, but the fabric of the targeted society was never at risk. The strategic environment may now have changed. If terrorists, the weakest players in the international system, can obtain the proliferating technologies required to make and effectively use weapons of mass destruction, they could bring a superpower to its knees. For example, an incident of bioterrorism—a biological agent sprayed by a terrorist group from a rooftop sprayer or crop-dusting aircraft—could kill hundreds of thousands of people in a U.S. city and result in pressure to curtail America's unique civil liberties in a vain attempt to prevent such future catastrophes. As noted earlier, technologies for weapons of mass destruction are becoming more easily available to such groups.

The new strategic environment has rendered U.S. security strategy obsolete. That strategy has its roots in the post–World War II reaction to the events of Munich in 1938. At Munich, Neville Chamberlain, the British prime minister, appeased Hitler by acceding to his conquest of the Czech Sudetenland in hopes that Germany's aggression would go no farther. Such appeasement only persuaded Hitler that Britain and France would do nothing to stop him if he continued his conquests. The United States learned a lesson from that chain of events, but learned it too well. During the Cold War, lest its resolve be questioned, the United States raced to counter perceived communist expansion anywhere in the world that it occurred. Thus, the United States saw the potential for "falling dominoes" everywhere, even if the conflict or region was unimportant to U.S. vital interests (all conflicts in Africa), the dominoes were unlikely to fall (Afghanistan, Nicaragua, or Grenada), or U.S. actions did more to help than hinder the communist movement (Cuba and Vietnam).

Despite the demise of international communism, the domino theory is alive and well in the post–Cold War world. Instead of encroaching communism, however, the enemy is spreading "instability." For example, the United States is meddling in the affairs of Bosnia and Kosovo to prevent a wider war in Europe. Yet the great powers of Europe, especially Russia in its weakened state, are unlikely to go to war over the developments in either place. Even a war between lesser nations in Europe, such as Greece and Turkey, would not adversely affect U.S. security. (Such a war would be unlikely to spread beyond the countries involved. Cyprus and the isles between Greece and Turkey—the most likely sites for the war—are not of strategic interest to the United States.) The United States should first let countries in a particular region attempt to solve a conflict therein.

"BALANCER-OF-LAST-RESORT" STRATEGY

In a post–Cold War world with no global adversary on the horizon for at least twenty or thirty years, the United States could rely on regional arrangements as the primary means of providing security, even in important regions like Europe and East Asia. The regional arrangements could include a regional security organization (such as any newly formed defense subset of the European Union), a great power policing its sphere of influence, or simply a balance of power among the larger nations of a region. Those regional arrangements would check aspiring hegemonic powers and thus keep power in the international system diffuse.[3] The United States would intervene only in the rare event that an aggressive great power threatened to destroy regional security arrangements and take over one of the two vital regions—that is, the United States would adopt a "balancer-of-last-resort" strategy.[4]

PROTECTION OF U.S. TRADE

Any aggressor nation or modern-day pirate must realize that the U.S. Navy will protect U.S. shipping and trade on the world's oceans. But the right to free passage on the seas should not be taken to excess. Prior to World War I, the United States insisted that its citizens had a right of safe passage aboard a belligerent's (Britain's) ships carrying munitions through a war zone. Today, private American trade transiting through war zones (the territorial waters of belligerent nations) in conflicts in which the United States is not a participant should not be protected by the U.S. Navy. Those private ships know the risks of trading with belligerents and should not draw the United States into an unnecessary conflict. On the other hand, if a belligerent nation attacks U.S. commerce in international waters or in the territorial waters of a nonbelligerent, the U.S. Navy should respond swiftly.

Protecting legitimate rights of free navigation on the world's ocean, however, is not an excuse for maintaining a navy that is forward deployed on a regular basis. The navy currently deploys a carrier battle group in East Asia 100 percent of the time and the North Arabian Sea and the Mediterranean nearly as much. The navy claims that such nearly continuous presence in three theaters reassures friends, deters potential aggressors, contributes to regional stability, and promotes better relations with countries in the region through port calls by ships. It is very difficult to prove such amorphous claims for forward naval presence; no empirical evidence exists to do so. Moreover, even if they could be substantiated, the demise of the Soviet Union brought about by the end of the Cold War renders the tremendous cost of such forward presence unnecessary. The United States no longer has to worry about communist encroachment around the world. The decrepit Russian navy—which was inferior to the U.S. Navy even during the Cold War—has dramatically curtailed its deployments overseas. No longer does the navy of a rival superpower threaten freedom of navigation in the world's oceans.

U.S. overseas naval presence in fact discourages U.S. friends and allies in three aforementioned regions—most of which are wealthy nations (the Western Europeans, the Gulf Cooperation Council states, and Japan, South Korea, and Taiwan)—from doing more to ensure their own security and the security of their regions against potential aggressors that pose little threat to the United States. Furthermore, it is unclear how U.S. naval deployments overseas contribute to internal stability within countries or regions. Sending U.S. Navy ships or marines is rarely a long-term remedy for instability, which is usually caused by political conflict, economic deprivation or exploitation, or ethnic disputes. Finally, many ways exist to improve relations with certain nations other than sending the U.S. Navy for port visits.

In the rare case that aggression or instability in a region does threaten U.S. vital interests, a more potent message will be sent if ships and marines are sent all the way from the United States rather than from their stations in the theater. For example, in 1996, when China tested missiles near Taiwan as an act of intimidation before the Taiwanese elections, the most potent message was delivered when the United States dispatched a second carrier from the United States to join the one already in the theater.

EVEN IN THE MOST IMPORTANT REGIONS OF THE GLOBE, U.S. ALLIANCES ARE OUT OF DATE

The first permanent alliance that the United States ever joined in its long history was the Rio Pact of 1947, which pledged that an attack against one American state was an attack against them all.[5] The same fears of communist expansion that led to that treaty then resulted in a plethora of U.S.-led alliances (multilateral and bilateral) encircling the Soviet Union and China, a regime that was called "Pax Americana." In those alliances, the United States extended its shield to protect many nations. Now that the Cold War is over and the chief U.S. rival has disintegrated, all of those alliances are out of date. In a world where uncertainty exists about which nation or nations (if any) will be the next threat to U.S. security, rigid alliances undermine the flexibility of foreign policy. Alliances threaten to undermine U.S. security rather than enhance it; they threaten to drag the United States into wars that are unnecessary to secure its vital interests.

A historical example provides ample evidence of this proposition. In the late 1800s and the first few years of the new century, the countries of Europe formed formal and informal alliances that became outdated in the years prior to World War I. In the end, the alliances dragged those nations into the war. Austria-Hungary used the assassination of Archduke Ferdinand as an excuse to give Serbia a reckless ultimatum. Russia then came to the aid of its Serb allies. Germany—which had become allied with Austria-Hungary, in part, to avoid war by moderating its ally's behavior— was dragged into a worldwide conflagration by the reckless behavior of that very ally. France, an ally of Russia, then came to Russia's aid. Great Britain, an informal ally of France's, then felt obligated to enter the fray. In the end, through those rigid alliance systems, the nations of Europe were sucked into a continent-wide war that no nation, not even Germany, wanted.

NATO helped contain a large Soviet army in the center of Europe during the Cold War, but that threat no longer exists. Yet the United States still provides a security shield for the now-wealthy European nations. (Even during the latter part of the Cold War, those nations became well to do and should have taken on more of the burden for European security.) The combined annual defense budget of the great powers of western Europe (Italy, France, Germany, and the United Kingdom) ($127.1 billion) is more than twice that of Russia's yearly budget for defense ($56 billion).[6] The combined annual defense budget of the nations of the European Union ($164.5 billion) is about three times Russia's yearly defense budget.[7]

Yet the major goal of the United States is to retain a hundred thousand troops in Europe so that the U.S. foreign policy establishment can maintain "leadership" on the continent. To sustain the rationale for continued U.S. military presence, an outdated NATO alliance had to be maintained despite the end of the Cold War. In the "expand or die" mentality that ensued, the alliance's territory and missions had to be enlarged, or, it was perceived, the alliance would have withered on the vine. In short, the U.S. troop presence in Europe and the NATO alliance have become ends in themselves, rather than means to achieving the goal of enhancing U.S. security, which was their original purpose. Like the alliances created prior to World War I, NATO is now detrimental to the security of its members. NATO membership has dragged the United States into ethnic conflicts, in Bosnia and Kosovo, that have little relevance to U.S. vital interests. Those brushfire wars can have high costs, both monetarily and in lives lost. Such wars can also cause inflation at home (for example, the Vietnam War).

Expanding NATO's territory toward Russia and giving the alliance an offensive mission—that is, conducting "out-of-area" military actions, such as the war in Kosovo—violated informal pledges the United States gave to Mikhail Gorbachev, the last president of the USSR, when Germany was reunited. Such policies have soured U.S.-Russian relations and clouded the prospects for a settlement on missile defense and further cuts in strategic nuclear weapons. They also have spurred increased military cooperation between Russia and China.

In Asia, the United States also continues to shield nations—Japan and South Korea explicitly, and Taiwan implicitly—that became wealthy during the Cold War. Japan has an economy that is much larger than China's ($4.3 trillion versus $.7 trillion) and an annual defense budget that is about the same ($40.8 billion versus $39.5 billion). South Korea now has an economy ($407 billion) that is almost thirty times the size of North Korea's (roughly $14.7 billion) and a defense budget ($12 billion) that is almost six times that of the North ($2.1 billion).[8] Taiwan is a wealthy nation that has a substantial defense budget ($15 billion) and a modern military;[9] it is the largest importer of weapons in the world (by far); and it has all of the advantages accruing from defending an island (as noted, amphibious assaults are difficult).

The U.S. defense shield obviates the need for Japan, South Korea, and Taiwan to do more for their own security. Japan has the second-largest economy in the world but spends less than 1 percent of its gross domestic product on defense. Today's South Korea has a formidable military and an economy that has outgrown that of North Korea by leaps and bounds.[10] Yet, as noted earlier, the U.S. defense shield makes it possible for South Korea to spend less on defense than it should, and to buy weapons and forces to counter Japan rather than North Korea.[11]

Taiwan would like to strengthen its defenses by buying diesel submarines, P-3 antisubmarine aircraft, and Aegis air-defense ships from the United States. Although the United States has recently approved of such purchases, it would seemingly prefer to provide an implicit security guarantee for Taiwan than permit that nation to have the capable means to defend itself. But even if China invaded and occupied Taiwan, it would not necessarily signal that China was trying to dominate Asia; China regards Taiwan as a renegade province. The security of Taiwan has never been a vital interest of the United States.

In the nonstrategic Middle East, the United States is once again supporting the wealthy nations against their much poorer rogue enemies. Israel, a covertly nuclear-armed state, has an economy ($99 billion) that is 2.5 times the size of that of its arch rival Syria ($39 billion) and an annual defense budget ($8.9 billion) that is four and a half times the yearly defense budget of its adversary ($1.9 billion). Even though Syria lost its Soviet sponsor and is not modernizing its military greatly, the United States continues to pour billions of dollars' worth of economic and military assistance each year into Israel. The wealthy sheikdoms and kingdoms of the Gulf Cooperation Council (Saudi Arabia, Kuwait, the United Arab Emirates, Oman, Qatar, and Bahrain) have a combined economy ($253 billion) more than 13 times greater than the economy of Iraq ($19 billion) and more than double that of Iran ($109 billion). The states of the council have a combined annual military budget ($31.6 billion) almost twenty-three times greater than the yearly defense budget of Iraq ($1.4 billion) and five and a half times as great as that of Iran ($5.7 billion). Saudi Arabia alone has an economy ($141 billion) that is more than seven times that of Iraq and about one-and-a-half times that of Iran. Saudi Arabia's defense budget ($21.8 billion), one of the largest in the world, is almost sixteen times that of Iraq and almost four times that of Iran.[12] Yet the presence of U.S. forces and prepositioned military equipment in the region and the United States' lavish

Table 4.1
Nations with Sizeable Deployments of U.S. Forces

Germany	66,195
Japan	41,208
South Korea	36,538
Italy	11,772
United Kingdom	11,313
Saudi Arabia	6,264
Bosnia/Herzegovina	5,679
Kuwait	3,754
Turkey	2,462
Spain	2,086
Other	61,358
Total in All Foreign Countries	248, 629
Afloat Pacific	18,698
Afloat Near East	15,680
Afloat Europe	4,778

Source: Department of Defense, Worldwide Manpower Distribution by Geographical Area (Washington, D.C.: DoD, June 30, 1999), pp. 1–8.

economic and military assistance to Israel permit the GCC nations and Israel to "underinvest" in their own security. For example, Kuwait promised to modernize its military forces after the Gulf War but has been slow to do so because of continued U.S. protection.

Even with the end of the Cold War, U.S. informal and formal alliances are responsible for the continued stationing of U.S. forces all over the world. Almost a quarter of a million U.S. troops are still stationed in foreign countries. In addition to peacetime naval presence overseas and troops stationed "temporarily" on foreign soil for peacekeeping missions, the United States still has sixty-one permanent military installations in nineteen countries. The principal countries in which the U.S. forces are stationed and the number of forces stationed in them are shown in table 4.1.

Because those formal and informal alliances impede the flexibility of U.S. foreign policy in a post–Cold War world, they should be gradually phased out. The phase-out would give wealthy allies time to build up their militaries before U.S. forces left (the gradualness of a U.S. withdrawal might be particularly important in Korea, where a more acute threat to an ally exists). The ending of those formal and informal alliances would not preclude political or economic cooperation with other democratic nations or the periodic training of the U.S. military with their armed forces.

The United States should retract its overextended and ever-enlarging defense perimeter. Many analysts would say that this policy change would mean the end of U.S. status as a superpower. Nothing could be farther from the truth. Unfortunately, during the Cold War, superpowers were defined by their military power; the Soviet Union was never a superpower in economic terms. In reality, all military power derives from the economy—as demonstrated by the overextension and collapse of the excessively large Soviet military machine. Similarly, the British became involved in two costly world wars and lost their empire. According to historian Paul Kennedy, the same could happen to the United States. The United States has as many military commitments around the globe as it did in the 1960s, when its GDP as a percentage of the world's GDP was much higher.[13] An excessively large defense perimeter, covering most of the world, could easily embroil the United States in needless wars that absorb even more resources than the already bloated defense budgets of today.

Furthermore, continued U.S. dominance of the world could trigger a union of powers opposing that dominance, making wars more likely. China and Russia are already increasing military cooperation in order to balance U.S. supremacy.[14] So, contrary to the knee-jerk reaction of many analysts that U.S. withdrawal from its alliances and adoption of a balancer-of-last-resort strategy would make a bid for hegemony by an opposing great power more likely, hegemonic behavior by the United States may lead to aggressive "balancing" behavior by other great powers. In contrast, with the United States acting as a balancer of last resort, such aggressive reactions by other great powers would be reduced, and regional security arrangements by former allies would be encouraged (for example, the efforts of nations in the European Union to augment their defense capabilities). The conventional wisdom is false that suggests that if the United States does not provide security to allies and friends around the world, hegemonic aggression or chaos will result. Rich, friendly powers can and should spend more on defense and act as the primary security guarantors in their own regions. Thus, the balancer-of-last-resort strategy would allow the United States to act as a back-up if the "going got tough."

In short, the United States should follow George Washington's admonition in his Farewell Address to "steer clear of permanent alliances." The entire spectrum of political opinion in the founding generation agreed with Washington: Alexander Hamilton and James Madison shaped the Farewell Address, and, at his inauguration, Thomas Jefferson warned against "entangling alliances." The view of the founders did not result from complacency about U.S. security or naivete about the international environment. In the Farewell Address, Washington noted America's "distant and detached position" and asked rhetorically, "Why forego the advantages of so peculiar a situation?"[15] Washington did not rule out "temporary alliances for extraordinary emergencies."[16] But current U.S. alliances originated a half a century ago and were designed to contain a hegemonic enemy that has disappeared. The alliances are no longer temporary, and the emergency ended a decade ago. The time has come to go back to the intelligent foreign policy of the founders: one that makes the most of the geostrategic advantages of the United States, which have not changed in two and a quarter centuries.

THE CONSTITUTIONAL DIMENSIONS OF U.S. FOREIGN POLICY

At the constitutional convention in 1787, one of the foremost complaints the nation's founders had against despotic European monarchs was that their subjects (the common people) ultimately paid the price for the kings' foreign military adventures. Abraham Lincoln reflected that view in 1848:

The provision of the Constitution giving the war-making power to Congress was dictated, as I understand it, by the following reasons. Kings had always been involving and impoverishing their people in wars, pretending generally, if not always, that the good of the people was the object. This, our Convention understood to be the most oppressive of all Kingly oppressions; and they resolved to so frame the Constitution that *no one man* should hold the power of bringing this oppression on us.[17]

As a result, the founders gave Congress two of the three most important security-related powers that had previously been reserved for monarchs: the power to declare war (the war power) and grant letters of marque and reprisal (to authorize military actions short of war); and the power to raise armies, provide a navy, and fund them. The president was given only the role of commander in chief of the army and navy.[18]

During the constitutional convention, Pierce Butler proposed giving the war power to the president, but his proposal died for lack of a second. James Madison, the father of the Constitution, argued that "executive powers do not include the Rights of war & peace."[19] He also noted: "In no part of the Constitution is more wisdom to be found than in the clause which confides the question of war or peace to the legislature and not to the executive department. The trust and the temptation would be too great for one man."[20] Madison and Elbridge Gerry wrote the language now in the Constitution that gives Congress the power to "declare" rather than "make" war. Madison made clear that this wording left "to the Executive the power to repel sudden attacks."[21]

Ryan Hendrickson, a professor of political science at Lambuth University, argues that "it is widely agreed among constitutional scholars that an 'offensive' use of force demands prior congressional approval, while the president has the authority to use force without the approval of Congress only for defensive purposes."[22] Therefore, congressional authorization should precede U.S. military operations, other than those to resist sudden attacks.

Congress's power to grant letters of marque and reprisal requires that even limited military actions overseas should get its approval. Shortly after the convention, Thomas Jefferson, then secretary of state, noted, "The making of reprisal on a nation is a very serious thing that is considered an act of war." He concluded, "The right of reprisal is expressly lodged with Congress by the Constitution and not with the executive."[23]

During the nineteenth century, Congress exercised its war powers, and no president claimed unilateral war powers as commander in chief.[24] Yet during the Cold War, presidents began to commit U.S. forces to battle overseas without declarations of war or any other authorization from Congress. Such unconstitutional practices began on a large scale when Harry Truman sent U.S. forces to Korea in 1950. This unfortunate precedent has motivated modern presidents to insist that they do not need congressional authorization before ordering military forces into harm's way overseas. During the Cold War, the rise of deterrence theory—the perception that the Soviet Union had to be dissuaded from aggression by swift U.S. actions—contributed to the accumulation of executive power.

The United States conducted an interventionist foreign policy and felt the need to respond rapidly to every action by the Soviet Union. The perceived requirement for rapid reaction caused authority to flow from the deliberative Congress to the action-oriented executive branch. The thinking was that there was no time for a declaration of war to be introduced, debated, and passed. Declaring war or granting letters of marque and reprisal simply fell out of the fashion in congressional circles.

Even since the Cold War ended, however, presidents have continued to flout the Constitution. President George H. W. Bush invaded Panama without congressional authorization. Also, he maintained that his authority as commander in chief, as well as a resolution by the UN Security Council, made unnecessary a congressional authorization of the Persian Gulf War; he sought congressional authority at the last minute, and only as a courtesy. President Clinton committed U.S. forces to Somalia, Haiti, Bosnia, and Kosovo without congressional authorization.

During the Cold War, presidents justified such executive actions by declaring the existence of inherent presidential power in relations with foreign nations. A 1936 Supreme Court decision, the Curtiss-Wright case, is cited to support such inherent power. Justice George Sutherland wrote for the Court: "In this vast external realm, with its important, complicated, delicate and manifold problems, the President alone has the power to speak or listen as a representative of the nation." Justice Sutherland also noted the "very delicate, plenary and exclusive power of the President as the sole organ of the federal government in the field of international relations."[25]

Yet using this decision is insufficient to justify unilateral presidential power to make war, for four reasons. First, saying that the president is the sole spokesperson for the United States in the international arena is much different from saying the president can unilaterally decide to make war without an approval by Congress. In fact, Justice Sutherland never argued for this position. In 1919, before joining the court, he argued, "The framers of our Constitution . . . provided that Congress, and not the President, should have the sole power to declare war. . . . The Constitution confers no war powers upon the President as such."[26] Second, according to Louis Fisher, a noted constitutional scholar at the Library of Congress, Justice Sutherland borrowed the phraseology of the power of the president as the "sole organ" of the nation in external relations from a speech given by John Marshall, later one of the most famous chief justices of the Supreme Court in U.S. history. The speech, however, indicates that Marshall argued that the president was the "sole organ" of implementing national policy, not making it. In 1981, a federal appellate court rejected any implication from Sutherland's phrase that "constitutes a blanket endorsement of plenary Presidential power over any matter extending beyond the borders of this country."[27] Third, the Court's 1936 opinion seems to contravene the intent of the founders. Alexander Hamilton, the most vociferous advocate of executive power among the founders, argued in "Federalist 75" that the president's power in foreign relations should be severely limited:

The history of human conduct does not warrant that exalted opinion of human virtue which would make it wise in a nation to commit interests of so delicate and momentous a kind, as those which concern its intercourse with the rest of the world, to the sole disposal of a magistrate created and circumscribed as would be a President of the United States.[28]

James Wilson, another founder who advocated a strong presidency, argued that the new constitutional system "will not hurry us into war. It is calculated to guard against it. It will not be in the power of a single man, or a single body of men, to involve us in such distress."[29] If Hamilton and Wilson held this view, the rest of the founders would have been even more skittish about presidential power in foreign affairs and war making. Evidence for that reluctance is contained in the proceedings of the convention and constitutional language emanating from it.

Fourth, President Franklin Roosevelt asked for a declaration of war against Japan even after that nation's surprise attack on Pearl Harbor in 1941. Only during the Cold War was the 1936 Curtiss-Wright decision dredged up and used to justify unilateral, unconstitutional interventions by the president.

Presidential usurpation alone, however, is not responsible for the erosion of the vast congressional war power in the Constitution; Congress has willingly abdicated its constitutional responsibilities on an issue that is vital to any republic. For a representative democracy, the potential ramifications of going to war are great—for example, the loss of life, economic damage, and the restriction of civil liberties. Yet Congress is often reluctant to take a stand on going to war. The members of the legislature do not want to be accused of "tying the president's hands" by voting against military action. They also want to avoid the blame for approving campaigns that are unsuccessful. For example, in the precedent-setting Korean War, President Truman asked congressional leaders if he needed to ask for a declaration of war; their answer was no. The problem is that members of Congress look out for their own reelection rather than defending the constitutional powers of their institution.

During the Vietnam debacle, Congress stiffened its backbone and attempted to reclaim some of the war power; in 1973, it passed the War Powers Resolution. The resolution required the president to consult Congress before introducing U.S. armed forces into a situation where hostilities were actual or imminent. If U.S. armed forces were introduced into such a situation without a declaration of war, the president, in every possible instance, was to notify the Congress within forty-eight hours. Within sixty days after that notification, the president was required to terminate the use of armed forces unless: Congress had declared war or enacted a specific authorization for their use, had extended by law the sixty-day period, or was unable to meet because of an attack on the United States; or unless the president certified to Congress that a maximum of thirty more days were needed to withdraw the troops safely. Regardless of the sixty-day period, if U.S. forces were engaged in hostilities outside the territory of the United States without a declaration of war or congressional authorization, Congress could at any time direct the president to remove the forces by a concurrent resolution.[30]

Not once since the passage of the War Powers Resolution in 1973 has a president fully complied with it. The fear of taking political responsibility for terminating military action has made Congress reluctant to invoke its authority under the resolution.[31]

Proponents of U.S. intervention overseas and almost all presidents since the passage of the War Powers Resolution have deemed the resolution unconstitutional. Their argument is based on the aforementioned mythical "inherent powers" of the commander in chief in the realm of foreign affairs. They claim that the resolution imposes illegal constraints on such powers.

The War Powers Resolution may in fact be unconstitutional, but for reasons quite the opposite of those that presidents and interventionists put forth. The resolution—because it allows the president to commit troops overseas initially without a declaration of war or other congressional authorization—violates the intent of the language in Article I, Section 8, of the Constitution, which gives Congress the power to declare war and grant letters of marque and reprisal. At the time the War Powers Resolution was passed, Senator Thomas Eagleton, who had sponsored legislation to circumscribe executive war-making power, believed that the resolution was counterproductive: "What had finally been agreed to in conference . . . turned the Constitution on its head." He added:

By failing to define the President's powers in legally binding language, the bill provided a legal basis for the President's broad claims of inherent power to initiate war. . . . Rather than tying the President's hands—as the White House surprisingly claimed—the bill would tie Congress' hands.[32]

The War Powers Resolution, by allowing the president to initiate the deployment of forces or actual hostilities without prior congressional approval, allows the president to present Congress with a fait accompli. The Congress could vote against funding for the ongoing military operation, but it rarely does. For example, Congress refused to approve the air war in Kosovo but passed funding for it anyway. Politically, voting against such funding is perceived by members of Congress as "failing to support our dedicated troops while they are engaged in combat." Historically, the Congress has approved funding for military operations that have resulted in the deaths of U.S. military personnel but had little to do with legitimate U.S. security interests—a curious form of "support."

Members of Congress sued to challenge military aid to El Salvador in 1982, the United States invasion of Grenada in 1984, U.S. naval protection of oil tankers sailing through the Persian Gulf in 1987, and the U.S.-led war in Kosovo in 1999; the federal courts have avoided ruling on such cases. The Supreme Court has never ruled on the constitutionality of the War Powers Resolution.[33]

EFFECTS OF A FAILED SECURITY STRATEGY

The drafters of the Constitution made every effort to give the primary war-making power in the republic to the branch of government most representative of the people, the Congress; the citizens of the United States are now paying a heavy price for the usurpation of that power by the president during the Cold War. The notion, which has now become commonplace, that the president can commit the nation's forces to war without the approval of the Congress takes us back to what Abraham Lincoln said was the founders' greatest fear: that the president, like the kings of old, would involve and impoverish the people in wars justified as being for the popular good. The American people saw thirty-three thousand U.S. military personnel die in Korea and another fifty-seven thousand die in Vietnam, in wars that had insufficient authorization, became unpopular, and had little to do with U.S. security. In addition, the economic dislocations from the Vietnam War contributed to the "stagflation" of the 1970s. More recently, the United States lost 241 marines in Lebanon and eighteen U.S. Army Rangers in Somalia in peacemaking ventures that had absolutely nothing to do with U.S. security.

Wars and smaller interventions overseas conducted by imperial presidents have contributed to big government and an erosion of civil liberties at home. At the turn of the twentieth century—before the Great Depression, two world wars, and the Korean, Vietnam, and Gulf Wars—the federal government accounted for less than 5 percent of the U.S. economy. At the turn of the twenty-first century—after all of those crises—the federal government makes up nearly 20 percent of the U.S. economy.

Part of this increased federal spending has been accounted for by huge defense budgets; U.S. annual defense spending equals what is spent per year by the next seven countries combined. Large military forces, paid for by the large defense budgets, generate pressure to employ them. For example, early in the Clinton administration, Secretary of State Madeleine Albright asked Gen. Colin Powell, then chairman of the Joint Chiefs of Staff, what good the marvelous U.S. military was if the United States was not going to use it. Wars, in turn, complete the cycle by building pressure to increase defense budgets. For example, the Korean War lead to the first large peacetime defense budgets in U.S. history; they became a permanent fixture during the Cold War and have remained since then. Also, additional money is often needed after the war to replace lost equipment and ammunition, fuel, and other supplies that were used. The Clinton administration asked for six billion dollars in emergency funding to finance the war in Kosovo and humanitarian aid for the Balkans. Congress used the war as an excuse to double the increase to twelve billion dollars, which included unneeded items. Thus, wars can be used to justify additional defense spending on pork projects.

Wars also lead to the erosion of civil liberties at home. Laws related to domestic security are tightened, citizens who are against the war are labeled as traitors, and Americans whose ancestry is of the opposing country are watched or have their rights taken away. For example, in World War II Japanese-Americans were interned in prison camps. Unnecessary wars erode the constitutional system that the U.S. government claims it is trying to defend. Therefore, the United States should enter only those wars needed to defend truly vital national interests.

Eventually, the exorbitant cost of maintaining high-tech defense forces will force a retrenchment of the U.S. defense perimeter. As weapons increase in complexity, the money needed to buy, operate, and support them rises dramatically. Annual procurement-cost growth is 5.1 percent, and per capita operation-and-support-cost growth is 1.6 percent.[34] Rising unit costs reduce the number of weapons that DoD can afford. Many of the new complex weapons are much more capable than their predecessors (good for fighting large wars), but the lower quantities mean that they can be in fewer places around the world at once. It would be much smarter to rethink the extended U.S. defense perimeter in a rational manner than have a contraction foisted on the nation in a haphazard manner by the rising cost of weapons.

CONCLUSION

Adopting a more restrained U.S. foreign policy and acting as a balancer of last resort (that is, shrinking the U.S. defense perimeter) would actually provide more security for the United States in the more benign post–Cold War world, save U.S. taxpayers money, and help safeguard civil liberties. The secure geostrategic position of the United States has not changed much since the founding of the nation. We need to rediscover the wise, minimalist security policy of the founders. That policy is even more relevant today in a world of few hegemonic powers but many smaller nations and terrorist groups that could obtain weapons of mass destruction and use them against U.S. soil. The United States, however, must equip and train its armed forces to *assist* friendly nations overseas in the unlikely event that any hegemonic power should arise and threaten to destroy the balance of power in Europe or East Asia.

NOTES

1. Quoted in Ivan Eland, "Does U.S. Intervention Overseas Breed Terrorism? The Historical Record," Cato Institute Foreign Policy Briefing No. 50, December 17, 1998, pp. 2–3.

2. National Commission on Terrorism, *Countering the Threat of International Terrorism: Report of the National Commission on Terrorism* (Washington, D.C.: Government Printing Office, 2000), pp. 6–7.

3. Barbara Conry, "U.S. Security Strategy," in Cato Institute, *Cato Handbook for Congress: 106th Congress* (Washington, D.C.: Cato Institute, 1999), pp. 463–464.

4. Ted Galen Carpenter, *A Search for Enemies: America's Alliances after the Cold War* (Washington, D.C.: Cato Institute, 1992), pp. 187–189.

5. Patrick Buchanan, *A Republic Not an Empire: Reclaiming America's Destiny* (Washington, D.C.: Regnery, 1999), p. 33.

6. International Institute of Strategic Studies, *The Military Balance 2000–2001* (London: Oxford University Press, 2000), pp. 58, 61, 66, 80, and 120.

7. Ibid., pp. 53, 56, 58, 61, 63, 66, 69, 74, 75, 80, 85, 94, 96, 103, and 120.

8. Ibid., pp. 194, 200, 202, and 203.

9. Ibid., p. 214.

10. Doug Bandow, *Tripwire: Korea and U.S. Foreign Policy in a Changed World* (Washington, D.C.: Cato Institute, 1996), p. 7.

11. National Defense University, *1997 Strategic Assessment: Flashpoints and Force Structure* (Washington, D.C.: National Defense Univ., 1997), p. 101.

12. *Military Balance 2000–2001*, pp. 136, 139, 140, 142, 144, 149, 151, 152, 153, and 155.

13. Paul Kennedy, *The Rise and Fall of Great Powers* (New York: Random House, 1987), pp. 515, 519, 521.

14. Reuters, "Military Links with Moscow Boosted," *South China Morning*

Post, January 18, 2000, p. 1. That cooperation has now extended to nuclear weapons. Bill Gertz and Rowan Scarborough, "Inside the Ring: Moscow-Beijing Axis," *Washington Times*, January 14, 2000, p. A10.

15. Quoted in Eric Nordlinger, *Isolationism Reconfigured* (Princeton, N.J.: Princeton Univ. Press, 1995), pp. 50–51, 186.

16. Quoted in Carpenter, p. 180.

17. Quoted in Stanley Kober, "Reclaiming the War Power," *Cato Handbook for Congress: 106th Congress*, pp. 512–513. Emphasis in original.

18. U.S. Constitution, Article I, Section 8, and Article II, Section 2.

19. Quoted in Kober, p. 512.

20. Quoted by Congressman David Skaggs, *Congressional Record*, June 24, 1998, p. H5248.

21. Quoted in Kober, p. 512.

22. Ryan Hendrickson, "Clinton's Legal Dominion: War Powers in the Second Term," *National Security Studies 5*, no. 1 (Winter 1999), p. 50. Hendrickson cites Louis Fisher, *Presidential War Powers* (Lawrence: Univ. Press of Kansas, 1995); David Gray Adler, "The Constitution and Presidential Warmaking," *Political Science Quarterly* 103 (1988), pp. 1–35; and Charles Lofgren, "Warmaking under the Constitution: The Original Understanding," *Yale Law Journal* 81 (1972).

23. Quoted in Skaggs, p. H5248.

24. Hendrickson, p. 50.

25. Quoted in Kober, p. 512.

26. Quoted in ibid.

27. Louis Fisher, *Congressional Abdication on War and Spending* (College Station, Texas: Texas A & M University Press, 2000), pp. 29–33.

28. Quoted in Kober, p. 517.

29. Quoted in Doug Bandow, "Warmaking Redux," *Washington Times*, November 20, 1998, p. A26.

30. "War Powers Act," Public Law 93–148, 93rd Congress, House Joint Resolution 542, November 7, 1973.

31. Editorial, "Ax the War Powers Law," *Los Angeles Times*, April 28, 1999.

32. Quoted in Kober, p. 517.

33. John Yoo, "War Powers: Where Have All the Liberals Gone?" *Wall Street Journal*, March 15, 1999, p. A19.

34. Daniel Gouré and Jeffrey M. Ranney, *Averting the Defense Train Wreck in the New Millennium* (Washington, D.C.: Center for Strategic and International Studies, 1999), pp. 75, 90.

5

The United States Must Revamp
Its Military Forces

A decade after the Cold War ended, the United States still has a security strategy and military forces that are left over from the Cold War. In fact, both the U.S. strategy and force structure have their roots even farther back, in World War II. As noted earlier, the Cold War strategy, which continues today, of intervening anywhere in the world at the slightest hint of aggression or instability is an overreaction to the ill effects of appeasing Adolf Hitler at Munich in 1938. The requirement to retain military forces to fight in more than one theater at the same time originated in the experience of fighting the Germans and Japanese simultaneously in World War II. During the Cold War, once again, the two most important theaters were Europe and East Asia (the Persian Gulf was only added in the aftermath of the 1973 oil embargo). After the Cold War, however, emphasis changed to fight two regional wars in the Persian Gulf and East Asia. But today, the U.S. military has a Cold War force structure that has merely been scaled back because of lower budgets.

THE EVOLUTION OF THE CURRENT U.S. FORCE STRUCTURE

The U.S. force structure at the end of the Cold War (in fiscal year 1990) is shown in the first column of table 5.1. The George H. W. Bush administration then began reductions to a "base force." The cuts had not been fully implemented when Bush left office in fiscal year 1993; the force structure at that time is shown in column two. The Clinton administration's Bottom-Up Review later in fiscal year 1993 planned to reduce forces

Table 5.1
Evolution of U.S. Military Forces

	End of Cold War	Bush's Last Force	Today's Force	Percentage Cut from Cold War
Army				
Active divisions	18	14	10	44
National Guard combat brigades	57	43	39 [a]	32
Air Force				
Active fighter wings	25	16	12.5	50
Reserve fighter wings	12	11	7.5	38
Navy				
Total ships	566	435	317	44
Aircraft carriers				
Active/reserve (or training)	15/1	13/0	12/0	20
Active/reserve air wings	13/2	11/2	10/1	27
Attack submarines	99	88	55	44
Marine Corps				
Active/reserve divisions	3/1	3/1	3/1	0
Active personnel	197,000	182,000	173,000	12
Reserve personnel	44,000	42,000	39,000	11

a. The army originally planned to reduce the number of National Guard combat brigades from forty-two to thirty and convert the other twelve units into support forces. The plan was suspended after only three combat brigades had been partially converted.

Sources: Congressional Budget Office, Budget Options for National Defense (Washington, D.C.: Congressional Budget Office, March 2000), p. 8 (based on data from the Office of the Secretary of Defense, Annual Report to the President and Congress for various years); Office of the Secretary of Defense, Annual Report to the President and Congress (Washington, D.C.: Department of Defense, 2001), pp. 52, 58, and 63; and data provided by Dave McGinnis, Chief of Staff, National Guard Association of the United States.

farther. Only minor adjustments have been made to those forces since then (during the Quadrennial Defense Review in fiscal year 1997 and subsequently). Column three shows today's relatively stable force structure.

Since the end of the Cold War, even though the threat environment has changed dramatically, the active forces of each of the major services have been reduced relatively evenly. Navy ships were cut by 44 percent, active army divisions by 44 percent, and active air force wings by 50 percent. (The U.S. Marine Corps, a much smaller service in the Navy Department, had its personnel cut by only 12 percent.) The relatively uniform cuts square with the way the services do business. Historically, a "gentleman's

Table 5.2
Forces Needed to Fight a Major Regional War

Four to five army divisions

Ten air force fighter wings

Four to five aircraft carriers

Four to five marine expeditionary brigades

One hundred air force heavy bombers

Special operations forces

Source: Department of Defense, Report of the Bottom-Up Review (Washington, D.C.: DoD, 1993), p. 19.

agreement" between the services—designed to limit bureaucratic conflict within the Department of Defense—has generated relatively constant budget shares over time for each of the services. During the past ten years the budget share of the services have been relatively constant: 25 percent for the army, 29 percent for the air force, 31 percent for the Navy/Marine Corps, and 15 percent for the defense agencies.[1] Similarly, in the post–Cold War military drawdown, each service was expected to take its share of the cuts. As a result, the current U.S. force structure arose from bureaucratic politics rather than an analytical assessment of the forces required for U.S. security in the new threat environment. (That premise is demonstrated by the slightly deeper cuts in air force active wings despite the dominance of airpower on the modern battlefield—as shown by the results of Desert Storm and the war in Kosovo.)

The existing force structure is incompatible with a desperately needed change in U.S. strategy—even with the existing strategy. The Bottom-Up Review specified that the United States should have the forces needed to fight two major regional wars nearly simultaneously—a requirement that was reaffirmed in the Quadrennial Defense Review. Although billed as illustrative, the two-war scenarios involving Iraq and North Korea have become enshrined in the security literature as the two most likely conflicts. For each theater, the DoD allocated identical blocs of forces (see table 5.2).

Insufficient heavy bombers and marine expeditionary brigades exist to fight two wars nearly simultaneously. Some of those assets would need to be deployed to the first theater and then swung to the second. In contrast, the navy has more than enough carriers to fight two wars nearly simultaneously. The navy maintains that the two carriers in excess of the ten required for both wars (the total force is twelve ships) are needed for overseas presence in peacetime.

Although some analysts argue that the U.S. forces structure is insufficient to fight two wars nearly simultaneously, others believe that the threats from Iraq and North Korea have declined in recent years (even though the war-fighting requirements of the services—for example, army troops and navy ships—are increasing).[2] According to Michael O'Hanlon of the Brookings Institution, "Various DoD models and simulations indicate that a force only about 80 to 90 percent as large as today's might well be able to handle two overlapping regional conflicts of the Desert Storm variety."[3]

At any rate, the force blocs do seem somewhat arbitrary. The Iraqi and Korean theaters have much different terrain, and would probably not require identical forces. A package with more emphasis on ground forces (particularly armored forces) would probably be needed for another war against Iraq, in the flat desert. In contrast, Korean terrain, which is less friendly to tanks, would require more emphasis on airpower.

The requirement for four to five aircraft carriers to fight in each theater borders on the ridiculous. Compared to land-based airpower, sea-based aviation is expensive and inefficient. The range and bomb-carrying capacity of aircraft taking off from carriers are less than for land-based air. During the Gulf War, fifteen carriers were in the fleet, but the regional commander requested only four.[4] For political reasons, he received six. (Using more carriers in wartime helps the navy justify the retention of an excessively large force.) Even then, some sea-based aircraft were moved to land bases to increase their efficiency or had to be refueled by land-based, air force tanker aircraft to increase their range. Such practices compromised one of the major benefits of sea-based air—freedom from dependence on land bases.

In addition to the high costs of the ship and aircraft, the carrier requires costly supporting assets—destroyers and cruisers for protection, logistics ships for resupply, and (for nuclear-powered carriers) shore infrastructure designed to handle the nuclear material for its reactors. Therefore, the carrier and its battle group are very expensive for the relatively small amount of ordnance dropped on target. In the Gulf War, the six carriers provided about 25 percent of the combat aircraft, but they flew only 7 percent of the combat missions.[5] Most estimates project the cost of carrier-based air power at several times that of land-based airpower.[6]

When fighting a major war, carrier-based airpower is viable only in the rare case when no land bases are available. Even if the questionable national strategy of fighting two regional wars simultaneously is accepted, land bases would most likely be available in the Persian Gulf and East Asia (in the wealthy Gulf states, and Japan and South Korea, respectively). DoD probably figured that it would be politically impossible to justify a twelve-carrier force on the basis of peacetime overseas presence alone, so it allocated four to five carriers for each of the two regional war scenarios. Even then, it had two carriers extra. Some carriers are needed to be ready to fight a major war (or *rare* contingencies short of war) in which no land bases are available, but retaining a twelve-carrier force is excessive and expensive for those limited purposes.

Aside from its bloated carrier force, the navy's total inventory of ships is also excessive. The Navy would like to have 360 or more ships. That goal would require as much as nineteen billion dollars, to build eleven ships annually.[7] But the navy cannot afford to build enough ships to satisfy even its current official goal of slightly more than three hundred ships. The Clinton administration's fiscal year 2001 budget requested eight ships, costing $10.7 billion.[8] With an average ship-life expectancy of thirty-five years, building eight ships per year will result in a fleet of only 280 ships. Because the navy chooses to build expensive, "high-end" ships, the number of ships in the fleet will continue to plummet. (Building capable ships is not necessarily bad, but the Navy must accept the consequences—a smaller fleet.) Fortunately, a two-hundred-ship navy would be much more affordable and would remain by far the world's most formidable fleet.

THE UNITED STATES SHOULD MOVE AWAY FROM PLANNING TO FIGHT TWO WARS

The National Defense Panel, an independent panel of former senior military officers and prominent civilians in national security, was asked by Congress to critique the Clinton administration's Quadrennial Defense Review and develop force structures as alternatives to the one offered in the review. The panel realized that the two-war "strategy" was merely a way to justify the existing U.S. force structure:

The panel views the two-military-theater-of-war construct as a force-sizing function and not a strategy. We are concerned that this construct may have become a force-protection mechanism—a means of justifying the current force structure—especially for those searching for the certainties of the Cold War era.[9]

The American experience of fighting enemies in more than one theater simultaneously during World War II allows the military to continue to use the two-war construct to justify excessive force levels. But even during the Cold War, when the Soviet Union might have been willing to cause trouble elsewhere as U.S. forces were engaged in a conflict, it never did so. Today, with no superpower to orchestrate such mischief, it is less likely that two minor powers (North Korea and Iraq or Iran) would synchronize their attacks. Even if such a synchronization occurred, the conservative U.S. military would probably be reluctant actually to fight two wars nearly simultaneously, its planning criterion notwithstanding. If both regional aggressors had to be defeated, that could be done, and probably would be done, sequentially.

More important, as noted earlier, fighting regional wars in Korea and the Middle East is not in the U.S. strategic interest. Therefore, the United States should avoid planning its force structure around doing so. Instead, it should structure its forces to carry out the strategy of being a balancer of last resort.

THE FORCE STRUCTURE NEEDED TO BE A BALANCER OF LAST RESORT

The balancer-of-last-resort strategy entails coming to the assistance of like-minded nations if the balance of power in Europe or East Asia is threatened by an aggressive hegemonic power. For the United States, shoring up the balance of power should not mean "taking the lead" in repelling aggression—as it has in many past military operations; a regional power (or powers) should take the lead in maintaining the balance of power in a particular region. The United States should lend assistance only if the hegemonic aggressor threatens to take over the resources of the entire region. If U.S. forces act in this supplementary role, and if (as many military analysts conclude) no hegemonic power will arise for twenty or thirty years, the United States could reduce and restructure its forces along the lines of table 5.3. That restructured force is slightly larger than the force the BUR allocated to fight one major regional war. (The restructured force includes greater numbers of tactical air wings, heavy bombers, and aircraft carriers than the BUR designated to fight a notional regional conflict.) Unlike some alternative force structures that advocate a "one-plus war" strategy, however, the "plus" in the balancer-of-last-resort force is allocated not to operations other than war but to hedge against a tougher opponent in a regional war.

As a balancer of last resort, the United States should emphasize airpower in its contribution to any conflict rather than ground forces. Most of the ground forces should be provided by the nations benefiting from U.S. intervention. Besides, the United States has a comparative advantage in airpower—its air services are by far the best in the world. As a result, an optimally restructured force would cut ground forces more than air and sea forces (which include aircraft carriers).

Ground Forces

A force that emphasizes air and sea power fits well with the U.S. geostrategic position. Surrounded by two great oceans (which makes an amphibious assault all but impossible) and weak and friendly neighbors

Table 5.3
Force Structure Designed to Carry Out the Balancer-of-Last-Resort Strategy

	Current Force Structure	Restructured Forces	Percentage Change
Army			
Active divisions	10	5	50
National Guard combat brigades	39 [a]	39	0
Air Force			
Air wings (active/reserve) [b]	12.5/7.5	5/9	30
Heavy bombers	208	187	10
Navy			
Total ships	317	200	37
Active/reserve aircraft carriers	12/0	4/2	50
Active/reserve carrier air wings	10/1	4/2	45
Attack submarines	55	25	55
Marines			
Active divisions	3	1	67
Reserve division	1	1	0

a. The army originally planned to reduce the number of National Guard combat brigades from forty-two to thirty and convert the other twelve units into support forces. The plan was suspended after only three combat brigades had been partially converted.

b. The air force recently reorganized from wings to air expeditionary forces. Using the wing metric, the Air Force currently has 12.5 active wings and 7.5 reserve wings. The restructured force would have five active wings and nine reserve wings.

Source: William Cohen, Annual Report to the President and Congress (Washington D.C.: U.S. Department of Defense, 2001), pp. 52, 56, and 58.

(which makes the probability of a ground invasion negligible), the United States does not need a massive army to defend itself.

The Marine Corps can also be cut significantly. The Marines specialize in small-scale interventions in the developing world, which would be drastically reduced if a balancer-of-last-resort strategy were adopted. The marines would still be needed for the evacuation of U.S. embassies abroad and for amphibious assaults during wartime. However, there has not been a large amphibious assault since that against Inchon during the Korean War. The advent of modern precision-guided munitions (including antiship cruise missiles) and satellite reconnaissance (which destroys the critical element of surprise), combined with sea mines and diesel submarines in coastal regions, have made large-scale amphibious assaults much more difficult. In the Gulf War, sea mines prevented an assault on the beaches of Kuwait.

Thus, a restructured force makes the greatest cuts in the ground forces—

the active Marine Corps by 67 percent and the active army by 50 percent. The proposal cuts two active divisions from the Marine Corps's current force of three active divisions and one reserve division. The remaining active division should be able to handle the severely circumscribed list of acceptable small-scale operations during peacetime—for example, rescuing endangered embassy personnel or conducting amphibious raids to retaliate against terrorist attacks against the United States. For any larger amphibious assaults during wartime, a reserve division could be called up to augment the active division.

The balancer-of-last-resort strategy allows the active army to be cut in half, to five divisions (the BUR requirement to fight one major regional war). Five army divisions should be more than enough to fight any war in which the major contribution of the United States is airpower. The United States currently has ten divisions, four of which are light and six of which are heavy. (Heavy divisions include large numbers of armored vehicles, which light divisions lack.) Because the balancer-of-last-resort strategy significantly reduces U.S. involvement in small-scale conflicts and brushfire wars, light divisions are cut more than heavy ones. Heavier forces will more than likely be needed to help fight any aggressive hegemon.

Currently, the army's light divisions include the 82nd Airborne Division (troops delivered by parachute), the 101st Air Assault Division (troops delivered by transport helicopters), and two light infantry divisions. Those four divisions can get to a conflict faster than heavier armored and mechanized infantry divisions but have less firepower when they get into battle. The proposed force cuts the two light infantry divisions from the force and pares down the specialized elite functions of airborne and air assault by combining them into one division. Of the four heavy mechanized infantry divisions and two armored divisions, two mechanized divisions are cut. Both mechanized infantry and armored divisions have armor, but the armored division has more of it. Therefore, the restructured active force consists of five divisions—four of which are heavy (two armored and two mechanized infantry) and one of which is light (one hybrid airborne and air assault).

If even more U.S. ground forces are needed to beat back a major adversary (for example, when an aggressor badly outguns a friendly nation, or nations, on the ground), more reliance can be placed on the thirty-nine combat brigades of the Army National Guard. In most cases, a larger threat that would require the use of the Guard divisions would probably also allow plenty of time for their mobilization. The National Guard, like the Army, would also contain primarily heavy forces and would receive more funds to augment its training and readiness for war. The National Guard can be a very effective fighting force when the army gives it the proper training and equipment. In fact, the army has attempted to undermine the National Guard (as it frequently does) by reducing the Guard's combat brigades from forty-two to thirty and converting the other twelve units into support brigades. The plan was suspended after only three of the brigades had been partially converted. That ill-advised plan should be terminated and the remaining thirty-nine combat brigades retained.

Although most of the light forces would be cut from the army, the heavy forces left would probably need to become more agile. The army chief of staff, Gen. Eric Shinseki, has admitted that "our heavy forces are top heavy and our light forces lack staying power."[10] A rare bolt-from-the-blue attack by a potential hegemon might require active army heavy divisions to be sent more rapidly to the theater and combined with the ground forces of friendly nations and U.S. airpower to fight a holding action. That holding action would keep the aggressor at bay until U.S. National Guard forces could be mobilized and transported quickly to the theater. Yet heavy army (and Guard) divisions—with their large logistical demands (fuel and ammunition)—require much time to transport via sealift from the United States, at a time when the U.S. military can rely less on deploying them over shorter distances from overseas bases. Since the Persian Gulf War in 1991, U.S. forces have withdrawn significantly from overseas and must increasingly project power from the United States.[11] Even during the Gulf War, deploying heavy ground forces required about six months. Lighter, more agile "heavy" forces that can be more quickly transported by sea will be in even greater demand if a balancer-of-last-resort strategy—which advocates a further withdrawal from overseas bases—is adopted.

General Shinseki, to his credit, is apparently taking steps to create a lighter army (but some analysts say that if only light units are converted to medium-weight units, the army could actually get heavier). But resistance is likely from an army that is institutionally biased in favor of heavy units. A lighter, more tactically mobile army on the battlefield would also be more strategically mobile (would require less time to be transported by sea and airlift to the theater). The marines already have "medium" divisions and the dedicated amphibious transport to get them to the theater. (As a hedge, some heavy units could be retained in the Army National Guard, because the Guard would be mobilized only in the rare case that a severe threat arose. The rapid movement to the theater by medium-weight active army and marine divisions and the longer warning time afforded by a more severe threat would allow heavy Guard divisions time to mobilize and get to the theater in time.)

More important, once American ground forces get to the theater, they will probably need to trade off firepower for more mobility. In modern warfare, victory goes to the swift. But the army's current tank is the heavy M1 Abrams, which weighs seventy tons. In addition, the army canceled the "armored gun system, which was a lighter, more thinly armored, tracked vehicle. General Shinseki, an ex-tanker, now wants a lighter (twenty-ton) tank that can move across the battlefield on wheels rather than tracks, but resistance will arise from those who favor heavy, tracked vehicles.[12] The fielding of this vehicle has been delayed by a disputed contract.

But some skepticism about wheeled vehicles is warranted. Some analysts believe that adopting a wheeled vehicle is the first step toward creating an army designed for peacekeeping rather than war fighting. They claim that wheeled vehicles cannot traverse rough terrain, or can do so only at slower speeds than tracked vehicles. In order to ensure that transitioning to a medium-weight force preserves and enhances war-fighting capabilities, any lighter tank should probably be tracked.

In addition to cutting unneeded and expensive divisions from the force, smaller active ground forces help to preserve the liberties laid down in the Constitution. Until the historical anomaly of the Cold War, the United States had a peacetime tradition of a small standing army supplemented by part-time militia. The founders of the United States realized that Britain's geographical position, removed from the main source of conflict—the European continent—had allowed the British the luxury of maintaining only a small standing army. Having a smaller army meant that English society could develop personal liberties that other societies with larger armies could only dream about. The founders realized that America's even more insulated geographical location, and the small standing army that it allowed, could safeguard those same English liberties, which had been transplanted to the United States.

But the U.S. Army and Marine Corps remain large by U.S. historical and world standards and are encroaching ever farther into law enforcement (for example, antidrug and anti-immigration missions) and defense of the American homeland. The large military bureaucracy, especially during times of reduced external threat, eagerly seeks such new missions. The *posse comitatus* law, which is supposed to prevent the military from engaging in law enforcement activities, has already been eroded. In a republic, using the military to perform police functions is an ominous development.

In addition, maintaining a smaller standing army and Marine Corps inhibits interventionist policy makers—such as the Clinton administration's Secretary of State Madeleine Albright—from conducting armed adventures overseas, which can ultimately undermine the constitutional system and civil liberties at home. As noted earlier, many post–World War II presidents have used the large military to engage in far-flung military adventures without getting approval from Congress.

Air and Sea Power

The restructured force makes smaller cuts in navy ships (37 percent) and even smaller cuts in air force wings (30 percent). The smaller, restructured navy would provide the ultimate defense against an unlikely amphibious invasion, would protect U.S. shipping in war and during peacetime, and would provide sea-based power projection, however inefficient, when air bases on land are unavailable in a major conflict. The need for sea-based power projection should be fairly rare, because like-minded nations faced with a severe threat from a hegemonic aggressor would probably open their air bases to U.S. airpower. In addition, the army, navy, and air force currently possess redundant capabilities for the strike mission that need to be trimmed. Thus, the number of aircraft carriers can be cut more severely (50 percent) than the number of total ships (37 percent).

In other words, the navy should be reconfigured to emphasize sea control—that is, the protection of U.S. shipping in both wartime and peacetime—and deemphasize power projection. The sea-control mission would fall more heavily on surface combatants (cruisers and destroyers) acting as convoy escorts rather than on aircraft carrier battle groups. Surface combatants today are much more capable than ever before. They have sophisticated air defense and antisubmarine warfare systems that allow them to operate independently without support by carrier-based aircraft. Some aircraft carriers would still be useful, however, to enhance the protection of shipping from dense air and submarine attacks.

Also, surface combatants have recently enjoyed a renaissance in an attack role. Surface ships, loaded with Tomahawk land-attack missiles, have become the weapon of choice to destroy enemy air defenses and other strategic targets on the first day of any conflict, when most manned aircraft are vulnerable to those air defenses. Tomahawk strikes are also very useful for punitive retaliation—for example, against nations or terrorists that strike U.S. embassies overseas. In both missions, using unmanned Tomahawks puts fewer valuable pilots and aircraft at risk.

During the Cold War, the U.S. nuclear-powered attack submarine force's primary missions were to protect the shipping of troops and war materiel to the European theater against Soviet attack submarines and to hunt Soviet submarines that fire nuclear-tipped ballistic missiles (SSBNs). With the abject demise of the Soviet submarine fleet, leading to a drastic reduction in deployments, and the consequent lessening of the need to perform those missions, far fewer U.S. nuclear attack submarines are needed. Foreign diesel submarines, confined mainly to the littorals of the world are quiet, but they can be isolated and "smothered"—that is, they can eventually be forced to come near the surface (to snorkel air to recharge their batteries), where they are vulnerable to attack. The advent of air independent propulsion will allow diesel submarines to stay underwater longer but they will eventually need to come near the surface. The length of time required to kill a diesel may be more of a threat to amphibious operations than it is to U.S. shipping. In any event, the need to destroy diesel submarines can be satisfied primarily by the antisubmarine capabilities of the surface fleet and P-3 antisubmarine patrol aircraft—thus requiring fewer U.S. attack submarines. Moreover, the worldwide threat from diesel submarines is not worsening appreciably.

Therefore, the U.S. nuclear attack submarine fleet could be cut by 55 percent, from the current fifty-five vessels to twenty-five ships. Some nuclear submarines need to be retained as a kernel of expertise to hedge against the unlikely resurrection of the Russian nuclear submarine fleet or the rise of a smaller Chinese force. That U.S. smaller submarine force would also gather intelligence (although the threat has been dramatically reduced, and the United States has plenty of other intelligence assets); insert, on rare occasions, special forces on commando missions; and be the ultimate defense of the moats surrounding the U.S. homeland.

The size of the navy, and in particular the number of aircraft carriers, can be reduced, because the balancer-of-last-resort strategy would cut back greatly on naval forward presence. Because the navy needs roughly four ships in the force for every one that is deployed overseas (4.5 nuclear attack submarines are needed for every one deployed), U.S. naval presence overseas is very inefficient and costly. To satisfy the requirements of overseas presence, the navy in many cases needs more ships than would be required to fight even two major theater wars at about the same time. For example, in the Bottom-Up Review, DoD maintained that fifty-five submarines were needed for overseas presence (this requirement was later reduced to fifty boats in the QDR with little analytical support, and was then raised with equally scant public justification) but that only forty-five would be needed to fight two wars (that goal was also raised without public justification). The Pentagon says that twelve carriers are needed to provide overseas presence but that only ten would be needed to fight two wars nearly simultaneously. Thus, in general, overseas presence requires a larger and more expensive navy.

Each active carrier battle group has an annual cost of almost four billion dollars per year; that sum includes procurement and operations and support costs for the carrier, the air wing, and all of the combatant escorts and support ships in the battle group. Therefore, keeping costly additional carriers above those required for war (as demonstrated earlier, the number of carriers needed for war fighting could even be reduced) to achieve amorphous and ill-defined foreign policy gains provided by overseas presence is questionable.

DoD asserts that naval presence overseas reassures allies, deters potential aggressors, and ensures regional stability by enabling quick responses to crises. Yet the Pentagon has provided little empirical data to substantiate most of those claims. (The implication from the analysis by Press and Gholz, cited in Chapter 2, is that even if naval presence does all of those things, its cost may be greater than the cost of the instability and wars it averts.) A carrier battle group can respond quickly only if it is in the right place in the theater at the right time. If the carrier is not in position, U.S. air force bombers and fighters may be able to get there more quickly. More important, as noted earlier, most foreign crises do not affect U.S. security, and the utility of most U.S. alliances need to be reexamined in the post–Cold War era. Using naval presence to meddle in such crises or to shore up the morale of rich allies that can afford to defend themselves is questionable.

It is doubtful whether regular U.S. carrier presence in three theaters (100 percent of the time in the Pacific and 84 percent each in the Mediterranean and the Arabian Sea) provides much deterrence against regional aggression that most often has local roots.[13] Besides, a carrier may now be less intimidating to growing regional air forces, because a substantial portion of the carrier's aircraft are devoted to defending the ships in the battle group. In the rare instance that the United States needs to send a warning to a foreign troublemaker, a much more dramatic message can be delivered by dispatching a "surge" carrier from the United States rather than by using one already on station.

A smaller "surge" navy of two-hundred ships (including six large *Nimitz*-class aircraft carriers) that conducts few overseas deployments other than those needed for training would still be the most powerful fleet on the planet. No other navy has six super aircraft carriers. The only other nations with carriers that are capable of handling aircraft that can take off and land conventionally are Russia (with one fairly large carrier that deploys only sporadically) and France (with one medium-sized carrier the size of one of the twelve smaller U.S. amphibious carriers). A six-carrier U.S. fleet (four active and two reserve *Nimitz*-class carriers) would be more than large enough to perform all wartime missions in a regional conflict. That force is even greater than the excessive BUR requirement of four to five carriers for one major regional war (as noted earlier, the experience of Desert Storm is illustrative). To be conservative, a carrier was added to the BUR requirement in case one carrier was in overhaul when a conflict broke out. (It has always been unclear whether the four to five carriers in the BUR force bloc included a carrier in overhaul.)

The restructured air force is designed to defend U.S. airspace (with fighters) and to provide a capability for a quick and efficient response (with both fighters and heavy bombers) to a major conflict. Combat experience in the Gulf War shows how devastating airpower can be against ground forces. Airpower is especially potent when used defensively, to pulverize an attacking force. Thus, the number of air wings is cut by only 30 percent, and the number of heavy bombers is cut only 10 percent.

In the rare instance when a limited punitive strike is needed quickly (one example might be strikes against terrorist training camps in Afghanistan after the bombing of the U.S. embassies in Kenya and Tanzania), stealthy

B-2 bombers can strike rapidly anywhere in the world from the United States. (If a navy ship happened to be in the region, it could complement the B-2 with Tomahawk strikes on targets.)

In a major conflict against a hegemonic power, the B-2s—in combination with the stealthy F-117s and Tomahawk cruise missiles fired from ships—could destroy enemy air defenses on the first day of the war or hit other strategic targets before the destruction of those air defenses made it safe for nonstealthy aircraft to attack them. In such a conflict, the nonstealthy B-1s and B-52s, which are large, efficient bombers, could be used to attack targets after air defenses are destroyed or when escorted by fighters and jamming aircraft. They also have long ranges, so they could operate from distant bases, which are less vulnerable to enemy attack than are bases closer to the front (on which shorter-range tactical fighter aircraft must rely).

Vulnerable Air Bases

One possible criticism of a force that emphasizes land-based airpower is that air bases near the front are becoming vulnerable to attack by enemy ballistic missiles. Reliance on heavy bombers that have the range to fly from more remote bases will mitigate this problem greatly. Unfortunately, since the Vietnam War, generals from the tactical fighter community have run the U.S. air force. As a result, improvements in the bomber force have taken a back seat to enhancements in the tactical fighter force. Improvements to the bomber force need a higher priority; among other things, a research and development program for a new bomber should be started immediately.

Even if the bomber force were improved, some air bases closer to the fighting would still be needed for tactical fighters. In the short term, to mitigate the problem of vulnerability to missile attack, the air force should concentrate on improving its command, control, communications, and intelligence systems so that effective offensive missions can be mounted against mobile ballistic-missile launchers. In the medium term, theater missile defense systems should be purchased to defend the bases against missile attacks. The Patriot air defense system currently has some capability against ballistic missiles, but more is needed. In the longer term, the air force should consider buying the short take-off and landing (STOVL) version of the Joint Strike Fighter, which can take off and land from dispersed, unprepared airfields. Such aircraft would not need to rely on large, vulnerable air bases.

Airlift and Sealift

Any force carrying out a balancer-of-last-resort strategy needs enough strategic mobility to get to the theater in question (Europe or East Asia).

Although the most probable U.S. contribution to friendly forces in any conflict would be airpower, the United States might also, on rare occasions, need to contribute some ground forces. To move such forces and their supporting elements, as well as the supporting elements for U.S. airpower, sufficient airlift and sealift capacity would be needed.

Airlift has much less carrying capacity than sealift but can arrive much faster in the theater of operations. If U.S. airpower needs to get to the theater quickly during a crisis, some of its support assets would need to be airlifted. Certain high-priority items for ground forces might also have to be airlifted—for example, air defense batteries. But the United States is only 20 percent short of having enough airlift capacity to carry troops, aircraft, and supplies for two Desert Shield–equivalent operations.[14] Thus, the air force has more than enough airlift to fight one war against an aggressive power.

Any large conflict with a potent aggressor in Europe or East Asia that requires a balancer of last resort would probably afford ample warning time. Such a large conflict might also require heavier American ground forces. Thus, sealift is more important in carrying out a balancer-of-last resort strategy than is airlift.

The navy is completing construction of nineteen new roll-on/roll-off ships for transporting tanks and other heavy military equipment. Under current plans, eleven of the ships will operate from the United States as surge sealift ships, to be used in transporting military equipment to foreign theaters after a conflict starts; the other eight will be prepositioned in foreign theaters in advance of any conflict, with military equipment already aboard. In any conflict, military personnel would be flown into the theater to operate the prepositioned equipment. Surge sealift ships and prepositioned ships are virtually identical, except for the air conditioning required to store military equipment on the prepositioned ships.

Prepositioning equipment ahead of time in theaters of interest saves time when a conflict arises but has important drawbacks. First, prepositioned equipment is a lucrative target for any hegemonic aggressor. Second, storing military equipment in the theater may involve the United States in conflicts that it might otherwise choose to avoid—especially if its prepositioned equipment is destroyed early on. Even in the absence of an attack by an aggressor on U.S. equipment stores, a long-term presence in a theater may imply a commitment to intervene in minor conflicts in that region. This implied commitment is even greater when equipment is prepositioned on land rather than aboard ship. (For example, stationing American forces and prepositioning U.S. equipment in Kuwait implies a commitment to defend that nation despite the absence of a formal commitment to do so.) Third, the more benign threat environment of a post–Cold War world, combined with a balancer-of-last-resort strategy that avoids unnecessary minor conflicts, lengthens the warning time that the United States would have before a war and obviates the need to preposition equipment overseas—either on land or aboard ship. All land-based or sea-based prepositioning stores can be returned to the United States.

Thus, the navy can convert the eight prepositioned ships into surge sealift ships, at little cost. In addition, the Marine Corps can convert the entire fleet of marine prepositioning ships into surge sealift vessels. The converted ships would not add any capacity to the fleet but would be more compatible with the balancer-of-last-resort strategy, which would project force from the United States.

The existing sealift fleet should be more than enough to transport enough military equipment to fight one major theater war. The amount of dedicated shipping should allow the army alone to transport five divisions—two heavy and three light—to a foreign theater in 2.5 months.[15] The balancer-of-last-resort strategy has a heavier force of four heavy divisions and one light division, so a somewhat longer period might be needed. But the new strategy is based on the longer warning times that would be afforded by avoiding all wars except those against a potential hegemon (of which none currently exist). In addition, in the future, lighter tanks should be purchased to make the heavy forces more agile.

If for some reason the dedicated military sealift fleet does not provide adequate capacity to fight one war, it can be supplemented with commercial shipping. During the Gulf War, a much smaller dedicated fleet was augmented by commercial shipping. In fact, during that conflict commercial shipping provided the bulk of the lift capacity to transport military equipment to the theater. The major drawback to the use of commercial shipping during wartime is that it can take time to transit to U.S. ports from around the world; in contrast, military ships are ready and waiting at the dock to be loaded, after some preparation. With longer warning times, such concerns about commercial shipping should evaporate. Thus, no increases in sealift capacity are needed to carry out the balancer-of-last-resort strategy.

In short, after the completion of the nineteen new ships, no additional dedicated military sealift needs to be purchased. Similarly, no additional C-17 airlifters are needed. Some airlift may be needed for unforeseen brush-fire crises that involve American vital interests or to transport key items quickly in a larger conflict, but longer warning times and the adoption of the balancer-of-last-resort strategy obviate the need for increases in the capacity of dedicated military airlift. If additional airlift is needed, the Pentagon can rely on commercial airlift that is pledged to the U.S. government in wartime. In wartime, commercial aircraft can be collected much faster than commercial sealift.

Readiness of U.S. Forces

The force structure changes made to comport with the balancer-of-last-resort strategy imply a move toward a "tiered readiness" posture. The restructured force cuts the active army by half (from ten to five divisions) and relies more on the Army National Guard. The air force is restructured from 12.5 active wings and 7.5 reserve wings to five active wings and nine reserve. The navy's carrier fleet is cut from twelve active carriers to four active carriers and two reserve carriers. Marine forces are reduced from three active and one reserve division to one active and one reserve division. Thus, in all services the new strategy relies more heavily on Guard and reserve forces for combat power.

Guard and reserve forces are less ready to fight than their active counterparts. In a post–Cold War world, the United States can afford to reduce the readiness of its forces. No global superpower rival exists to require all forces to be on the razor's edge of preparedness. The new strategy does not require forces to stamp out brushfires quickly in the third world and anticipates long warning times for the rise of a "near peer" competitor. Thus, some forces can now be left less ready than others.[16]

The readiness of U.S. forces has slipped a little since its peak during the George H. W. Bush administration, but as Michael O'Hanlon has shown, the mission-capable rates for tanks, aircraft, and other major systems are still about 70 to 80 percent—about what they were during the Reagan administration, at the height of the Cold War.[17] Yet the Cold War is over, and no major threat to U.S. security looms on the horizon.

Readiness scores cannot be examined in isolation or even compared solely with the readiness scores of the same U.S. military units in the past. At each point in time, the potential threat must be identified and the degree of readiness needed to deter (or fight) it determined. For example, because the threat level is much lower now than during the Reagan administration, many units of the U.S. military could have lower readiness ratings than they did during the 1980s without jeopardizing U.S. national security.

Lawrence Korb, an assistant secretary of defense for readiness during the Reagan administration, has asked, "Who is out there that is more ready than we are?"[18] The answer is that no country even comes close. The Russians have a decaying military that undertakes few deployments. The Chinese have an antiquated military that has pockets of modernization but will take twenty to thirty years to be able to project sustained force in the East Asian region.[19] The so-called rogue states (Iraq, Iran, Syria, Libya, North Korea, and Cuba) are all poor, spend only about fourteen billion dollars per year combined on defense (compared to the $300 billion spent by the United States), and have the obsolescent forces to show for it. When the secure geostrategic position of the United States (the United States has friendly neighbors and is oceans away from the major areas of conflict) is added to the equation, a reduction in the readiness of much of the U.S. military can be allowed without compromising security.

Senator John McCain has proposed a tiered-readiness system in which some forces are made more ready than others, or more forces are placed in the reserves, or both.[20] The late James L. George proposed a tiered-readiness system that does both. He proposed to cut active army, navy, and air force units and rely more heavily on the reserves. In addition, only a portion of the remaining active forces would need to achieve the high states of readiness that were required during the Cold War. George noted that the proposed force structure would be more than sufficient to fight a regional war and respond to any crisis in the more benign post–Cold War environment. According to George, even if China becomes a threat by 2010, a U.S. military that reflected a tiered-readiness posture could use the long warning time to rebuild itself.[21]

Strategic Forces and National Missile Defense

With the end of the Cold War, much of the conventional wisdom on nuclear weapons and missile defense has become outdated. During the Cold War, each superpower put large numbers of warheads on accurate missiles that were designed to target the other superpower's nuclear forces—that is, the weapons were designed to carry out a counterforce nuclear doctrine. Thus, nuclear forces had to be in high states of readiness to ensure that they were not destroyed before they could be launched. Also, each superpower needed enough warheads to survive an enemy's first strike to be able to annihilate the opponent (called an "assured destruction" capability).

Conventional Wisdom on Missile Defense Is Out of Date

During the Cold War, the conventional wisdom was that defensive systems designed to shoot down incoming enemy missiles—antiballistic missile (or ABM) systems—would lead to an offensive arms race by threatening the opponent's assured destruction capability. In other words, if superpower A had a missile defense system but superpower B did not, superpower A might be tempted to launch a first strike, knowing that its defenses could destroy many of the surviving warheads that would constitute superpower B's retaliatory strike. Therefore, defenseless superpower B would probably increase the number of its offensive warheads to overcome superpower A's defenses, thus safeguarding its assured destruction capability, while working on its own defensive system. As superpower B developed a defensive system—which could in turn threaten superpower A's assured destruction capability—superpower A would have an incentive to augment its own offensive nuclear forces to negate B's defenses. Thus, according to this line of reasoning, an offensive (and possibly a defensive) arms race would have begun.

It was never clear that the conventional wisdom held even during the Cold War. Henry Kissinger, who negotiated the ABM Treaty with the Soviet Union in 1972, has stated that he did not conclude the agreement to enshrine severe limits on missile defenses in order to forestall an offensive arms spiral between the superpowers. Instead, his purpose was to constrain

Soviet defenses at a time when Congress was severely limiting funds for a U.S. missile defense system. Kissinger wanted to avoid a situation in which the Soviets had effective defenses but the United States did not.[22] In other words, Kissinger wanted to avoid a defensive arms race that the United States was likely to lose. Kissinger's account was confirmed by James Woolsey, President Clinton's Director of Central Intelligence.[23]

Some even argue that the ABM Treaty allowed the Soviets to acquire more offensive warheads than they would have had without the agreement. According to that line of reasoning, after the treaty was signed the Soviets took the money they would have used for defenses and bought offensive nuclear weapons.[24] Yet it is difficult to know how many offensive weapons the Soviets would have purchased had the treaty not been enacted, especially with their propensity to spend a large portion of their GDP on defense.

Regardless of whether the conventional wisdom—that is, the idea that deploying missile defenses would lead to a spiral in offensive nuclear weapons—was true during the Cold War, it is probably not now. Russia, currently in the greatest economic depression of any country in world history, cannot afford an offensive nuclear arms race with the United States even if U.S. missile defenses were deployed. The Russian nuclear arsenal is decaying, and the number of warheads Russia possesses is likely to decline precipitously whether or not the Strategic Arms Reductions Talks (START) II treaty ever enters into force. In the long term, the Russian nuclear arsenal could decline to as low as a thousand warheads. According to Bruce Blair, then at the Brookings Institute, and Harold Feiveson and Frank Von Hippel, scholars at Princeton University, the number of survivable Russian nuclear warheads deployed at sea or on mobile land-based missiles away from their bases has already declined to about two hundred.[25]

The deployment of a national missile defense (NMD) by the United States is unlikely to lead to a Russian buildup of nuclear weapons, especially if the United States can assure the Russians that the system will be a limited one, designed to counter small missile strikes from rogue states (for example, North Korea and Iran). But it is important not to build a defense large enough to threaten Russia's assured-destruction capability. Any vulnerability of this capability—when combined with the decrepit Russian early-warning system—could cause the Russians to launch their weapons quickly in a crisis so as not to lose them (a "use or lose" situation). A U.S. defensive system that is designed to intercept up to about twenty incoming warheads using a hundred interceptors—the first phase of a three-phase Pentagon plan—would not seriously compromise a Russian attack of two hundred or more warheads. The system's small capacity would send the Russians a signal that it was not aimed at them. In addition, the Russians—unlike rogue states, which will probably have only crude missiles with single warheads and crude (if any) decoys—have advanced missiles with multiple warheads and sophisticated decoys that could overcome a limited missile defense.

Phases two and three of the Pentagon plan would add more radars, greater numbers of interceptors at a second launch site and a full constellation of the Space-Based Infrared System (SBIRS) low system—a satellite network in low earth orbit that detects and tracks missiles at long ranges.[26] That system might alarm the Russians, because it might allow the United States to "break out" by creating a more robust defense that could threaten the Russian assured-destruction capability. Once these satellites were in orbit, a "breakout" could be achieved by rapidly adding more U.S. interceptors. Also, "SBIRS-low" is designed to help intercept missiles with sophisticated decoys, which could cause the Russians to doubt that the system was designed only to counter missile attacks from rogue states. A more capable defense of this nature could lead to what the arms control community fears—Russia's scrapping of the START process and retention of destabilizing land-based ICBMs with multiple warheads. Therefore, phases two and three of the program should not be undertaken.

To show good faith (after unnecessarily ruffling Russian feathers by expanding NATO and conducting a war against Russia's Serb allies in Kosovo), the United States could share at least some technology for NMD with the Russians. The U.S. assured-destruction capability would not be harmed if the Russians also built a limited NMD. Although the Russians might not be able to afford to move from a missile defense that protects only Moscow to a national system (just as they cannot afford an offensive arms race), sharing technology would be an even stronger signal that U.S. defenses were not aimed at them.

Missile Defense Has Utility Despite Its Inability to Counter All Threats

NMD cannot counter the most likely threats of biological, chemical, or nuclear weapons delivered by means other than long-range missiles (by ship, aircraft, sprayer, short-range missiles, etc.), but the U.S. government should take what actions it can against other threats to the American homeland. NMD is a back-up system in case powerful U.S. offensive nuclear forces fail to deter a rogue state with nuclear weapons and long-range missiles from attacking the United States. The defense could be used against small attacks, intentional or accidental. In fact, the potential for an accidental launch by a rogue state with newly acquired weapons and long-range missiles may be the best reason for deploying a limited, land-based NMD. Those nations would probably have inadequate command and control, nuclear doctrine, and nuclear safeguards. DoD should spend some money on defending the homeland; it now spends vast sums defending rich allies and regions where the United States has no vital interests.

Opponents of missile defense claim that such expensive defenses can be countered with inexpensive decoys or numerous bomblets containing chemical or biological weapons. But developing decoys may not be that easy—especially not the means to dispense them in space—for rogue nations that cannot carry out great numbers of missile tests. The superpowers did not develop the ability to launch multiple warheads from one missile until a decade or so after perfecting long-range missiles. Although dispensing decoys along with a warhead from a missile is somewhat easier than multiple warheads, the technology is similar.[27] In addition, Boeing, the contractor for NMD, maintains that the system will not be fooled by simple decoys. But a thorough testing of the system against missiles with decoys to prove the contractor's claim is needed before a decision to purchase is made.

Chemical and biological bomblets on missiles are less dangerous than a nuclear warhead. Missiles are not the ideal means of delivery for biological and chemical weapons; the explosion upon impact can incinerate the chemical or biological agents. In addition, chemical weapons are less lethal than nuclear and biological weapons; biological weapons must be released at the right altitude and temperature—two factors difficult to control when using missiles. Also, biological weapons are best when the adversary is not aware that they are being used; by the time the symptoms become apparent (several days), antibiotics are much less effective. A missile strike should be a warning to any government that biological agents could be present; antibiotics could immediately be distributed.[28]

Combine Missile Defense with Deep Cuts in Offensive Forces

Deep cuts in U.S. offensive nuclear forces—accomplished either unilaterally or through mutually reciprocal cuts—would also ease tensions with Russians and provide assurances that the United States was not attempting to achieve nuclear domination over them in their weakened state. Russia knows that its only claim to status as a great power derives from its nuclear arsenal. Russia measures its nuclear forces against those of the United States. If the United States significantly reduced its nuclear arsenal unilaterally, the Russians might have an incentive to get rid of a substantial portion of their dangerous, decaying arsenal (the more warheads they retain, the more that can be stolen or sold to rogue nations or terrorists).

The United States could cut its nuclear forces deeply even without reciprocal reductions in Russia's large arsenal. As noted earlier, Russia's decaying force probably can muster only a few hundred invulnerable warheads. As a candidate, President George W. Bush hinted that he would consider unilateral cuts in the U.S. strategic arsenal. But it might be smarter for the United States to negotiate deep reciprocal reductions with Russia. Although unilateral U.S. reductions would give the Russians some incentive to cut a substantial part of their decrepit force, actually locking them into reciprocal verifiable reductions would require them to find and allocate the scarce funds for actually decommissioning the warheads. Mutual, verifiable reductions in warheads would also be more acceptable to Congress than unilateral U.S. reductions.

Whether reducing its forces unilaterally or reciprocally, the United States should go below the three thousand to 3,500 strategic warheads in the START II agreement, even below the two thousand to 2,500 warhead level agreed to by Russia and the United States as a framework for negotiating a START III agreement.[29] In a post–Cold War world with a decaying Russian nuclear force, the United States could probably safely cut its nuclear force to about 1,500 warheads, which the Russians have proposed.

The Pentagon is resisting reducing the number of strategic warheads below two thousand. DoD currently maintains 2,260 warheads on alert to strike Russian targets. According to defense experts, the Standard Integrated Operating Plan (SIOP)—the U.S. plan to fight a nuclear war—allocates about 1,100 warheads to nuclear sites, five hundred to conventional military targets, five hundred to defense factories, and about 160 to "leadership" targets, such as bunkers. Only a few more warheads are kept on alert to hit targets in China and the "rogue" states.[30] If the United States changed its nuclear doctrine from war fighting to deterrence, it could easily make do with 1,500 warheads. In a post–Cold War world, there is now little need, if there ever was one, for enough weapons to carry out a warfighting doctrine. In fact, the destructive power of nuclear weapons has always made "winning" impossible.

In addition, the level of redundancy in U.S. nuclear systems during the Cold War is no longer needed. Then, a "triad" of nuclear-capable bombers, land-based intercontinental ballistic missiles (ICBMs), and submarine-launched ballistic missiles (SLBMs) was thought needed to ensure that at least some U.S. warheads would survive a Soviet first strike and be launched in retaliation. In a less threatening post–Cold War world, the triad could now be pared down to a "dyad" of bombers and SLBMs.

It is tempting to eliminate nuclear warheads based on both bombers and ICBMs, leaving only the warheads on SLBMs, which are least vulnerable to preemptive attack. But the United States will retain nuclear-capable bombers for conventional missions anyway. Besides, even in the more benign threat environment, some redundancy of nuclear systems may be desirable. The United States is working on technology to detect submarines below the surface of the ocean. Other nations may be working on similar technology, which in the long term might make ballistic missile submarines and their SLBMs more vulnerable to attack. In addition, in times of tension, bombers can take off to reduce their vulnerability to attack, but—unlike ICBMs or SLBMs when launched—they can be called back to base if tensions decrease.

Thus, the future U.S. nuclear force of 1,500 strategic warheads should consist of about 1,200 warheads on ten Trident ballistic missile submarines (down from the planned START II–compliant force of fourteen boats) and

Table 5.4
Proposed Nuclear Posture for the United States (number of warheads)

	Likely START II Compliant Force	START III Force	Proposed Future Force
ICBMs 500 Minutemen x 1 warhead	= 500	TBD	0
SLBMs 14 subs x 24 missiles x 5 warheads	= 1,680	TBD	10 x 24 x 5 =1,200
Bombers 76 B-52s (with 984 warheads) 984	984	TBD	0
21 B-2s x 16 warheads	= 336	TBD	300
Total Warheads	3,500	2,000–2,500	1,500

Note: TBD—to be determined. Presidents William Clinton and Boris Yeltsin issued a joint statement in March 1997 expressing their intent eventually to begin negotiating reductions to a START III level of two thousand to 2,500 warheads for each nation. The details of a START III agreement have not yet been finalized.

Source: First two columns of the table derived from William Cohen, Annual Report to the President and Congress (Washington, D.C.: Department of Defense, April 1998), pp. 58–59; William Cohen, Annual Report to the President and Congress (Washington, D.C.: Department of Defense, 1999), chapter 6; and William Cohen, Annual Report to the President and Congress (Washington, D.C.: Department of Defense, 2001), pp. 90-92.

about three hundred warheads on twenty-one B-2 stealth bombers (see table 5.4). So U.S. strategic forces would be cut from the 3,500 warheads under START II to 1,500 warheads—that is, a reduction of four submarines with almost five hundred warheads, five hundred Minuteman III ICBMs (one warhead apiece), and almost a thousand air-delivered nuclear weapons carried by bombers (the aircraft would be retained for conventional bombing missions). The five hundred warheads on Minuteman missiles should be eliminated, because keeping them over the long term would mean an expensive replacement of their guidance and propulsion systems.[31]

According to William Perry and Ashton Carter the *Nuclear Posture Review*, DoD's assessment of its nuclear forces, argued that a nonstrategic arsenal of 1,500 to two thousand tactical bombs and cruise missiles (on attack submarines) would suffice.[32] The United States should unilaterally or bilaterally (with Russia) reduce its force to that number of warheads.

Modifying the ABM Treaty to Allow NMD

The attempt by the Clinton administration to negotiate modifications to the ABM Treaty to allow a limited national missile defense—rather than withdraw from the pact unilaterally and immediately—reflects the right approach. Technically, the ABM Treaty is null and void; the United States signed the treaty with a state that is now defunct, the Soviet Union. The Clinton administration signed agreements with several states of the former USSR to modify the treaty so as to make it multilateral, but those agreements have not been ratified by the Senate. But it may be wise in the aftermath of NATO expansion and the war in Kosovo to avoid needlessly aggravating the Russians yet again.

Because the Russians still have an arsenal of 6,000 to 7,500 deteriorating nuclear warheads, a top priority of U.S. foreign policy should be a good relationship with that nation. The United States needs a good relationship with the Russians to exert maximum leverage on them to stem the proliferation of weapons of mass destruction and to dismantle their dangerously decrepit nuclear arsenal. Equally important, any U.S. effort to build a limited missile defense should ideally be undertaken with the acquiescence of Russia, because the Russians could sell rogue states sophisticated decoys that could defeat the system. The Russians have also threatened to rescind their compliance with other arms control treaties if the United States unilaterally abrogates the ABM Treaty. For example, Russia could retain the land-based missiles with multiple warheads negotiated away under START II. Those missiles are thought to be destabilizing, because they offer both sides lucrative multiple targets bunched together in single silos. Each side may have an incentive to initiate a preemptive first strike to kill multiple enemy warheads before the missiles can leave their silos and become harder to destroy, and to launch its missiles quickly to avoid losing them in a similar manner.

Besides, it may not be very difficult to get the Russians to agree to modify the treaty to allow a limited NMD, especially if they can be convinced that the defenses are truly limited and not aimed at them. Before leaving office, the first Bush administration made considerable progress in renegotiating the ABM Treaty to win Russian acceptance of the Global Protection against Limited Strikes (GPALS) missile defense system. GPALS consisted of space-based sensors and weapons and ground-based interceptors that would have provided worldwide protection against limited nuclear strikes. The Russian receptivity to negotiation was especially interesting because the GPALS system was much more ambitious than any NMD system the Clinton administration proposed.[33] The Clinton White House did not attempt to sustain the progress with the Russians, because it was much less enthusiastic about missile defense than had been the Bush administration.

A North Korean missile test near Japan, and increased congressional pressure, made the Clinton administration more receptive to missile defense and renegotiation of the ABM Treaty with the Russians to allow it. The negotiations during the George W. Bush administration will likely be more productive if the Russians realize that the United States is prepared to withdraw unilaterally from the treaty if they do not agree to amendments allowing limited defenses.

In the end, Russia will probably realize that renegotiating the treaty is in its best interest. Negotiated modifications allowing limited land-based U.S. defenses that do not threaten the Russian assured-destruction capability would be better for Russia than the unconstrained U.S. development of NMD without a treaty, during a time of Russian financial and military weakness.

Also, retaining a modified ABM Treaty would constrain ardent proponents of missile defense in the United States. Those proponents would prefer to have no treaty limiting NMD. Their long-term goal is a more ambitious and much more expensive NMD system that includes space-based weapons (GPALS or even a return to the grandiose Reagan "Star Wars" scheme). Amending the ABM Treaty to allow limited land-based defenses, rather than scrapping it, would fend off those expensive and unneeded dreams. GPALS and Star Wars were really "international missile defense" systems rather than "national missile defense" systems, because they were designed to use space-based weapons to provide global protection. Spending billions of taxpayer dollars to defend wealthy friends and allies against a narrow range of threats is ill advised.[34]

Furthermore, building wider and "thicker" missile defenses—as the George W. Bush administration seems to favor—rather than the limited ground-based system proposed by the Clinton administration would embolden U.S. proponents of an activist foreign policy to intervene against rogue states possessing WMD and long-range missiles. With such a robust defense, the interventionists would have much less fear of effective retaliation against the U.S. homeland. The Heritage Foundation, one of the foremost advocates of building an expansive NMD system, implies that an American NMD would facilitate interventions by protecting the United States and its allies from retaliatory strikes with ballistic missiles:

The existence of longer-range ballistic missiles—particularly ones armed with nuclear weapons—would have made the situation in the Gulf intolerably unpredictable, possibly precluding the use of U.S. military force. . . . With long-range ballistic missiles Saddam Hussein could have held cities throughout Europe at risk. It probably would have been impossible to form an allied coalition with Europeans had Saddam possessed the capability to target European cities with ballistic missiles, especially if they had been armed with chemical, biological, or nuclear warheads. The U.S. Congress would have been hard-pressed to sanction the use of force had Iraq possessed ballistic missiles with intercontinental range.

These lessons will not be lost on rogue leaders. A former Chief of Staff of the Indian Army expressed his view that "The Gulf War emphasized once again that nuclear weapons are the ultimate coin of power. In the final analysis, they [the Americans] could go in because the United States had nuclear weapons and Iraq didn't."[35]

Thus, retaining the ABM Treaty may have even more important positive effects domestically than it does vis-à-vis Russia. In short, a "national" missile defense should be just that—not a global defense or a wide and robust shield that facilitates U.S. interventions around the world.

The ABM Treaty allows Russia and the United States each to have one land-based missile defense site of a hundred interceptors that protects a local area—that is, Moscow and the U.S. intercontinental ballistic missile fields at Grand Forks, North Dakota (the Grand Forks ABM site has been dismantled). Missile defense systems that are designed to protect the entire territories of the two nations are prohibited. Thus, any NMD system would violate the treaty. The treaty would have to be modified to allow national protection.

Also, the number of sites and interceptors that are allowed under the treaty might be expanded. The Clinton administration upon leaving office had not yet decided how many sites ultimately to build or how many interceptors to buy, but there had been talk of anywhere from one to two sites (Grand Forks, North Dakota, or Alaska, or both) and a hundred to 250 ground-based interceptors. As noted earlier, to ensure that no "break out" capability could threaten the Russian assured-destruction capability, the number of interceptors should be limited to one hundred, at the Alaska site; also, the SIBRS-low satellite network should not be deployed. (That is, phases two and three of the Pentagon plan should be scrapped.) Thus, the treaty's limit of one hundred interceptors should be retained.

Many proponents of sea-based NMD advocate scrapping the ABM Treaty altogether and believe that building such a system would require that end (the treaty forbids sea-based and space-based antiballistic missile systems). Once the treaty was terminated, their goal clearly would be to deploy weapons in space. (A sea-based system cannot provide a stand-alone missile defense of the United States—because of gaps in coverage—and is not as cheap or as rapidly attainable as its proponents claim.[36]) Of course, such robust NMD systems are not required to achieve the stated goal: defending against a small (a few warheads), unsophisticated missile attack from a rogue state or a limited accidental launch. The unstated goal of advocates of grandiose defenses is to intercept larger potential missile attacks from China (however, at present, even the Clinton administration's limited land-based system could probably intercept China's entire strategic arsenal of about twenty long-range warheads). Yet China—unlike the poor rogue states—probably will have the money and sophisticated technology (for example, missiles containing multiple warheads or sophisticated decoys) to defeat even most large NMD systems. In any arms race with China, which could be caused by the deployment of robust U.S. missile defenses, the advantage would probably lie with cheaper offensive missiles. Thus, spending the additional exorbitant sums of money to build sea-based and space-based NMD systems to combat a limited threat seems unnecessary, unwise, and may even be counterproductive.

Benefits of a Much Smaller Nuclear Arsenal Coupled with a Limited NMD[37]

A limited NMD would allow the United States to defend against a small, intentional or accidental, long-range ballistic missile attack launched from a rogue state (and small numbers of such warheads accidentally launched from Russia or China). The possibility of an accidental nuclear launch from rogue states with underdeveloped command and control, security, and nuclear doctrine may be the best reason to deploy a limited defense. A limited NMD would provide no protection against the more likely threat from weapons of mass destruction delivered by shorter-range missiles, ballistic or cruise, from a ship off the U.S. coast or by devices delivered by a small aircraft or ships. Such threats are more likely and harder to combat; still, the U.S. government should counter the threats that it can—provided that expenditures on NMD are limited and commensurate with the narrow threat that is being countered.

If NMD provided high confidence that the United States could be defended against limited attacks from long-range ballistic missiles, perhaps the nation would be more willing to reduce substantially its offensive nuclear deterrent. As noted earlier, substantial reductions in the U.S. offensive arsenal—whether done unilaterally or reciprocally with Russia—would provide incentives for Russia to reduce and dismantle its own nuclear arsenal. Those dangerous and decrepit weapons are in danger of proliferating to rogue nations and terrorists (the most serious security threat the United States faces).

Substantial reductions in the U.S. nuclear arsenal might in turn make a U.S. NMD system more acceptable to the Russians. Reductions in the U.S. nuclear force would drastically lower the threat to Russia's already decaying assured-destruction capability. Russia's effective nuclear force will dwindle to low levels whether the United States reduces its forces or not. With fewer U.S. nuclear missiles to threaten the remaining Russian offensive forces, more of their warheads would survive any U.S. first strike. The larger number of surviving Russian second-strike warheads would not be threatened by a limited U.S. missile defense designed to destroy twenty warheads launched from a rogue state.

A limited missile defense might also reduce public pressure in the United States to annihilate, using nuclear weapons, any rogue state that launched one or more long-range missiles armed with WMD at the United States. If those missiles were intercepted before causing catastrophic damage in the

United States, less public pressure for revenge would arise. Thus, the United States government might be able to retaliate with surgical strikes using conventional weapons against military targets in the rogue state rather than devastating the target nation's civil society with nuclear weapons.

NMD Must Be Thoroughly Tested before Purchase

The Clinton administration's cautious approach to NMD was a wise one. The administration planned to renegotiate the ABM Treaty to allow a land-based, single-site NMD in Alaska that included a hundred interceptors (which could target a few incoming warheads from rogue states). As the threat grew and technology advanced, the United States would further amend the treaty to allow a greater number of land-based interceptors at at least two sites and the use of space-based sensors.[38] Yet even more caution should be exercised.

NMD has always been a risky undertaking. Reagan's space-based Strategic Defense Initiative (dubbed "Star Wars" by its critics) was grandiose, unaffordable, probably unworkable, and detrimental to nuclear stability. The more limited NMD now being developed is more feasible but still faces tough technological hurdles. Intercepting an ICBM with another missile ("hit to kill") has been compared to hitting a bullet with another bullet, but it is even more difficult than that. ICBMs are seventeen times faster than a bullet (about fifteen thousand miles per hour).[39] Even more challenging may be integrating NMD satellites, radars, command elements, and missile sites in far-flung locations into a working system. NMD is the most complex weapons project ever undertaken.

Historically, many missile defense projects have looked good on paper but proved failures. The hit-to-kill technology was demonstrated—never reliably—in only a couple of experimental programs in the 1980s.[40] Technology, however, has improved, and many experts say that the hit-to-kill technology being developed is likely to be successful (despite the mixed test results to date). The main challenges are in system integration (putting all the high-tech parts of the system together and making it work) and the ability of the system to destroy the incoming warhead when faced with decoys.[41]

Congressional pressure could drive an NMD deployment before it is technologically and operationally ready. In 1998, Gen. Larry Welch, former air force chief of staff, warned that the ambitious NMD schedule could lead to a "rush to failure."[42] Since the Welch report, the theoretical deployment date has been delayed from the original 2003 goal to as late as 2005. Because of test failures and delays in developing the interceptor booster, that date may slip to 2007 or later.

A second Welch report in the fall of 1999 stated that the NMD program was plagued by management lapses, inadequate testing, and hardware shortages. Some effort was made by the Clinton administration to address those issues, but there are still too few tests scheduled before the deployment decision. Philip Coyle, then–DoD's chief weapons tester, said that the Clinton administration's schedule, which would have compressed ten to twelve years of development and testing into eight years or less, put "undue pressure" on the NMD program "to meet an artificial decision point in the development process."[43]

When the Pentagon decides to produce weapons that have not been subjected to full developmental and operational testing, problems often arise later that require substantial amounts of time and money to fix.[44] For example, even Lt. Gen. Lester Lyles, then director of the Ballistic Missile Defense Organization, admitted that aggressively adhering to the schedule of the Theater High Altitude Air Defense (THAAD) system (a theater missile defense system designed to defend U.S. forces and allies against shorter-range ballistic missiles) led to increased costs and poor performance.[45]

The bureaucracy at the Pentagon regularly attempts to rush the development and production of weapons systems for political reasons. Getting approval for the latter stages of development and production turns on the spigot of funding to defense contractors around the nation, making a weapon system very hard to terminate. In the case of NMD, the Congress is assisting DoD in raiding the taxpayers' wallet by demanding a more ambitious schedule than even the Pentagon wants. NMD's technical complexity demands more testing and a more cautious schedule than other weapons systems, not less testing and "a rush to failure."

In other words, pushing the schedule now may ultimately lead to a delay in fielding the system or deploying a system that does not work.[46] NMD must be tested against missiles with decoys under conditions approximating the system's operational environment. A *decision* on whether to produce the system may have to be delayed until as late as 2003. But an NMD that experiences a long delay or fails to work does not defend the homeland. NMD should remain a research program until it is technologically proven.

CONCLUSION

The United States, by adopting a balancer-of-last resort strategy, can reduce its military forces significantly. The move to a smaller military would save money and reduce the temptation of the political leaders to embroil the United States in unnecessary and bloody conflicts, thus ensuring that America will be a superpower for a long time to come. Maintaining a smaller military returns to the enlightened view of the nation's founders, that possessing a small military and avoiding foreign conflicts best preserves the Constitution and the liberties and prosperity of the American people.

In particular, a small army best preserves liberties. Fortunately, because of America's secure geostrategic position, oceans away from the centers of conflict, the nation's external security can be assured even with much smaller ground forces—the army and marines. In short, small ground forces fit well with a balancer-of-last-resort strategy. Although the threat of U.S. ground forces manipulating the American political system currently seems remote, the record of the twentieth century—during which governments repressed and killed millions of their citizens—should cause Americans to be ever vigilant of their liberties. Unfortunately, the U.S. Army and Marine Corps remain large and are getting ever more involved in domestic law enforcement (antidrug and anti-immigration missions)—an ominous development. Making substantial cuts in the active army (50 percent) and Marine Corps (67 percent) would best fit with American geostrategic advantages and help safeguard U.S. liberties.

With two great oceans separating America from some of its major trading partners, the United States is a maritime nation. The United States must have a capable navy to protect both peacetime and wartime shipping (carrying military supplies to the theater of combat during any major conflict with a hegemonic aggressor) and provide airpower for the rare war in which no land bases are available. But the current fleet of twelve aircraft carriers is designed to maintain a dubious near-continuous presence in three foreign theaters and project power during brushfire crises. Such a large navy merely tempts politicians to embroil the United States in unimportant turmoil in remote regions of the world. The navy should feel moderate cuts— from 315 ships to two hundred ships (37 percent)—and be reconfigured to emphasize sea control (the protection of sea lanes for shipping).

Both Kosovo and the Gulf War showed the efficacy of land-based airpower, already an American comparative advantage. Thus, in a rare war against a major aggressor, the balancer-of-last-resort strategy would provide primarily airpower to assist friendly nations. Because land-based airpower is more efficient than carrier-based aviation, the air force should be cut back less than the navy and the ground forces. The air force eventually needs to change its emphasis from shorter-range fighters—which rely on vulnerable air bases close to the front—to longer-range bombers.

Much of the Cold War thinking on ballistic missile defense is now outdated. The United States should continue developing a limited, land-based national missile defense until thorough testing shows that the technology works. The Pentagon should couple a limited NMD with deep cuts in offensive nuclear forces to make missile defense more palatable to the Russians and enhance nuclear stability.

The adoption of a balancer-of-last-resort strategy, and a reduction in force structure that the strategy allows, has important implications for the development and procurement of U.S. weapon systems.

NOTES

1. Jeffrey Barnet, "Funding Two Armies: Why Paying for the Army's Transformation Could Spark an Interservice Brawl," *Arms Force Journal International*, May 2000, p. 14.

2. Carl Conetta and Charles Knight, "Bigger Budgets Will Not Cure the Pentagon's Ills," *Boston Globe*, October 8, 2000.

3. Michael O'Hanlon, *How to Be a Cheap Hawk: The 1999 and 2000 Defense Budgets* (Washington, D.C.: Brookings Institution, 1998), p. 70.

4. Les Aspin, "An Approach to Sizing American Conventional Forces for the Post-Soviet Era," Armed Services Committee, U.S. House of Representatives, Washington, D.C., January 24, 1992, p. 13.

5. Thomas Keaney and Eliot Cohen, *Gulf War Air Power Survey, Summary Report* (Washington, D.C.: Government Printing Office, 1993), p. 184, cited in Volney Warner, "Technology Favors Future Land Forces," *Strategic Review* 26, no. 3 (Summer 1998), p. 45.

6. Ibid., p. 43. As evidence, Warner cites one example of a study that showed carrier-based airpower to be two to three times more expensive than land-based airpower. Rebecca Grant, ed., *Origins of the Deep Attack Weapons Mix* (Washington, D.C.: IRIS Independent Research, 1997), p. 12.

7. Chuck McCutcheon, "The Shrinking Navy: Build-Down to Breakdown?" *Congressional Quarterly*, April 15, 2000, p. 876.

8. Steven Kosiak, *Analysis of the FY2001 Defense Budget Request* (Washington, D.C.: Center for Strategic and Budgetary Assessments, 2000), p. 31.

9. National Defense Panel, *Transforming Defense: National Security in the 21st Century* (Arlington, Va.: National Defense Panel, December 1997), p. 23.

10. Quoted in Sean Naylor, "U.S. Army Sees Future of Armor in FCV," *Defense News*, September 20, 1999, p. 66.

11. Bryant Jordan, "U.S. Mobility Falls Short in Two-War Scenario," *Defense News*, September 20, 1999, p. 64.

12. Sebestyen Gorka, "Cold War Thaw: U.S. Army Finally Crossing the Millennial Bridge," *Washington Times*, February 22, 2000, p. A15.

13. Congressional Budget Office, *Improving the Efficiency of Forward Presence by Aircraft Carriers* (Washington, D.C.: CBO, August 1996), p. 9.

14. O'Hanlon, *Cheap Hawk*, p. 63.

15. Rachel Schmidt, *Moving U.S. Forces: Options for Strategic Mobility* (Washington, D.C.: Congressional Budget Office, 1997), p. 79.

16. For a more detailed discussion on the advantages of "tiered readiness," see James L. George, "Is Readiness Overrated? Implications for a Tiered Readiness Force Structure," Cato Policy Analysis no. 342, April 29, 1999.

17. Easterbrook, p. 25.

18. Jaffe, p. A36.

19. For a more detailed discussion, see Ivan Eland, "Tilting at Windmills: Post–Cold War Military Threats to U.S. Security," Cato Policy Analysis no. 332, February 8, 1999, pp. 21–23, 26–29.

20. John McCain, "Ready Tomorrow: Defending American Interests in the 21st Century," March 1996.

21. George, p. 20.

22. Comments by Henry Kissinger, former national security advisor and secretary of state, at a Heritage Foundation conference, "Defending America: Meeting the Urgent Missile Threat," March 23, 1999.

23. Comments by Jim Woolsey, former Director of Central Intelligence, at a Heritage Foundation conference, "Defending America: Meeting the Urgent Missile Threat," March 23, 1999.

24. Comments by Peter Huessy, National Defense University, at a National Defense University Foundation National Missile Defense breakfast, June 4, 1999.

25. Bruce Blair, Harold Feiveson, and Frank Hippel, "Redoubling Nuclear Weapons Reduction," *Washington Post*, November 12, 1997, p. A23.

26. Elizabeth Becker, "Missile Defense May Have a Price of $60 billion: Cost and Reliability to Figure in Plan's Fate," *New York Times*, April 26, 2000, p. A1.

27. Michael O'Hanlon, *Technological Change and the Future of Warfare* (Washington, D.C.: Brookings Institution, 2000), p. 101.

28. Ibid., pp. 101–102.

29. William Cohen, *Annual Report to the President and the Congress* (Washington, D.C.: Department of Defense, 1999).

30. Walter Pincus and Robert Suro, "How Low Should Nuclear Arsenal Go?" *Washington Post*, May 12, 2000, p. A4.

31. William Perry and Ashton Carter, *Preventative Defense: A New Security Strategy for America* (Washington, D.C.: Brookings Institution, 1999), p. 90.

32. Ibid., p. 86.

33. Charles Pena and Barbara Conry, "National Missile Defense: Examining the Options," Cato Institute Policy Analysis no. 337, March 16, 1999, p. 4.

34. For a complete discussion of that argument, see Ivan Eland, "Let's Make National Missile Defense Truly 'National,' " Cato Foreign Policy Briefing no. 58, June 27, 2000.

35. Heritage Foundation, *Defending America: Ending America's Vulnerability to Ballistic Missiles* (Washington, D.C.: Heritage Foundation, 1996), pp. 16–17.

36. For a more detailed critique of sea-based missile defense, see Charles Pena, "From the Sea: National Missile Defense Is Neither Cheap Nor Easy," Cato Institute Foreign Policy Briefing No. 60, September 6, 2000; and Joseph Cirincione, "Lost At Sea," Carnegie Endowment Non-Proliferation Project Issue Brief, Vol. III, no. 27, September 12, 2000.

37. For a complete discussion of the advantages of making deep reductions in offensive nuclear weapons paired with a limited land-based NMD, see Charles Pena, "Arms Control and Missile Defense: Not Mutually Exclusive," Cato Institute Policy Analysis no. 376, July 26, 2000.

38. Bradley Graham, "U.S. to Go Slowly on Treaty: Quick ABM Overhaul Rejected by Clinton," *Washington Post*, September 8, 1999, p. A13.

39. Richard Roesler, "Missile Threat: Scaled-Down Versions of Star Wars in the Works to Protect U.S. and Troops Overseas," *Pacific Stars and Stripes*, August 8, 1999, p. 3.

40. Bradley Graham, "Navy Will Get a Shot at Missile Defense," *Washington Post*, November 11, 1998, p. A1.

41. Paul Richter, "Missile Test Failure Points to Bigger Problem," *Los Angeles Times*, January 22, 2000, p. A1.

42. John Donnelly, "Patriot Missile Costs Double, BMDO Cracks Down," *Defense Week*, January 4, 1999, p. 12.

43. Pat Towell, "Pentagon's Chief of Testing Reinforces Bipartisan Movements to Postpone Anti-Missile System," *Congressional Quarterly*, February 19, 2000, p. 1231.

44. John Deutch, Harold Brown, and John P. White, "National Missile Defense: Is There Another Way?" *Foreign Policy*, Summer 2000, p. 94.

45. Bradley Graham, "Low-Tech Flaws Stall High-Altitude Defense: In Rush to Deploy Novel Missile Shield, Lockheed Is behind Schedule, over Budget," *Washington Post*, July 27, 1998, p. A1.

46. Deutch, Brown, and White, p. 94.

6

Weapons Unnecessary for a Balancer-of-Last-Resort Strategy

According to DoD's own Defense Science Board (DSB), the U.S. military is preparing to fight the last war and is spending too much of its funding on a Maginot Line of Cold War weapons that future adversaries will be able to circumvent. According to Donald Hicks, the Pentagon's former research director and head of the DSB Task Force on Globalization and Security,

The result is severely depressed U.S. military technological innovation and a defense industry devoted primarily to the development of [armed] service-preferred legacy system replacements—not necessarily what the services need to meet emerging strategic challenges.[1]

Many weapons the Pentagon is currently procuring were originally designed during the Cold War (for example, the navy's *Nimitz*-class aircraft carrier and the Marine Corps's V-22 tiltrotor transport aircraft). Many weapons now in development began that process during the Cold War (for example, the air force's F-22 fighter and the army's Comanche helicopter). In addition, the tradition-bound military services are buying successors to Cold War systems (for example, the Navy's *Virginia*-class submarine, the future large aircraft carrier (CVNX), and F-18E/F aircraft). Some weapons are too costly (for example, the F-22) or are inappropriate for their service's future concept of war (the army's heavy Crusader artillery system). Finally, the Pentagon buys some unneeded weapons to provide pork for various states and congressional districts (for example, the air force's C-130 airlift aircraft and the navy's third *Seawolf* submarine). Thus, inertia, tradition,

Table 6.1

Total Program Costs for DoD's Most Expensive Programs

Rank	Program	Cost (in billions)	Recommendation
1.	Joint Strike Fighter (2,852 aircraft)	$250.0	Delay
2.	Virginia-Class submarine (30 submarines)	65.2	Buy only four submarines
3.	F-22 fighter (341 aircraft)	62.7	Cancel
4.	DDG-51 destroyer (58 ships)	54.0	Buy only 57 ships
5.	F/A-18E/F fighter (548 aircraft)	47.0	Cancel
6.	C-17 airlifter (135 aircraft)	44.9	No additional procurement
7.	B-2 bomber (21 aircraft)	44.4	No additional procurement
8.	Comanche helicopter (1,292)	43.0	Cancel
9.	V-22 tiltrotor aircraft (458)	36.2	Cancel
10.	D-5 Trident II missile (453 missiles)	27.4	Stop procurement
11.	Seawolf submarine (3 submarines)	13.4	No additional procurement
12.	LPD-17 (12 ships)	9.9	Buy only 6 ships
13.	CVN-77 aircraft carrier (1 ship)	5.2	Cancel

Source: Costs compiled by the Center for Defense Information, from DoD Selected Acquisition Reports and Congressional Budget Office cost estimates for the Joint Strike Fighter and Comanche programs. Recommendations are the author's.

and pork undermine the rational development and procurement of weapon systems.

A rational plan for the acquisition of U.S. weapons should reflect the U.S. geostrategic situation and a U.S. military strategy that considers such geostrategic factors. As noted earlier, the nation's secure geostrategic position will allow the adoption of a balancer-of-last-resort strategy. That strategy would in turn allow the force structure (the number of divisions, air wings, and ships) to be cut and the budgets for weapons acquisition (development and procurement) to be reduced. Within the smaller acquisition budgets, a substantial number of weapons programs under development and in production should be terminated or delayed, and a smaller number of programs should be started or accelerated.

Table 6.1 lists the total program costs of the most expensive weapons programs in the Department of Defense budget. The table also indicates what the author recommends for that program. An explanation for those recommendations follow the table.

WEAPONS TO BE TERMINATED OR DELAYED

Some weapons are unneeded, redundant, too costly, represent pork, or are relics of the Cold War. All such weapons should be terminated. Other weapons are needed, but their purchase could be delayed.

Tactical Fighters

The current generation of American aircraft (the air force's F-15 and F-16 and the navy's F-14 and F-18C/D) will enjoy crushing air superiority over all other air forces for the foreseeable future. According to Eliot Cohen, director of the Strategic Studies Program at Johns Hopkins University's School of Advanced International Studies and an acknowledged expert on airpower, "There's not anybody who's going to be comparable to us for as long as you can see."[2]

But the U.S. military services are currently developing or purchasing three new fighter aircraft (the air force's F-22, the navy's F-18E/F, and the multiservice Joint Strike Fighter) at a cost of about $360 billion. The three new fighter aircraft alone will consume a quarter of the Pentagon's annual budget for procuring new weapons and crowd out weapons that should have a higher priority—for example, a modestly priced replacement for aging U.S. bombers.[3] By 2006, the navy and air force would each be spending about 8 percent of their budgets on fighters, or twice the average of the past quarter-century.[4]

Even John Murtha, ranking minority member of the House Appropriations defense subcommittee, normally an advocate of increased defense spending, has stated, "There's no way that you can buy these three fighters as planned. The money's just not there."[5]

Thus, two of the three aircraft—the F-22 and F-18E/F—should be terminated, and the Joint Strike Fighter (JSF) should be delayed.[6] (Congress will probably produce all three aircraft in insufficient quantities instead of killing one or more of the programs. That outcome will result in a reduction in combat power.)

F-22 Raptor

The F-22 will be far superior to any air-to-air fighter in the world.[7] According to Tony Cappacio, a defense reporter, the Raptor was originally designed during the Cold War to combat two futuristic Soviet fighters that were never built.[8] The aircraft incorporates stealth technologies (making it difficult to detect with radar), cruises (that is, flies without a fuel-guzzling afterburner) at one and a half times the speed of sound, and incorporates state-of-the-art electronics.

The problem is that the F-22 will replace probably the best fighter aircraft in the world today, the F-15. The existing Russian-built MiG-29 and Su-27 and the new European-built Eurofighter may be the F-15's rough equivalent; that is in dispute.[9] However, no aircraft that the Russians, Chinese, or Europeans build would stand much of a chance when flown against large numbers of upgraded F-15s flown by well-trained American pilots.[10]

Political adversaries are not improving their air forces quickly. Russian aircraft are reasonably good, but that nation's economic crisis severely limits the quantities that it can purchase and the all-important training it can give to pilots. China is modernizing its antiquated air force only slowly, and its pilots receive substantially less training than do U.S. pilots.[11] In addition, the destitute rogue states could not afford to buy many MiG-29s, Su-27s, Eurofighters, or French Rafales to contend with the very large U.S.

air force. The Iraqi air force was decimated by the Gulf War, and the Iranian and North Korean air forces are antiquated and not likely to experience rapid modernization.[12]

Moreover, the United States can integrate its air operations the way no other nation in the world can. The U.S. Airborne Warning and Control System (AWACS) is unparalleled for providing early warning of an attack by enemy fighters and is a tremendous force multiplier in air-to-air combat. Thus, the absence of any near or medium-term threat from an enemy air force that can compete with the U.S. Air Force renders the advanced capabilities of the F-22 unneeded. (Furthermore, according to James Stevenson, former editor of *Top Gun Journal* and author of the book *Pentagon Paradox*, despite the F-22's ability to minimize the probability of radar detection, its relatively large size for a fighter might make it more vulnerable in an air-to-air engagement with a more primitive enemy aircraft. At the Top Gun fighter school, the bigger planes were always shot down first, because they were seen by the naked eye first.)[13]

If the air force needs anything (and its dominance in Kosovo and the Gulf War indicates that it might not), it is more ground-attack capability. With the absence of any substantial threat from enemy air forces, hitting targets on the ground has become more important. The F-22 program only belatedly added a modest ground-attack capability. Larger bombers with greater bomb payloads are more efficient than smaller fighter/attack aircraft against such targets. Bombers have a much larger internal bomb capacity than the F-22. In order to maintain its stealth, the F-22 can carry only two precision-guided munitions (Joint Direct Attack Munitions, or JDAMs) internally and cannot deliver laser-guided bombs or Maverick air to ground missiles like standard tactical aircraft. Furthermore, as noted earlier, land bases in close proximity to any conflict—which are used by fighter aircraft like the F-22—are becoming vulnerable to enemy ballistic missiles. Bombers have a much longer range than tactical fighters and can operate from less vulnerable theater bases farther from the conflict or even from the United States.

At a unit cost of $160 million, the F-22 is a very expensive plane, over triple the $47 million of an F-15E.[14] The F-22 would be the most costly fighter aircraft ever developed and is the third-largest program in the DoD budget. The aircraft's cost has more than doubled because of problems in development.[15] The program has also experienced delays in its schedule;[16] the plane will be delivered at least a decade late. Since it will most likely find itself in a ground-attack role most of the time, the F-22 is exorbitantly priced and not optimally designed. The United States already has two expensive stealth aircraft designed explicitly for the air-to-ground mission—the F-117 strike fighter and the B-2 bomber. The U.S. Air Force needs only a small "silver bullet" force of such aircraft to take out dangerous enemy ground-based air defenses in the first few days of a war and to destroy other targets before such defenses are obliterated. (The United States certainly should not need stealthy F-22s to escort such stealthy ground-attack aircraft to their targets; if it does, much money has been wasted on stealth technology for those strike aircraft.) Once enemy air defenses are destroyed, less expensive nonstealth fighter and bomber aircraft can take over the bulk of the air-to-ground missions. Therefore, the $63 billion F-22 program should be terminated.

If the U.S. military decides that improvements in tactical fighter aircraft are needed before the advent of the multirole JSF, the F-15E—using upgraded electronics and weapons and operated by the best pilots in the world—would allow the United States to maintain its dominance in air-to-air combat over any adversary for the foreseeable future. In an age when success in warfare depends more and more on electronics and weapons, quantum improvements in the air platforms that carry them are less necessary.[17] In addition, in contrast to the F-22's capabilities, the F-15E was designed primarily to attack ground targets and only secondarily to fight other aircraft. Thus, the F-15E better satisfies U.S. needs in a post–Cold War world where the United States already has air dominance. An upgraded version of the F-15E (with enhanced air-to-air capabilities) should be purchased instead of the exorbitantly priced F-22. (Alternatively, if the air force is adamant that further advances in dedicated air superiority technology are needed, an upgraded version of the F-15C could be purchased, either instead of or in combination with the upgraded F-15E.)

F-18E/F Super Hornet

The navy's F-18E/F Super Hornet should also be canceled. The F-18E/F is significantly different than the C/D model of the same aircraft (the Hornet) and costs twice as much, but the E/F is only a slight improvement for the extra money.[18] The General Accounting Office (GAO), Congress's auditing arm, agrees that only marginal improvement will be obtained for the high cost.[19] The F-18E/F is supposed to have a greater range and payload than the F-18C/D (according to navy officials, a 40 percent increase in range and about 22 percent greater payload).[20] The Super Hornet is also supposed to be more survivable than the Hornet. Finally, the E/F can land on a carrier with three times more ordnance than the C/D, saving on bombs that have to be dumped in the ocean.

Yet independent experts have criticized the F-18E/F program for falling short of its objectives. The GAO has repeatedly questioned the navy's reasons for buying the aircraft and whether it offered much improvement compared to the F-18C/D in range, speed, and air-to-air combat capability.[21] GAO recently testified that the Super Hornet has failed to meet all of its performance requirements, has seen its schedule slip, and costs more than planned. The navy claims that the aircraft has a range of 525 nautical miles, but GAO argues that test data indicate that the E model will have a range of only 434 nautical miles. This reduced range is only about 15 percent more than that of the C model and could go even lower. In addition, the GAO found that only a small portion of the F-18E/F's unused volume could be used for future growth in aircraft systems—a major selling point for the Super Hornet—and that most of the upgrades would fit in the C/D models.[22] (The Navy had claimed that the C/D models are stuffed to capacity with electronics systems.)

The Pentagon's own weapons testers have been even more damning. In one phase of operational testing (OT-IIA), Navy operational testers found sixteen major deficiencies in the Super Hornet and concluded that the single-seat E version was actually less capable than the single-seat C version in some areas, including the fighter-escort mission. When carrying a light load of air-to-air missiles, the E model was slightly less capable than the C model in instantaneous or sustained turn performance or in some instances of unloaded acceleration.[23]

A little later in the testing process, the aircraft appears to have improved only marginally. According to a classified operational test report (on the Operational Testing OT-IIB phase of testing) written by navy officials, in several measures of flying performance the Super Hornet offers only "marginal" improvement over the Hornet. The Navy's operational testers recorded twenty-nine major deficiencies in the E/F that result in only marginal improvements over the C/D model in particular missions. The testers said that the greater payload of the E/F barely outweighed deficiencies in climb performance, maximum altitude for combat, slow maximum speed, and slow acceleration. Echoing this finding, a report by Philip Coyle noted that for fighter-escort and combat-air-patrol (air defense of a carrier) missions (both involving air-to-air combat), the increased weapons load and fuel capacity of the Super Hornet barely overcame several shortfalls, including deficiencies in high-altitude climb performance, maximum altitude for combat, maximum velocity and acceleration, and the problem of wing buffet.[24]

The navy testers reportedly stated that the E/F was only "marginally effective in [the] ACM [air combat maneuver] mission against the projected threat." Similarly, they said that the Super Hornet was "marginally effective in the FE [fighter escort] mission against the projected threat."[25] Aerodynamically, the F-18E/F does not compare well with the Soviet-built MiG-29, which was fielded in the mid-1980s.[26] Philip Coyle confirmed that conclusion, noting that the MiG-29 and Su-27 can accelerate faster and out-turn the F-18E/F in most scenarios.[27]

In other words, in air-to-air combat, the E/F model is only marginally superior—or even inferior—to the C/D model and marginally effective against potential threats. According to internal navy documents reviewed by *Inside the Pentagon*, during the OT-IIB tests among the "top concerns" of test officials was "taking a step backward in aircraft performance."[28] Franklin "Chuck" Spinney, an analyst in the Pentagon's Office of Program

Analysis and Evaluation, thinks that the E/F's flying performance "is almost unambiguously a step backward."[29] In addition, navy officials privately concede that the twin-engine E/F is underpowered. The aircraft's engines do not provide adequate "get-up-and-go."[30]

Despite the low marks in operational testing to date, Coyle is optimistic that further testing will resolve most of the Super Hornet's performance challenges.[31] But even in the best case, the Super Hornet is only a marginal improvement over the Hornet and twice as expensive (the E/F model costs a whopping eighty million dollars per aircraft, while the C/D model costs forty million dollars each).

Yet comparing the E/F and C/D models of the F-18 is somewhat misleading. The F-18C/D was designed to be a multirole complement to the more capable F-14 air-superiority fighter and the A-6 attack aircraft. The F-18E/F will replace all three of these aircraft. But the F-18E/F has less range and payload than the A-6 and less range and fewer air-to-air capabilities than the F-14.

The real reasons that the navy hitched its aviation wagon to the F-18E/F had less to do with the aircraft's performance than with politics. In 1993, an evaluation of the F-18E/F against nine other aircraft by navy leaders rated it as "poor" and recommended "canceling the program." But the navy was desperate to replace the aging aircraft on carrier decks after the cancelation of the first replacement for the A-6—the stealthy A-12 attack aircraft. In addition, in 1991, the financial problems of the A-12's manufacturer, McDonnell Douglas, led the Department of Defense and Congress to shore up the contractor by buying the F-18E/F aircraft.[32] Although significantly different than the F-18C/D, the new aircraft was given the designation F-18E/F, implying that it was merely an upgrade to an existing model. Under Pentagon rules for weapons procurement, McDonnell Douglas would not have been guaranteed the right to build an aircraft designated as "new." Thus, the F-18E/F moniker became a way to hide corporate welfare.

The decrease in range associated with the F-18E/F versus the F-14 and the A-6 comes at a bad time for the navy. It needs longer-range aircraft as the carrier gets pushed farther from the world's coasts by threats from land-based and ship-based antiship missiles, mines, and diesel submarines in coastal areas.[33] Even before the advent of the shorter-range F-18E/F, the Navy had problems with the range of its aircraft. To reach their targets in the Gulf War, carrier-based Navy aircraft often had to be flown from land bases or refueled by land-based air force tankers, compromising the carrier's major advantage of being independent of terrestrial bases.

With the more limited threat from enemy air forces in the post–Cold War world, the F-18C/D would probably suffice for air superiority operations. Overall, the F/A-18/C remains superior to China's Su-27 and Iraq's MiG-29 (even without considering U.S. advantages, which include pilot training, aircraft maintenance, and airborne fighter control), according to the Office of Naval Intelligence.[34] After all, the F-18 E/F may even be worse than all three aircraft at those missions.

For the attack mission, the navy should purchase a "navalized" version of the F-117 aircraft. The conditions at sea are challenging for the upkeep of stealth technology, but the navy was planning to surmount them with the A-12 aircraft and will have to surmount them if a stealthy version of the Joint Strike Fighter is eventually purchased. Until the navy version of the JSF is ready for production, a navalized F-117 could provide the range and payload necessary to give the aircraft carrier some relevance to the battle on land as the battle group is pushed farther out to sea. Buying a navalized version of the F-117 is especially critical because the navy JSF program (as well as the marine and air force versions) should be delayed.

Joint Strike Fighter

The JSF is a multiple-service research and development program that is designed to produce three different aircraft having 80 percent of their parts in common. (Common parts should reduce costs by reducing the burden on the military supply and maintenance systems.) Unlike the F-22 and F-18E/F, which are nearing or are in production, the JSF program will not begin production until 2005. Even if the F-22 and F-18E/F are produced in the numbers currently planned (339 and 548 aircraft, respectively), the JSF will become the backbone of U.S. combat airpower; its production run of 2,852 planes will dwarf that of the other two types of aircraft.[35] In short, the JSF is the most expensive aircraft program in history.[36] Also, at a total cost of $250 billion, the program is by far the highest-cost weapon system in the DoD budget.

Given the divergent requirements of the three services for their JSF aircraft, some doubt exists about whether the ambitious goal of 80 percent commonality can be achieved. The navy wants a high-end stealth JSF aircraft to fill the void (left by the stealthy A-12 cancelation) on its carrier decks; the Marine Corps wants to replace its F-18C/D multirole fighter and AV-8B vertical-take-off-and-landing close air support aircraft with the short-take-off-and-landing (STOVL) version of the JSF; and the air force wants a low-end (compared to the F-22) aircraft to replace the less-expensive multirole F-16 and A-10 close air support aircraft and the more expensive F-117 and F-15E strike aircraft. The navy's desire for a long-range stealth aircraft would necessarily dominate the design of the aircraft and could drive costs up. The air force has indicated that it will not support an aircraft that is designed to meet navy requirements; for the air force, the airplane must be cheap and lightweight.[37] But using the JSF to replace both low-end and high-end aircraft in the Air Force indicates just how fuzzy the JSF concept is in one service—let alone across services.[38]

Yet the program is fairly young, and the designers eventually may be able to make the three designs congruent. But the airplane is likely to cost much more than the $28 million to $36 million per unit advertised and will probably take longer to develop than planned.[39] Fortunately, any threat from a hegemonic power with state-of-the-art aircraft is at least twenty years away. Thus, a delay in the JSF production schedule is warranted.[40]

The GAO agrees. The GAO warns that the two contractors competing for the JSF contract are not making enough progress in developing critical technologies for the aircraft. According to GAO, "To allow the JSF to proceed as planned—without maturing critical technologies—would perpetuate conditions that have led to cost growth and schedule delays in many prior DoD weapons system acquisition programs."[41] In other words, slowing the program now will help reduce cost growth and obviate even longer delays in the future caused by the use of technology that is not ready for production.

The navy JSF can be delayed longer than the air force and marine versions, but all three services will need an interim solution until the JSF can be fielded. As noted earlier, a navalized F-117 can provide a longer-range strike aircraft until the navy JSF is operational. Alternatively, the navy could adopt the cheaper solution of producing F-18C/Ds until the advent of the new aircraft. In the current relatively benign threat environment, the air force can continue to fulfill the requirement for a low-end multirole fighter by buying the most recent version of the F-16. Similarly, the Marine Corps can continue to buy the F-18C/D until the JSF is ready.

In addition, the air force and Marine Corps may want to consider consolidating their versions of the JSF. The air force has recently exhibited more interest in a STOVL aircraft. STOVL aircraft could disperse to unprepared airfields rather than remain concentrated at large, vulnerable air bases. The air force, however, must be ready to accept limitations on other aspects of aircraft performance to garner the benefits of STOVL.[42]

Thus, the radical proposal to terminate the F-22 and F-18E/F and produce the JSF (albeit with a delay) is a good one. But why terminate two of three aircraft programs when the balancer-of-last resort strategy depends so much on supplementing ground forces from friendly nations with U.S. airpower? In short, the reason is that the United States is unlikely to face a hegemonic threat for decades, and U.S. airpower will remain dominant even without the purchase of the F-22 and F-18E/F. Furthermore, at a time when success in warfare depends more on electronics and precision weapons, it is less imperative to modernize airframes rapidly.

If a new threat arises in twenty years and a new aircraft is needed, the technology in the F-22 and F-18E/F will probably be out of date anyway. The JSF, which will not begin production until 2005 at the earliest (later, if delayed as recommended), would be more up to date than the other two aircraft when any future threat arose. (The JSF will be able to take advantage of the technology developed in the F-22 program and improve upon it.) The National Defense Panel "believes that the services must demonstrate how these two systems [F-18E/F and JSF], and the F-22, can operate effectively in the 2010–2020 environment, which will be characterized by new challenges to our power projection capability."[43] The JSF might be the best aircraft of the three to meet those challenges. As noted earlier, the F-22 must operate from forward air bases that are becoming vulnerable to attack by ballistic missiles, and the F-18E/F has a shorter range than the aircraft it is replacing (the A-6) at a time when the threat from mines, diesel submarines, and antiship missiles is pushing the aircraft carrier farther from shore. The air force should consider adopting a STOVL version of the JSF to lessen reliance on forward air bases. The navy's higher-end version of the JSF is likely to have greater range than the F-18E/F.

The air force maintains that if the F-22 were canceled, the service would need to redesign its version of the JSF as a high-performance aircraft with enhanced air-to-air capabilities. But with the absence of severe threats from other air forces, the F-15C or even F-15E should suffice for the air-to-air mission. Thus, the air force (and marine) JSF could still be a low-end workhorse (like the F-16 today) with STOVL capabilities.

A hegemonic threat is unlikely to arise sooner than twenty years hence. The current abysmal states of the militaries of the two most likely candidates (Russia and China) and the fact that it takes longer and longer to develop sophisticated, modern weapons—especially when a nation is coming from behind—ensure that threat interregnum will be lengthy. Even in the unlikely event that the United States is surprised earlier by a substantial threat, the JSF program, which is developing more than one type of aircraft, will be ready in about a decade to modernize U.S. airpower adequately. The United States simply does not need to buy three new kinds of fighter aircraft (F-22, F-18E/F, and JSF) when its airpower has bone-crushing dominance—as the wars in the Persian Gulf and Kosovo demonstrated clearly— in a relatively benign international threat environment.

Airlift Aircraft

The United States is committed to buy 120 of the new C-17 transport aircraft to replace the aging C-141 airlifter (and maybe fifteen more C-17s configured for the use of special operations forces). In the past, heavier airlift aircraft, the C-5 and C-141, provided strategic lift to transport military provisions from the United States to major air bases in a foreign theater. From there, the supplies were usually transferred to smaller tactical airlift aircraft—C-130s—that can land at more austere airfields. Although a heavy airlifter (the C-17 has a greater payload than the C-141 but less than the C-5), the C-17 can fly straight to the austere airfields to deliver its cargo.[44]

Boeing, the producer of the aircraft, has floated a proposal to sell the air force sixty additional C-17 aircraft so as to replace the C-5 as well. This proposal should be rejected and procurement ended after the 135 aircraft are delivered. Even at the unrealistic $150 million price per unit advertised by the contractor (the cost is likely to be higher), the C-17 is still an expensive aircraft; an F-16 fighter costs about twenty million dollars.

More important, the balancer-of-last-resort strategy would require less airlift capacity than does the current U.S. interventionist foreign policy. The United States would drastically cut back on interventions in small, brushfire conflicts—for which the C-17 is ideally suited, being designed to land light forces at austere airfields or airdrop supplies in remote areas that have no airfields. In fact, the restructured force designed to implement the balancer-of-last-resort strategy cuts out three of the four light divisions in the U.S. Army. Only the hybrid airborne/air mobile division remains, and that capability relies partly on helicopters for tactical mobility.

Instead, the new strategy might possibly require the United States to send heavy ground forces to supplement those of friendly nations engaged in a major conflict in Europe or East Asia. Although some airlift would be needed to transport high-priority items (particularly for air force units that would arrive before army units), most of the heavy equipment would be transported via sealift. In two recent major wars, Desert Storm and Vietnam, about 95 percent of military equipment and supplies were delivered by sea.[45]

After the Persian Gulf War, the chairman of the Senate Armed Services Committee, Sam Nunn, argued that the conflict had demonstrated that the requirement for an outsized airlifter such as the C-17 was overstated and that sealift and commercial airlift could be more cost-effective than such aircraft. If civilian aircraft that can be requisitioned by the government (the Civilian Reserve Aircraft Fleet, or CRAF) during a major conflict are deemed insufficient to supplement the 135 C-17s, the air force should retain and modernize the nearly 126 C-5s already in the force (at the much lower cost of thirty to forty million dollars per copy). Alternatively, the air force could buy civilian aircraft for dedicated military use to replace the C-5s. Each C-17 has only 65 percent of the mammoth C-5's payload and unrefueled range. Buying sixty more C-17s would provide only about one-half of the capacity of 76 C-5As and severely erode the air fleet's capacity to lift "outsized" (very large) cargo.[46] The modernized C-5 does have one advantage over large commercial aircraft—the capability to drop cargo while in flight—but this feature is less likely to be needed if a balancer-of-last-resort strategy is adopted. Even the army's current requirement for enough lift capacity to airdrop a brigade can be fulfilled using about a hundred C-17s.[47]

V-22 Tiltrotor Aircraft

The V-22 is a propeller-driven aircraft that takes off like a helicopter, shifts its propellers (rotors) from a horizontal to a vertical plane, and then flies like a normal fixed-wing aircraft. The aircraft is designed to transport marines or their light equipment from amphibious ships off the coast to the shore during an amphibious assault. Each V-22 can transport twenty-four marines or ten thousand pounds of their equipment. The V-22 can fly faster than the medium-lift helicopters (C-46s) now used for the mission, making the aircraft somewhat less vulnerable to enemy fire. Also, the aircraft can fly greater distances than helicopters without refueling. Unlike helicopters, which take up space on airlift aircraft and sealift ships while being moved to distant theaters, the V-22 can self-deploy. Those added capabilities make V-22s substantially more expensive than helicopters.

But the V-22 is not especially fast, large, efficient, or stealthy. Its enhanced survivability when compared with helicopters has been exaggerated. The V-22 is more survivable than helicopters with similar countermeasures only when under attack from small-arms fire.[48] Unlike the CH-53 helicopter, the V-22 cannot carry heavy equipment, and it is twice as expensive.[49] The V-22 costs eighty million dollars per aircraft, which is much more than an F-16 and about the same as the new Joint Strike Fighter.[50]

In the 1980s and 1990s, senior officials from the Reagan, Bush, and Clinton administrations recommended killing the program. Because of the V-22's exorbitant cost, the Bush administration tried to terminate the program.[51] But for political reasons, Congress insisted that the aircraft be built. (The contractors, Boeing and Bell Helicopter Textron, had spread subcontracts around to about forty states to ensure that the program would not be terminated.) The Clinton administration agreed that the aircraft should be built, but the 1997 Quadrennial Defense Review later cut the planned purchase by the marines from 425 to 360 planes.[52] The navy plans to buy a small number of V-22s for search and rescue and logistical support for the fleet. The special operations forces may also buy a small number of the aircraft.

Because David Chu, the chief weapons evaluator during the Reagan-Bush years, told the marines that the V-22 was too expensive to ferry marines and their equipment the relatively short distances from amphibious ships to the beach, and because the Iraqi antiship missiles, mines, and beach fortifications prevented the amphibious assault during the Gulf War, the marines developed the concept of "Operational Maneuver from the Sea." The doctrine deviates from the traditional mode of launching an amphibious assault, wherein a large fleet approaches the coast, launches a massive amphibious assault, and builds up forces on the beach before advancing inland. The new concept involves keeping the amphibious flotilla a safe distance from the coast, while using the longer-range V-22s to fly over coastal defenses and transport marines directly to the targets inland.[53] The longer-range requirements to execute the new doctrine are convenient for justifying the need for the aircraft.

But according to critics, the new doctrine is risky, because V-22s cannot carry heavy equipment or large amounts of supplies. The marines must still rely on slower, heavy helicopters (for example, the CH-53) and air-cushion landing craft to carry heavy equipment to land.[54] An unsupported assault inland by marines using V-22s is every bit as risky as an unsupported airborne assault by light army troops using parachutes. Since the end of World War II, large airborne assaults have been rare (the reason for consolidating airborne and air assault divisions in the restructured force). For equally compelling reasons, inherently risky amphibious assaults have also been rare. It seems unwise to add even more risk by landing unsupported marines inland, with only light equipment, against a reasonably capable foe.

The Marine Corps should rethink the "Operational Maneuver from the Sea" doctrine, which seems, at least in part, contrived to justify the procurement of an unneeded aircraft. Landing marines with heavy equipment and supplies on the beach from over the horizon (to reduce the vulnerability of amphibious ships) may be a good idea, but risky, unsupported landings inland via V-22 are less attractive.

Furthermore, the balancer-of-last-resort strategy, which focuses on assisting friendly nations against large-scale aggression by a great power, will require fewer amphibious assaults of any kind and only one active marine division and one reserve division to carry them out. Thus, the diminished need for the aircraft and its high cost are compelling reasons to stop production.

Instead, an alternative discussed by the Congressional Budget Office should be adopted. Rather than continuing production of the V-22, more of the less expensive CH-53E heavy-lift helicopters should be produced.[55] Alternatively, the marines could buy the army Blackhawk helicopter for about a sixth of the cost of the V-22.[56] The small number of V-22s already purchased might be used for search and rescue or special operations (for example, rescuing hostages).

The Comanche Helicopter

The Comanche is a stealthy, light reconnaissance and attack helicopter that can operate at night and in all weather. It would replace the OH-58 Kiowa scout and AH-1 Cobra light-attack helicopters. The Comanche program was begun in 1983 during the Cold War and was originally designed to combat Soviet tanks in Central Europe. The army and other advocates of the Comanche now argue that the helicopter can act as the "quarterback of the digital battlefield" by rapidly collecting and disseminating tactical reconnaissance. They maintain that the armed reconnaissance helicopter will help the army fulfill its strategic vision for the next century, which emphasizes the dissemination of timely information about the situation on the battlefield.[57]

But the Comanche is very expensive for a helicopter (about thirty million dollars a copy), and will have been in development over twenty years when low-rate production begins in 2004. The cost to develop, procure, and operate the Comanche over its lifetime is estimated at about $100 billion.[58] The National Defense Panel tacitly acknowledged that the army cannot afford both of its two highest procurement priorities—the Comanche and the Crusader self-propelled howitzer—in the quantities now planned. The panel implied that fewer Commanches and Crusaders should be purchased.[59] Richard Aboulafia, an analyst specializing in aircraft at the Teal Group, was more blunt: "It's all a question of money. The Army cannot afford Comanche, Crusader and the AH-64D [Apache Longbow attack helicopter]."[60]

The Apache is a heavy, tank-busting attack helicopter that is being upgraded with the Longbow radar, digital technology, and increased firepower in a dramatic enhancement of its effectiveness.[61] Although the Comanche was originally justified as inexpensive to purchase, operate, and maintain, the new helicopter is now more expensive than the Apache. But the Apache is bigger and heavier than the Comanche and has similar capabilities. In the Gulf War, the Apaches were used without scout helicopters; therefore, no Comanches need to be purchased for that role.[62] In the future, greater use of unmanned aerial vehicles (UAVs) and improved DoD information networks should further render a reconnaissance role for the manned helicopter questionable.[63] Indeed, Eric Labs and Joann Vines of the Congressional Budget Office have developed and analyzed an option for using UAVs instead of helicopters. UAVs are in some ways more capable reconnaissance platforms than the Comanche. They are about 15 percent faster, can observe an area five times longer without need to refuel, and can eliminate the risk to pilots in hazardous missions.[64]

Enough Apaches have been purchased to provide the required number of attack helicopters for all but five of the army's divisions (the other five divisions have the AH-1 Cobra light attack helicopters, which would be replaced by Comanches). But the balancer-of-last-resort strategy cuts the army force structure by five divisions. Thus, there is no need to purchase Comanches to replace Cobra helicopters in those divisions. If any additional attack helicopters are needed, the army can purchase additional Kiowa Warriors (an armed version of the scout helicopter), which were very effective in the Gulf War.

After the Cold War, some analysts would argue that the threats the army is likely to face would not require the advanced stealth, electronics, and other technologies that the Comanche would incorporate.[65] The Apache, with its highly successful performance in the Gulf War, earned a reputation as the most formidable tank-killing helicopter in the world. (The failure to use the Apaches during the war in Kosovo was mainly caused by commanders' fears of casualties, and by inadequate training.) With the addition of the sophisticated Longbow millimeter-wave radar, the Apache can operate at night and under most weather conditions, using the Hellfire missile.[66] A force of Apaches (especially when upgraded to the Longbow configuration), supplemented by more Kiowa Warriors if needed, should be adequate in the post–Cold War environment.

Crusader Self-Propelled Howitzer

The Crusader self-propelled howitzer is the army's other high-priority item for procurement. As noted earlier, the National Defense Panel implied that both the Comanche and the Crusader should be purchased, but in smaller quantities. The Pentagon consistently tries to stuff more weapons into the defense plan than it can afford (this is called "overprogramming"). Then, when budgets decline or costs of weapons inevitably increase, the Pentagon merely cuts the quantities of each weapon system to be purchased; the political constituencies supporting them are too strong to eliminate any of them. This inefficient solution leads to even higher unit costs for each system, because overhead costs—for example, the cost of setting up the production line—are spread over fewer units. The Pentagon's practice no longer surprises anyone, but the timidity of the independent panel's critique of the two programs and its backhanded endorsement of poor procurement practices is disquieting.

Like the Comanche, the Crusader should be terminated. The Crusader combines an artillery system and a reloading vehicle—each with a crew of three—that will be fielded by 2005. The army originally wanted to purchase about 1,100 units.[67] The system will replace the M109 Paladin self-propelled howitzer, which has been in the inventory since the early 1960s.[68] But the Crusader is too heavy and does not make use of "leap-ahead" technologies. The Crusader clearly did not fit well with the National Defense Panel's recommendations to "evolve to lighter, greater range, more lethal fire support systems" and "reduce systems that are difficult to move and support; shift to lighter, more agile automated systems."[69] The Crusader, with its rapid rates of fire and longer range, is more lethal over longer distances than the Paladin. Also, the Crusader has automated the firing of artillery, previously a labor-intensive activity. But both the House and Senate Armed Services Committees agree that the fifty-five-ton Crusader does not fit into the army's plan for a more agile force.[70] (With its supply vehicle, the whole system weighs over a hundred tons.)[71] RAND concurs with that assessment.[72] Nevertheless, the National Defense Panel lacked the courage to recommend terminating the program.

Since the panel's report, General Shinseki has made the creation of a lighter, more agile force a high priority. In the past, army leaders have talked about making divisions lighter and more deployable, but every major unit has increased in weight since the Gulf War. The Crusader program endures. The program has been incrementally revised in an attempt to save it from the budget axe. The howitzer has been reduced in weight, size, and capacity so that its transport weight (empty) is about forty tons. But when fully loaded, the vehicle could still weigh as much as fifty tons. (With its supply vehicle, the system will still weigh about eighty tons). The redesign to reduce the weight caused development costs to soar by 48 percent.[73] To save money only 480 systems will be purchased instead of the planned 1,138.[74]

Although the army has called the Crusader's technological development "revolutionary," Congress declared it to be "evolutionary" and demanded a rationale for adhering to the program's planned schedule. Congress, not the army, seems to be correct. The army decided against using a more technologically risky cannon with liquid propellant (a series of chemicals that could send a shell up to thirty miles) in favor of employing a less-advanced gun using solid propellant. Also, the army spurned a more expensive turbine engine for a cheaper diesel power plant. As a result of those compromises, some in the army's ground-vehicle community believe that the Crusader is an expensive way to make only marginal improvements (the same problem found in the navy's F-18E/F aircraft).

In other respects, the Crusader may have too much technology. According to the General Accounting Office, because the Crusader's autoloader has no backup, the crew cannot get into the rear of the vehicle to load the cannon manually.[75]

A replacement for the Paladin is needed, but a new self-propelled artillery piece should be lighter than even the modified Crusader so that it can be a part of the more agile army of the future. An R&D program for a lighter self-propelled gun should be started immediately.

Upgrading the M1A1 Tank

The army is upgrading some of its M1A1 Abrams tanks to an M1A2 version. The M1A2 adds a commander's independent thermal viewer, enhanced armor, more advanced electronics, enhanced reliability, and fully integrated weapons stations so that targets can be engaged more quickly. In short, the M1A2 is more lethal and survivable than the M1A1.[76]

Yet the M1A1 is already the best tank in the world. In the Gulf War, the Abrams literally blew the turrets off Soviet-made T-72 tanks. Thus, much sentiment exists even in the army to discontinue the upgrades and transfer those funds to research on future weapons. This course of action should be taken immediately.

Some of the funds saved should be used for research and development on a much lighter tank. In the future, even "heavy" units (armored or mechanized infantry) will need to be more agile on the battlefield. They will need to have greater speed and will require a logistical tail (for example, petroleum and ammunition supplies) that is leaner and less vulnerable to missile attack. The heavy (seventy-ton) M-1 tank, dominant on the plains of Central Europe, is too big to navigate narrow mountain roads and bridges and tight urban streets (the world has become more urban, and major conflicts will increasingly take place in built-up areas).[77] Roads must often be reinforced before the M-1 can traverse them, undermining the shock value of rapid armored assault. Heavy forces must also be more rapidly transportable to the theater using airlift and sealift. Lighter armor could be transported more quickly; less fuel must be hauled for lighter tanks, and more of them can fit into fewer ships and aircraft. Thus, saved funds should be used to develop a lighter tank—which has all of those qualities—rather than throwing it away on improvements to a heavy system.

Unneeded Antitank Weapons

DoD is spending $11.1 billion to produce ten antitank weapons and $3.5 billion to develop nine new systems. U.S. inventories of antiarmor weapons are almost as large as they were during the Cold War. Yet the major threat that existing and developmental antitank weapons were designed to counter—a massed Soviet tank attack in Europe—is gone. According to the General Accounting Office, "Plans to acquire large quantities of new and improved antiarmor weapons do not appear consistent with the reduced size of the armored threat and the existing large and capable inventory of antiarmor weapons.[78] The report concluded that the number of tanks and other armored vehicles in potential areas of conflict has declined to less than 20 percent of what it was at the end of the Cold War.[79]

Antitank weapons are a low-cost way of countering armored forces, particularly when used as a defensive weapon. In fact, in the battle against the tank, antitank weapons may be gaining the edge. In the future, the United States would probably want to use antitank weapons to help defend against the massed armored offensive of an aggressive great power. But the current armored threat has declined so much that ten existing and nine developmental programs cannot be justified. Most of those weapons will be obsolete by the time any new armored threat might arise, in twenty to thirty years. Thus, the army should prune the numbers of such systems under development and concentrate its resources on only the most promising systems. Not all of the nine new systems need to be purchased.

Advanced Amphibious Vehicle

The Advanced Amphibious Assault Vehicle (AAAV) is designed to replace the Amphibious Assault Vehicle (AAV). Both vehicles are amphibious personnel carriers that transport marines and their equipment from amphibious ships to shore by "swimming." Once they reach the shore, they traverse the land using tanklike treads.

The AAV is very slow on land (fifteen to twenty miles per hour) and on the water (six to eight miles per hour). The slow speed over land means that the AAV cannot keep up with a main battle tank, which travels at about thirty miles per hour. The snail's pace over water means that too much time is spent traveling from the ships twenty-five to fifty miles off shore to the coastline; the AAV requires three or more hours to go twenty-five miles. This glacial pace impedes the rapid buildup of forces on the shore—which is vital to surprising the enemy and to the success of the amphibious assault—and exposes the marines in the AAVs to more enemy fire.

To overcome the AAV's limited speed on water, the navy could bring the amphibious ships closer to the shore—making them more vulnerable to enemy mines, patrol boats, aircraft, diesel submarines, and precision-guided munitions—or it could transport the AAVs on air-cushion landing craft (LCACs). But the LCACs are designed to transport nonamphibious heavy equipment, such as tanks and artillery, to the shore. Taking up space on the LCACs to transport AAVs would impede the rapid buildup of amphibious forces on the shore.[80] Besides, it seems silly to transport on a boat a vehicle that is supposed to be able to swim to shore.

The AAAV, currently under development, is designed to speed up amphibious operations. The Marine Corps maintains that the AAAV will be able to travel over land at up to forty-five miles per hour and over water at up to twenty-nine miles per hour. If the AAAV achieves those speeds, the amphibious fleet will be able to avoid the aforementioned threats in coastal waters and hold more of the enemy coastline at risk by staying farther offshore.[81] In addition, the AAAV is designed to be more survivable and lethal than the AAV. The AAAV will substitute a twenty-five-millimeter cannon for the .50-caliber machine gun on the AAV.[82] The AAAV is designed to defeat enemy light armored vehicles during the 2005–2025 period; the AAV cannot defeat the light armored vehicles of today.[83]

The AAAV is needed, because the AAV severely limits amphibious assaults from over the horizon. (The LCAC, already in the inventory, is also needed for such long-range assaults. Although the Marine Corps argues that the V-22 is necessary as well for that mission, helicopters have the range to get to deliver troops inland from ships twenty-five to fifty miles out to sea, albeit at a slower speed than the V-22. The V-22 can best be used to transport marines and light equipment farther inland, but that is a risky mission.) But as argued earlier, reconnaissance by satellites and unmanned aerial vehicles, precision-guided munitions, and mines may have rendered large-scale amphibious assaults obsolete. More important, the balancer-of-last-resort strategy will require that fewer amphibious assaults of any size be undertaken. Cutting the Marine Corps from three active divisions and one reserve division to one active division and one reserve division should cut the number of AAAVs needed to well below the thousand vehicles being planned.

Nimitz-Class Aircraft Carrier and Future Carriers

The tenth and last *Nimitz*-class aircraft carrier, the CVN-77, was funded by Congress in 2001. Because aircraft carriers are relatively inefficient tools of power projection during a major war (except in the rare case when no land bases are available), the balancer-of-last-resort strategy cuts the carrier force from twelve to six ships.

The CVN-77 will be a "transition" to a class of more stealthy carriers. In plain English, the CVN-77 is another of the large, vulnerable ships of the past. The ship would be easily spotted on radar and may be vulnerable to small numbers of antiship cruise missiles or torpedoes. Cruise missiles can be fired from underwater, from small ships, or from land. Vulnerable carrier battle groups spend a significant amount of their resources defending themselves, leaving fewer aircraft and ordnance for attacking the enemy.

Furthermore, carriers are becoming even more inefficient in projecting power inland as they are pushed farther and farther from shore by the danger of mines and antiship missiles. Thus, the navy needs a longer-range aircraft than the F-18E/F—which, as a noted, has a shorter range than the A-6 aircraft that it will replace—to hit targets inland. Aircraft carriers were somewhat more useful for power projection when they had the A-6. But as the Gulf War showed, when forward land bases are available in theater, as they most assuredly would be in any war with a hegemonic power, land-based airpower is superior to that based on carriers. In fact, also as noted, during the Gulf War, some U.S. carrier aircraft were flown to land to operate from longer runways, thus improving their range and payload. Also, aircraft that did operate from carriers were refueled from tankers operating from land bases, negating the independence of carriers from land bases (a major advertised advantage).

Therefore, a six-carrier force should be more than enough to hedge against the remote possibility that no land bases will be available and should also ensure U.S. control of the seas. Only two other nations have aircraft carriers that can launch conventional (nonvertical-takeoff-and-landing) aircraft. The French have one carrier at thirty-three thousand tons, which carries thirty to forty fixed-wing aircraft; the Russians have only the 68,000-ton *Kuznetzov*, which carries twenty fixed-wing aircraft.[84] The operation of the Russian ship has been hampered by the severe funding constraints brought about by the Russian economic depression. All other aircraft carriers in the world are smaller ships that can carry only vertical-takeoff-and-landing (VTOL) aircraft. Thus, even a reduced American force of six *Nimitz*-class ships at about a hundred thousand tons apiece—each carrying seventy fixed-wing aircraft—would clearly dominate the world's oceans.

In the unlikely event that the U.S. Navy needed more than six carriers during a conflict to control the seas or to substitute for absent land bases, large flat-deck amphibious ships could be easily converted into smaller aircraft carriers that would supplement the larger ships. The amphibious flat decks (LHDs and LHAs) displace about forty thousand tons, making them larger than the medium-sized French carrier that can carry conventional aircraft. Normally, the flat decks carry helicopters and six AV-8B Harrier jets (vertical-takeoff-and-landing aircraft). According to navy and Marine Corps officials, if the flat decks were needed for the sea control mission, the helicopters could be taken off and fourteen more Harriers added. Of course, the smaller flat decks control less air and sea space and carry less ordnance than a *Nimitz* supercarrier.[85] But the flat decks are well suited to be supplements to the larger carriers for the sea control mission. If land bases were not available during a war, Harriers from the smaller flat decks could provide air defense for a task force of multiple *Nimitz*-class super-carriers. That air defense umbrella would free up all of the super carriers' longer-range aircraft to attack targets on land.

Maintaining a fleet of six *Nimitz*-class carriers would not require the U.S. Navy to deploy a new carrier until at least 2031. The oldest of the six most recent *Nimitz*-class carriers was commissioned in 1986, and carriers have a normal service life of at least forty-five years. (In fact, six carriers—including the three oldest *Nimitz*-class ships—would need to be decommissioned early to reduce the carrier fleet to six ships.) Thus, the navy does not need yet another *Nimitz*-class ship. Congress appropriated the money for the CVN-77 in 2001 but the ship can still be canceled.

Each nuclear-powered carrier costs almost six billion dollars (fiscal year 2000 dollars) to procure; its air wing costs slightly more. In addition, operating and maintaining one ship and its air wing costs over $600 million a year.[86] This vast sum does not even include the six surface ships and two submarines designated to protect the carrier and the logistics ships that supply it. Carriers are expensive and inefficient means of projecting power during a major war. Significant sums could be saved by reducing the carrier force and forgoing procurement of the CVN-77.

With a smaller force of six carriers, the procurement of a future, more stealthy class of aircraft carriers could be delayed from 2008 to 2031. Originally, the navy planned to introduce a revolutionary smaller, and thus stealthier, carrier in 2008, but the seven billion per ship price tag and the reduced number of daily strike missions that could be accommodated on a smaller deck led to a modification of the project. Now the new class of carriers will incorporate only incremental changes in stealth technology. For example, the new carrier would have a smaller "island" to reduce the carrier's radar signature; fewer antennas to reduce its electronic signature; and electromagnetic catapults instead of steam catapults, to lessen its noise signature.[87] In short, the new class of carriers would be only marginally more stealthy than the relatively vulnerable *Nimitz* class. If the new class was delayed, new stealth technologies might be developed that could revolutionize carriers at an affordable price. Secondly, STOVL or VTOL technology for aircraft might be improved so much that smaller carriers could deliver the same number of bombs on target as the large *Nimitz* platforms of today. (That is, range and payload of penalties of STOVL and VTOL aircraft might be reduced.) Alternatively, improvements of STOVL or VTOL technology might render the carrier obsolete as the new aircraft were dispersed to smaller, less vulnerable surface combatants—destroyers and cruisers.

Virginia-Class Submarines

The nuclear-powered attack submarine force is in the same situation as the carrier force. The submarine force needs to be reduced in size, thereby obviating the need to buy new submarines that are now beginning to be built (the *Virginia* class).

The 1997 Quadrennial Defense Review decided that the post–Cold War drawdown of nuclear attack submarines from about a hundred vessels would stop at fifty ships. Also, the Joint Chiefs of Staff had a requirement for ten to twelve of those ships to be very quiet by 2012. Recently, with budget surpluses looming as far as the eye can see, DoD has decided to return to the upper end of the goal of forty-five to fifty-five ships enunciated in the 1993 Bottom-Up Review and may go even higher. According to a study by the Joint Staff and others, the United States should have fifty-five to sixty-eight submarines by 2015 (eighteen of which should be *Virginia*-class submarines "to counter the technologically pacing threat"); it should have sixty-two to seventy-six boats by

2025.[88] Although Gen. Henry Shelton, the chairman of the Joint Chiefs of Staff, has not endorsed the upper end of the study's goals, the need for even fifty-five boats is questionable.[89]

Although still a formidable naval weapon, the nuclear attack submarine had its heyday during the Cold War. U.S. attack submarines were assigned to hunt Soviet attack submarines that would be attempting to sink U.S. convoys of war materiel going to any land war in Europe. They were also assigned to trail and destroy Soviet nuclear ballistic missile submarines (larger submarines that can launch long-range nuclear missiles) under the polar ice cap. With the abject demise of the Soviet submarine fleet (lack of funds makes deployments rare and training meager), the need for U.S. submarines to do both of those missions has evaporated.

The end of the Cold War should obviate the need for U.S. attack submarines to hunt Soviet ballistic missile submarines in the Arctic. Even during the Cold War, rendering a substantial portion of the adversary's nuclear force vulnerable to attack was considered by many analysts to be destabilizing. In a nuclear crisis, such vulnerability might cause the adversary to use the weapons so as not to risk losing them. In the post–Cold War world, the Russians may be even more likely to be trapped into a "use or lose" (that is, launching weapons on warning of attack) situation if a significant number of their few remaining survivable nuclear weapons—those on ballistic missile submarines—are targeted. The erosion of the Russian early-warning system makes Russia even more paranoid about losing its weapons to a surprise U.S. nuclear attack, thereby creating an even more dangerous situation.

The United States has apparently never been very good at finding Soviet subs in the Arctic, where the defense has the advantage of thousands of miles of shallow, ice-filled seas in which to hide. U.S. scientists have had limited success in designing a sonar that can compensate for conditions in those shallow seas—that is, temperature and salinity layers, the noise of ever-present storms, the sound of ice crunching, and the barks of seals and walruses. Thus, tracking Soviet subs in Arctic regions is generally difficult.[90]

Yet according to a Russian security official, after the end of the Cold War, American submarines have continued to try to tail Russian ballistic missile submarines closely. That cat-and-mouse behavior could result in a crisis if there is a collision or a skirmish between the two vessels. Two such collisions in 1992 and 1993 caused Russian president Boris Yeltsin to make a personal appeal to president Bill Clinton to end such underwater tailgating.[91] President Clinton was furious when a U.S. sub—the *Grayling*—hit a Russian ballistic-missile submarine (SSBN) in 1993. Since 1993, U.S. officials say that U.S. attack submarines have maintained a distance of at least 5 miles. Yet Russian officials say that the trailing of Russian SSBNs presents the appearance, if not the reality, that the U.S. is training to neutralize

Russia's sea-based nuclear deterrent.[92] In the post–Cold War era, such risks are no longer worth the rewards (if they ever were).

The discarding of this dangerous and unneeded mission should naturally lead to the scrapping of the original requirement to have ten to twelve very quiet submarines by 2012. The official reasons given by the Joint Chiefs of Staff for that quantity of very quiet boats was to attack Russian ballistic-missile submarines and provide submarine presence overseas.

In the long term (twenty to fifty years), if surface vessels become more vulnerable to enemy attack or a new near peer competitor arises (similar to the Soviet Union), much of the navy may have to be put under water. Of course, the *Virginia*-class submarines, now beginning to be built, will be out of date by then or may be the wrong kind of submarine. For example, in the long term, the navy may want to design a large futuristic submarine that is designed to carry large numbers of conventional missiles for attacking targets ashore. But in the near to medium term, no major undersea threat exists that would preclude a reduction in the submarine force.

Yet the navy is desperately seeking new missions for the attack submarine, to justify keeping as many vessels in the force as possible during that period. The Bottom-Up Review completed in 1993 called for forty-five ships to fight two theater wars nearly simultaneously and fifty-five vessels to meet requirements for overseas presence. Four years later, the Quadrennial Defense Review, without much justification, chose the midpoint and declared that the attack submarine force would consist of fifty ships. Thus, the requirement for overseas presence is softer than it first appears. A deeper analysis shows that it is quicksand.

The original requirement of ten to twelve very quiet submarines to provide overseas presence was always overkill. Two of the few legitimate overseas-presence missions for submarines are collecting intelligence and the rare insertion of special forces off coasts of adversarial nations. In most cases, to do those missions, U.S. nuclear submarines must avoid diesel submarines in coastal areas. Such evasion is not hard to accomplish, because the much smaller diesel submarines usually have limited sensors and weapons. Also, surface navies in the third world have primitive antisubmarine warfare systems. Thus, existing U.S. submarines can handle the legitimate overseas missions very well. At present, no new very quiet submarines need to be procured.

But generally, the submarine force has never been much good at conducting overseas presence missions (the collection of intelligence and insertion of special forces excluded). "Showing the flag" is usually best carried out by surface ships that can be seen by the country that is the object of the coercion. Furthermore, the balancer-of-last-resort strategy calls for a substantial reduction in U.S. naval presence overseas.

Also, the post–Cold War practice of deploying fairly regularly two submarines to guard aircraft carrier battle groups was always questionable. Even during the Cold War, when a substantial threat existed to carrier battle groups from Soviet nuclear attack submarines, U.S. attack submarines rarely operated with the battle groups. The Silent Service was renowned for its independent operations. Strangely, as the threat from the Soviet submarine force declined and the navy began to focus on operating in littoral areas of the third world, the navy began sending more regularly two submarines to ride shotgun (conduct direct-support missions) with every battle group.[93]

Yet diesel submarines owned by rogue nations are much less of a threat to the battle groups than were their Soviet nuclear brethren. The smaller diesel boats carry fewer sensors, less data processing equipment, and fewer weapons. They are also vulnerable to attack when they come near the surface to recharge their batteries by taking in air through a snorkel. Diesel submarines are a greater threat to commercial shipping than they are to nuclear submarines or to surface warships, both possessing their own sophisticated antisubmarine warfare systems. Furthermore, the Office of Naval Intelligence admitted that the number of modern diesel boats worldwide was not increasing rapidly.[94] It is curious that, as the post–Cold War threat from enemy submarines decreased dramatically, the need for underwater protection of battle groups seemingly increased.

In addition, it is questionable how much protection U.S. attack submarines provide the battle group. Although U.S. attack submarines are fast enough to keep up with battle groups, most cannot use their sensors at that speed. Moreover, the attack submarines may actually hinder the operations of the battle group. Some submarine officers, including a submarine commander, argue that the submarine's limited ability to communicate with other ships in the battle group increases the potential for collisions and even fratricide (mistakenly attacking one's own forces).[95] In fact, Kevin Peppe, the submarine commander, made the following frank admission:

It's a dirty little secret, one of those things most in the business know but are too polite to say: U.S. nuclear-powered attack submarines (SSNs) no more support the carrier battle group commander than wet roads support traffic safety. . . . The heart of the problem is that no one really seems to know what the submarine is supposed to do for the carrier battle group.[96]

The commander then candidly admitted that the added mission as escorts to battle groups was designed merely to justify a larger submarine force.

How does the [submarine] force continue to play a vital role in shaping the future if we continue to be less than fully integrated into what the American people pay their naval forces to do—maintain peace and stability through the presence of forces forward, the centerpiece of which is and will remain the carrier battle group. . . .

Submarines remain critical to this nation's maritime future. But if we decide that this future in fact requires a decreased level of effort or even precludes us from conducting direct support operations, where will the informed arguments for a strong submarine force come from? We might be able to continue to argue within the community for sufficient platform strength, but drumming up support outside the force will be difficult.[97]

Sending two attack submarines with each battle group was undertaken less to fend off the threat, to the battle group from rogue state diesel subs than to fend off the threat to cut the U.S. submarine force after the Cold War.

If the two submarines the navy allocates to escort the twelve battle groups were eliminated from the fleet, about half of the fifty-ship QDR force would remain. That force would be adequate to conduct legitimate overseas presence missions, which include transporting special forces near the shores of potential adversaries and collecting electronic and communications intelligence off their coasts. Recently, the navy has shifted emphasis from protecting the battle group from diesel submarines to gathering intelligence as the rationale for more submarines (the navy now claims that only three of sixty-eight submarines it says it needs would be used in direct support of carrier operations).[98]

A submarine force of twenty-five ships could keep at least five to six submarines continuously deployed worldwide for collecting intelligence. (For every submarine that is deployed overseas, the navy needs 4.5 in inventory, because some submarines are training their crews and others are in port for crew rest, maintenance, or overhaul.) Five or six submarines on station collecting intelligence should be sufficient, given the benign threat environment of the post–Cold War world, the many other U.S. intelligence assets available, and the desirability of a U.S. foreign policy of military restraint. Submarines would be used in key regions (East Asia and Western Europe) to fill holes in the coverage of other intelligence assets. If a severe crisis occurred that the United States needed to monitor, however, many more submarines could be deployed overseas quickly (that is, "surged") to gather intelligence.

After the Cold War ended, U.S. naval intelligence recommended cutting drastically the number of surveillance missions off the Russian coast; a constant watch was no longer needed.[99] Strangely, however, despite the dramatic decline in the threat, the number of total intelligence-collecting missions has doubled since 1989.[100] Valid intelligence requirements should have some proportionality to the threat. According to the U.S. Navy, the doubling of missions has been caused by the "national need for unique intelligence in many new trouble spots around the globe."[101] Yet the navies of China, North Korea, Iran, and Iraq existed during the Cold War and today are mere shadows of the Soviet navy of old—the principle target of snooping by U.S. submarines. Furthermore, it is questionable that all (or even any) of the new trouble spots are crucial to a narrower list of U.S. vital interests.

Yet despite the abject demise of the Russian navy and the reduction in intelligence missions in Russian waters, DoD is justifying its preferred goals—fifty-five to sixty-eight boats by 2015 and sixty-two to seventy-six by 2025—on the basis of further increasing requirements for intelligence collection (which, of course, are highly classified). How can the DoD predict such requirements so far out into the future? Even if increased intelligence collection is required (a dubious proposition) to buy expensive submarines (at $1.8 billion a piece) primarily to collect intelligence off the coasts of rogue nations in the third world—particularly when the United States has a plethora of other intelligence-gathering platforms—it is a waste of taxpayer dollars. Many versatile intelligence collection assets—such as human agents, satellites, and manned and unmanned aircraft—could be purchased for the price of augmenting the fleet of submarines, collection assets which have a reach limited to littoral areas of target nations.

With the collapse of the Russian submarine threat and slow modernization of the Chinese navy, suspicions should also be raised about the unspecified "technologically pacing threat" that now requires eighteen *Virginia*-class boats. Adding in the three existing *Seawolf*-class submarines, the navy now wants twenty-one very quiet ships by 2015 instead of the original ten to twelve very quiet submarine requirement by 2012. Once again, the post–Cold War undersea threat—if there is one—remains stagnant, but the requirements for submarines are increasing.

According to the BUR in 1993, forty-five submarines were "capable of" fulfilling war-fighting requirements—that is, fighting two major theater wars nearly simultaneously.[102] Today, DoD states that a force of fifty-five submarines would be "sufficient" in 2015 to meet the modeled war-fighting requirements.[103] (Such careful wording might indicate that even forty-five may not be the minimum needed to meet the two-war requirement). The actual threat has not increased since 1993, but the federal budget surplus that could be used to buy more submarines has. Furthermore, the "technologically pacing threat" is largely a fiction.

Assuming conservatively that the BUR's requirement of forty-five boats for fighting two wars is accurate (it may have been padded), a force of about twenty-five submarines would be more than enough to fight one such conflict. So a force of twenty-five vessels is sufficient to carry out the balancer-of-last-resort strategy.

For the navy to grab more of the excess government cash, it must retain more existing submarines—the *Los Angeles* (SSN 688) class—to justify eventually replacing them with new *Virginia*-class boats. Meeting the goal of eighteen *Virginia*-class ships in the near term, or the minimum goal of sixty-two vessels by 2025, would require the construction of three submarines a year (compared to one per year currently being produced). Those two additional submarines per year would cost four billion dollars a year for fourteen years.[104] If the goal was sixty-eight or seventy-six submarines, up to four submarines per year could eventually be needed.[105] Even if the additional submarines were needed, the navy's budget would not allow such profligate spending. The navy's budget, which is unlikely to go up significantly, now allows the purchase of only one submarine per year. (Congress may be willing to add a few submarines, but that action may come at the expense of other programs—something that other parts of the navy fear.) At that rate, the submarine force will eventually be reduced to twenty-eight boats—close to twenty-five ships needed for the balancer-of-last-resort strategy. As long as the navy continues to buy expensive submarines and ships, the fleet, including submarines, will dwindle. The navy is pushing for the requirement for submarines to be increased at a time when it can be reduced.

If the force were cut to twenty-five ships, no more new *Virginia*-class submarines would need to be procured (three of the boats have already been funded by Congress and a fourth is included in a multi-year contract). A force of four *Virginia*-class ships, three *Seawolf*-class submarines, and eighteen of the most modern "688I" *Los Angeles*–class vessels—with highly trained crews—would dominate the oceans for years to come. The 688I boat, the backbone of the submarine force, is the best submarine in the world today, with the exception of the truncated *Seawolf* class. The 688I has about the best mix of mobility, weapons, and sensors ever built into a submarine.

Much has been made of a few recent Russian boats—both in the water and on the drawing board—that are quieter at certain speeds and under certain conditions than the 688I. This situation was heavily publicized by the navy to justify the purchase of the *Virginia* class. According to the navy, the most modern Russian boats are quieter than the 688Is at the tactical speed of five to seven knots at one specific sonar frequency. But at slightly greater speeds, or over a full spectrum of sonar frequencies, the Russian boats become much noisier.[106] In short, problems with Russian quieting technology still exist.[107] Furthermore, technology is being developed that will restore the 688I's lead in quieting.[108]

Russia, in an economic depression, cannot afford to build many modern attack submarines, operate and maintain them, or adequately train their crews. From 2005 to 2010, the Office of Naval Intelligence admits, the number of modern Russian attack submarines will drop to barely over twenty. The vast preponderance of that force will be models currently in the fleet.[109] The few new quiet submarines that Russia can afford will not make up for the poor operational state of the Russian submarine force.

Although the absolute level of quieting is important for submarines, the key issue is whether U.S. vessels can hear the enemy before the enemy hears them. Even if Russian boats are quieter under certain circumstances, U.S. submarines have great advantages in sensor and computer-processing technology that enable them to hear Russian submarines before the Russian boats hear them. As noted earlier, U.S. submarines also have advantages in mobility, weapons, and the all-important training of crews.[110] Therefore, the unspecified "technologically pacing threat" that now requires eighteen *Virginia*-class submarines is fantasy.

A force of twenty-five U.S. attack submarines would provide an adequate submarine-based intelligence-gathering capability, a substantial capability to launch special forces ashore in the rare cases that they are needed, and a sufficient capability to launch Tomahawk missiles in a surprise attack on the first day of any war. Also, a twenty-five-ship force would hedge against the unlikely resurgence of a Russian submarine force or the equally unlikely rise of a significant Chinese submarine force. As noted earlier, submarines are needed to collect intelligence and insert special forces, but those limited needs cannot justify an excessive force of fifty submarines or greater.

Similarly, the United States may want to launch a covert Tomahawk strike—either a limited punitive attack in retaliation or as a surprise attack on the first day of a war (when enemy air defenses make missions with nonstealthy manned aircraft dangerous). A twenty-five-ship force would provide an adequate covert Tomahawk strike capability. The United States also has stealthy B-2 and F-117 aircraft to evade enemy air defenses and attack targets on the first day of a war. In most cases, overwhelming U.S. naval power (protection for surface ships making noncovert Tomahawk strikes) or the period of rising tension before a military strike (especially likely before a major war, which is the planning scenario for the balancer-of-last-resort strategy) will make large numbers of covert Tomahawk strikes unnecessary (even on the first day of the war).

Besides, if a greater covert strike capability were needed, more Tomahawks could be launched for the money by proposals to convert four Trident ballistic-missile submarines to Tomahawk carriers than by building new *Virginia*-class boats. But even without the four converted Tridents, the smaller restructured fleet would contain the capability to launch a maximum of about 8,500 Tomahawks, including about 750 Tomahawks launched covertly (from vertical launchers and torpedo tubes) from the twenty-five submarine force. Therefore, even spending the money to convert the Tridents to obtain about six hundred more launch cells is unnecessary. Furthermore, keeping the four Tridents in the fleet could count toward U.S. weapon ceilings in the existing Strategic Arms Reduction Talks II (START II) agreements, even though the boats would no longer carry nuclear weapons.[111]

Noncovert Tomahawk attacks (the vast majority) are best done by surface ships, because they have greater missile capacity and are therefore more efficient. The submarine community alleges that surface combatants are increasingly vulnerable to antiship missiles. But cruisers and destroyers have smaller radar silhouettes than aircraft carriers, and have the sophisticated Aegis air-defense system to destroy incoming antiship missiles. In the long term, the threat facing U.S. surface ships may become so severe that new behemoth (Trident-like) underwater missile carriers may be needed to replace the entire surface fleet. But that day is a long way off and should not preclude canceling the *Virginia*-class submarine—with its comparatively meager capability to carry Tomahawks—and passing up the conversion of Tridents, which would have limited life spans.

Using foreign submarine threats to justify building *Virginia*-class boats is even more shaky. The longer the Russian submarine force lacks funds for operations and maintenance, the more unlikely a resurgent threat becomes. Most of the Russian boats are rusting at the pier, along with the skills of their crews. A point of no return will be reached, if it has not already passed.

On paper, the Chinese have a formidable submarine force of eighty-five vessels. But most of them are not operationally maintained and would require much time and effort to overcome technical obstacles to reactivation.[112] In that fleet, the Chinese have five Han-class nuclear attack submarines, which were first introduced in the 1970s. Unlike U.S. submarines, the Han class must surface to fire missiles, making it very vulnerable to counterattack.[113] Many of the Han boats are inoperable. The addition of a few of the Russian-built Kilo-class diesel submarines will not solve the problems of the Chinese submarine force or threaten significantly the modern U.S. nuclear attack submarine force.

In the unlikely event that a resurgent Russian or rising Chinese submarine threat comes to fruition, it will do so only over a long period of time (twenty to thirty years). If new submarines are needed, the United States will have plenty of time to produce them. (A force of twenty-five submarines would provide a kernel of expertise around which a larger force could be rebuilt, in the unlikely event that it is needed.) In fact, as with other military technologies (for example, tactical fighters), the *Virginia*-class submarines would be obsolete, or at least obsolescent, by the time any serious threat could arise. (In the meantime, *Virginia*-class boats are exorbitantly priced platforms for collecting intelligence off the coasts of rogue nations.) During the hiatus in the threat, the United States should continue research and development on submarine technology but delay the production of new submarines until existing submarines are about to wear out.

Reducing the force of attack submarines to twenty-five would allow the DoD to cancel the *Virginia*-class program (after the four submarines that are already under contract) and not build a new class of submarines until at least 2014. With a force of 4 *Virginia*-class ships, three *Seawolf*-class boats, and eighteen 688I submarines, the last remaining 688I would need to be retired around 2021 (the ship was built in 1991, and the navy's notional service life for attack submarines has been thirty years). A new submarine program would probably need to start about seven years before the first new ship was needed to replace the first retiring 688I. Recently, there has been talk about extending the life of 688s to thirty-three years. If that could be done, a new submarine building program could be postponed until 2017. In the current benign threat environment, delaying a new submarine program until 2014 or 2017 would pose little risk.

The planned thirty-ship *Virginia* class is certainly no bargain. At sixty-five billion dollars in total program cost, the submarine is DoD's second-largest program. The *Virginia* class will be less capable in most respects than its predecessor, the *Seawolf*. The *Virginia* class will be as quiet as the *Seawolf* but inferior in size, speed, diving depth, and weapons capacity.[114] The *Virginia* class's main advances are in the ability to operate in the shallow waters off the coast of the third world and to insert special forces into coastal regions—missions that would be deemphasized in a balancer-of-last-resort strategy. The cost of the *Virginia* class is already escalating and could eventually be almost as much as that of the *Seawolf*, which was canceled for its exorbitant cost (the fifth *Seawolf* was projected to cost over two billion).[115]

The navy would argue that waiting until 2014 or 2017 to produce a submarine would devastate the submarine industrial base. But the major problem is that the navy has too large a submarine industrial base to support. The navy produces submarines at two locations: the General Dynamics Electric Boat facility in Connecticut, which only produces submarines, and Newport News Shipbuilding in Virginia, which produces aircraft carriers and submarines. Both shipyards have very little commercial business and are therefore wards of the state. The navy pays almost the entire overhead to keep both shipyards producing submarines. Congressional insistence that both yards be kept open, to safeguard employment and votes in both states, has led to the ridiculous situation in which one prime contractor produces part of the submarine and the other produces the rest.[116]

Terminating the *Virginia* program would, in effect, lead to a much-needed rationalization of the submarine industrial base. The smaller Electric Boat would probably close down, because it would have very little to produce. Until new submarines are needed, Newport News—the largest private shipyard in the United States—would still construct and overhaul aircraft carriers and could also be given maintenance business from government-run shipyards. The government shipyards—which, among other maintenance tasks, perform the overhaul work on nuclear submarines—should be closed.

The advantage of using a large shipyard that can produce both carriers and submarines is that the workforce can be shifted between the two production activities. One of the most critical difficulties in maintaining the industrial base is keeping skilled labor when a production run ends. It is difficult and costly to find, rehire, and retrain those workers. At Newport News, workers could produce or overhaul carriers or overhaul submarines until new submarine production is needed. The submarine design base could be kept alive by developing new submarine technologies and by contributing to the overhaul and modernization of existing hulls.[117]

Only a small percentage of the submarine subcontractors might need government intervention to stay viable (the rest make products that are variants of products sold elsewhere). If the navy does feel that government action is needed to shore up subcontractors, it might stockpile components in advance of production, allow subcontractors to revitalize or modernize equipment on existing submarines, or shift the work of failing subcontractors to the prime contractor.

Rationalizing the submarine industry will obviate the need to buy unneeded submarines to prop up a bloated industrial base. The *Virginia*-class submarines are not needed for military or industrial reasons. The navy should terminate the class after finishing the four ships that are already under contract and instead develop new technologies that can be used on future submarines. As Norman Polmar, a consultant to three secretaries of the navy, a former member of the Navy's Research Advisory Committee, and a harsh critic of the *Virginia*-class submarine, noted, "We have time to push the envelope [in research and development] now because we don't have the Soviets breathing down our necks."[118] The navy, by retaining more submarines than are needed for today's mild threat environment, is soaking up funds that could be used to develop advanced technologies that could be deployed if the threat worsened in the future.

Surface Combatants

The navy originally planned to build fifty-seven DDG-51 *Arleigh Burke*–class destroyers, but added an additional ship for the dubious purpose of preserving the industrial base. Those destroyers are expensive multimission ships. The fifth ship cost $1.5 billion, but many ships later the price is still high, at $850 to $950 million per vessel. The DDG-51s have the sophisticated Aegis air defense system as well as vertical-launch system (VLS) cells that can launch a variety of different missiles (including the Tomahawk for land attack). Those ships will be added to the twenty-seven *Ticonderoga* Aegis cruisers already in the force. The CG-47 cruisers are larger multimission ships that are even more capable than the DDG-51 (among other attributes, they have more VLS cells). Together, those Aegis surface combatants will form the backbone of the U.S. surface fleet well into the next century.

As of fiscal year 2001, fifty-one of the planned fifty-eight DDG-51s have been purchased. The six remaining ships that have been scheduled through 2005 should be purchased, to round out a potent eighty-four-ship force.[119]

Most other navies do not have such deluxe ships. Most are "frigate navies," based primarily on those smaller, less capable ships. Some of those navies contain some destroyers, but few have cruisers. The United States has by far the largest and most capable surface combatant ships in the world. The Aegis air defense system is so good that U.S. surface combatants can conduct independent operations without the protection of an aircraft carrier and its aircraft.

Yet despite this dominance, the navy is planning to purchase about thirty DD-21 destroyers for twenty-five billion dollars, beginning in about 2004.[120] The vessel will not have the Aegis air defense system, because its primary mission will be to attack targets on land. The ship is supposed to be half as expensive than the DDG-51 (the fifth ship will cost $750 million), but the history of repeated design changes and cost escalation in modern weapons systems makes this outcome questionable.[121] (The DDG-51 was supposed to be a more affordable version of the CG-47 but ended up costing almost as much.)

Like its predecessor the arsenal ship—which was also a single-mission land-attack vessel—the DD-21 should be cancelled. Although the U.S. Navy can dominate the world's oceans (no other nation's navy can even come close to challenging U.S. sea control) and the navy has been focused on projecting power ashore, the land attack mission should be done by multimission ships. Today, the cost of warships is so high that they should be able to perform a variety of missions well: antisurface warfare, antisubmarine warfare, and air defense, as well as land attack. With ninety-one and 122 VLS cells each, respectively, the multimission DDG-51 and CG-47 ships have ample magazine capacity (almost eight thousand cells) to dedicate a substantial part of it to land-attack missiles; those vessels also have five-inch guns that can be fired at targets ashore. The three varieties of submarines in the fleet (688I, *Seawolf*, and *Virginia*) also have VLS cells or torpedo tubes that can launch land-attack missiles. Thus, the U.S. Navy will possess formidable land-attack capabilities even without the DD-21. In fact, the military services already have redundant capabilities for striking deep targets. The DD-21 will have both Tomahawk strike missiles and guns, but is primarily a strike ship because the navy would rather perform that mission than provide fire support to the Marines. A few barges or simple ships with guns would better meet any needs for fire support than the expensive DD-21.

Furthermore, the U.S. Navy currently cannot afford to build enough ships to maintain a fleet of more than three hundred ships. The fleet is dwindling, because the navy is building ever more expensive ships. A balancer-of-last-resort strategy and a force of two hundred ships would be more affordable. But with fewer ships in the navy, each needs to be capable of doing multiple missions. The DD-21, lacking the Aegis system, will be vulnerable to attack from the air unless other ships protect it. With only two hundred ships in the fleet, hulls cannot be wasted on surface combatants that cannot operate independently or are designed with one mission in mind (land attack).

The first CG-47 cruiser will need to be replaced in 2018. Production of a CG-47 replacement (CG-21) ship would need to be started in 2012. The first DDG-51 will not need to be replaced until 2026. To retain the capable eighty-four-ship core of a two-hundred-ship American navy that will remain dominant on the planet, CG-47s and DDG-51s should probably be replaced one for one with sophisticated multimission ships.

Several technological developments could alter that policy prescription. In the long term, if vertical-takeoff-and-landing technology is so perfected that VTOL aircraft no longer have severe range and payload penalties, naval aircraft may be dispersed from the vulnerable aircraft carriers to surface combatants. If that occurred, more than eighty-four multimission surface combatants might be needed in the fleet—and more could be afforded if expensive aircraft carriers were eliminated. On the other hand, if surface ships become very vulnerable to enemy attack, fewer than eighty-four multimission surface combatants may be needed. Instead, large missile-carrying submarines may be needed to replace some or all of the surface navy.

LPD-17

The LPD-17 is an amphibious ship from which marines and their equipment can be transported to shore via air-cushion landing craft and from which helicopters and vertical-takeoff-and-landing aircraft can operate. The ship is designed to be part of a future amphibious ready group (ARG) of three ships. The LPD-17 is designed to complement a large flat-deck amphibious ship—a medium-sized aircraft carrier that hosts many helicopters and Harrier aircraft—and an LSD, which has less capacity than the LPD-17 for aircraft but more capacity for air-cushion landing craft, or cargo.[122] As of fiscal year 2001, the navy has purchased six LPD-17s and plans to purchase six more through fiscal year 2004. Those twelve ships will fill out twelve ARGs (one to patrol with each of the twelve carrier battle groups).[123]

But the balancer-of-last-resort strategy questions the need for near-continuous naval overseas presence, eschews U.S. involvement in brushfire conflicts that are a specialty of the Marine Corps, and is skeptical that a large-scale amphibious assault can be conducted in an age of satellite reconnaissance, precision-guided weapons, and proliferating sea mines. Adopting that strategy would allow cuts of 50 percent in both the number of carrier battle groups (from twelve to six) and the number of marine divisions (from three active and one reserve to one active and one reserve). Therefore, the number of ARGs should also be cut in half, from twelve to six. So only six LPD-17s are needed, one for each ARG. The production line of the LPD-17 ought to be terminated after the sixth ship is built.

Theater Missile Defense

Iraqi launches of Scud missiles during the Gulf War caused the U.S. military to realize that its forces and infrastructure in any regional war might be vulnerable to enemy ballistic missiles.[124] In the war, the Scud's inaccuracy rendered it mainly a political (terror) weapon. More accurate missiles will probably pose an increasing military threat in the future. To counter the new threat, however, the military overreacted in planning new defense systems. There are currently six theater missile defense systems in development—the navy's Area (lower-tier) and Theaterwide (upper-tier) defense; the army's Patriot PAC-3, Theater High Altitude Air Defense (THAAD), and Medium Altitude Air Defense System (MEADS); and the air force's Airborne Laser. Some of the systems are redundant (THAAD), some are designed primarily to protect wealthy allies (THAAD and Airborne Laser), some are unneeded (MEADS), and some are vulnerable to attack (Airborne Laser). The rest of the programs (area and theaterwide, and PAC-3) are needed and should be continued.

Retain the Navy Area and Theaterwide and Army PAC-3 Programs

If the United States had to intervene in Europe or East Asia to stop an aggressive great power, it would most likely be given access to regional ports and airfields. Those ports and airfields would probably be prime targets for the enemy. Killing military forces piecemeal as they disembark from air or sea is easier than fighting a complete force, assembled and prepared for battle. In the war of the future, ports and airfields will be lucrative targets for accurate enemy ballistic missiles launched from afar.

So even before U.S. forces are landed at ports and air bases, such nodes will need protection. To protect them, navy systems are the only assets available. Both the navy Area and Theaterwide systems take advantage of the existing Aegis/Standard air-defense system on destroyers and cruisers and the support structure (training, logistics, and engineering) that goes with it. Both the Aegis radar and Standard Missile 2 will be modified to conduct area defense. Area defense means protecting ports, airfields, and amphibious assaults by attempting to destroy incoming missiles during their third and final (terminal) phase of flight.

Navy Theaterwide also upgrades the Aegis radar but uses a more advanced version of the Standard missile (the Standard 3) that is designed to destroy the incoming missile in the first (boost) or second (midcourse) phases of flight. Deploying both the Area and Theaterwide systems provides a layered defense that would allow two shots at any incoming missile. The navy Theaterwide system will defend a larger area than the navy Area system. The major limitation of the Theaterwide system is that its coverage diminishes as military forces move inland. Therefore, some land-based theater missile defense is needed.

The PAC-3 provides a terrestrial area (terminal) defense, much like the navy area system provides from the sea. This deployable system can protect important nodes—for example, headquarters, airfields, supply depots, etc.—farther inland on the battlefield. Like the navy systems, PAC-3 takes advantage of an existing air defense system and its support structure. Improvements will be made to the Patriot radar and missile.

Terminate THAAD, MEADS, and Airborne Laser

THAAD, at almost thirteen billion dollars, is the most expensive theater missile defense program. Although, like navy Theaterwide, THAAD is designed to intercept the incoming missile in the midcourse phase, the system covers less area and is therefore less cost-efficient. THAAD is also large and not readily deployable. During expeditionary operations, THAAD relies on navy Theaterwide to protect the ports and airfields through which it might deploy into a theater of operations. More than likely, THAAD would be transported to the theater via scarce airlift or sealift; navy systems transport themselves. But THAAD is mainly a system designed to protect U.S. forces already deployed overseas, or wealthy allied nations—neither of which fits well with the balancer-of-last-resort strategy. That strategy does not rely on U.S. forces based overseas. If rich allies want missile defense, they should buy it themselves rather than rely on the United States.

Furthermore, THAAD has been a troubled program. Its first six attempts to intercept incoming missiles were failures. The next two intercepts were successful, but they were "tightly scripted" and not "operationally realistic," according to Philip Coyle, then–DoD's chief weapons tester. Coyle noted that the testing conditions were contrived, a different THAAD missile was tested than the one that would be purchased, and the target missiles were of shorter range than those the system might face.[125]

MEADS is designed to provide terminal defense for army forces in the field. Although the PAC-3 is transportable (that is, can be taken down and moved, over a period of time) while MEADS is truly mobile and provides 360-degree coverage, the two systems have similar capabilities (in fact, MEADS uses the PAC-3 interceptor missile). In fact, John Hamre, as deputy secretary of defense, once sheepishly admitted that while "MEADS is an important program, it's last in [DoD] priorities because it duplicates capabilities we already have."[126]

Yet compared to PAC-3, MEADS will probably cost more—about eleven billion dollars (if the projected cost of MEADS's defunct predecessor Corps

SAM is any guide) versus $6.2 billion. Also, MEADS provides a smaller radius of defense than PAC-3, five to six miles versus twenty-five to thirty miles. The threat from enemy missiles is most severe to fixed, high-value targets (for example, headquarters, logistical bases), which PAC-3 can best protect. Missile defense for forces in the field is less urgent, because they can rely on mobility and dispersion to increase their survivability against missile attacks.

The low priority of MEADS is reflected by the actions of DoD and Congress. DoD has had difficulty coming up with the funding to keep this international program alive.[127] U.S. stinginess has led its international partners, Italy and Germany, to question its commitment to the program. The program has experienced years of delay. In fiscal year 1999, Congress terminated the program. DoD then announced that it had chosen a contractor to develop MEADS and finally pledged to provide $260 million over three years. The House Appropriations Committee accused DoD of ignoring the congressional intent to terminate the program by misdirecting two million dollars from another program to keep MEADS on life support. The committee, angered by this alleged action, refused to appropriate any money for the program in fiscal year 2000.[128] Tax dollars should not be wasted on a high-cost weapon system that even the deputy secretary of defense admits is redundant, and that is effectively merely a way to foster international military cooperation.

The air force Airborne Laser is fired from a commercial aircraft and is designed to shoot down an enemy missile during the boost phase—that is, when the projectile is on an upward trajectory, just after launch. The major advantages to a boost-phase intercept are that the missile is most visible and vulnerable during this period, the missile can be destroyed before chemical or biological submunitions are released, in which case those potent agents would fall over the enemy's territory. The major disadvantage of boost-phase intercept is that it must be done quickly, because the boost phase is brief—North Korea's Taepodong missile, for example, burns for just under three minutes.[129]

But the Airborne Laser depends on access to air bases in the theater that might be vulnerable to attack from the very missiles that the laser is trying to shoot down. If enemy missiles could destroy the base while the laser was on the ground or before it had been deployed, the laser would be effectively neutralized as a weapon. Even when the Airborne Laser is conducting its mission, the large commercial aircraft housing it would be vulnerable to air-to-air and surface-to-air missiles. Thus, the United States must have air superiority or at least assign fighters to protect the laser.

Even if protected, the Airborne Laser may not be able to achieve the requirement to shoot down enemy missiles four hundred miles away. A report by the Congressional Research Service indicates that the system might have trouble tracking missiles that are as close as two hundred miles away. Even then, the system may be vulnerable to countermeasures, such as a missile that rolls through the air, is polished to reflect a laser beam, or is hardened to withstand it. The laser might also have trouble killing multiple targets at one time.[130]

There are many technical challenges facing the Airborne Laser. The General Accounting Office and DoD's office of Program Analysis and Evaluation have raised many concerns, and the Senate Armed Services Committee has declared the program to be an undertaking of high risk.[131] The laser beam must be corrected if precipitation or turbulence is present in the air. Imaging and tracking must account for the relative motion of the laser and its target. The most challenging technical obstacle may be fitting the large laser into a Boeing 747 aircraft. Also, Philip Coyle has raised concerns about the laser's weight, susceptibility to countermeasures, and ability to stay locked onto the target.[132]

Finally and most important, one gets the idea that the Airborne Laser, like THAAD, is being designed to provide U.S. allies with a missile shield against threats from nations in their neighborhoods. Spending large sums of money to protect wealthy allies does not fit well within the balancer-of-last-resort strategy or serve genuine American interests.

A good estimate for the total cost of DoD's theater ballistic missile program is $47.3 billion. Of that sum, the PAC-3 and navy Area and Theaterwide programs account for only $17.4 billion. Thus, eliminating THAAD ($12.8 billion), MEADS (an estimated $11 billion, based on the costs of the Corps SAM program), and the Airborne Laser ($6.1 billion) will reduce costs by almost thirty billion dollars (or 63 percent). Costs can be reduced so much because some of the most expensive systems provide the least security or are simply unneeded.

CONCLUSION

Many complex and expensive weapon systems that were designed for the Cold War, or are simply unneeded, could be terminated. Instead, given the lower threat environment, many existing weapons could be upgraded with new electronics and computers until a new threat arises, if it ever does. A small portion of the savings generated from those policies could be used to fund vital but unglamorous items that the military services often neglect. But the vast bulk of the savings would be returned to the American taxpayer. With a more benign post–Cold War threat environment (which provides longer warning times of a major threat arising) and a new foreign policy of military restraint compatible with that reduced threat, those gold-plated weapon systems can be eliminated from the budget without endangering the national security. In fact, staying out of useless brushfire wars and using a small amount of the budgetary savings to fund critical but neglected items should enhance U.S. security.

NOTES

1. Quoted in George C. Wilson, "Why Is the Pentagon Ignoring the Defense Science Board?" *National Journal*, February 7, 2000, p. 1.

2. Quoted in Steve Vogel, "Dogfight: Of Three New Fighter Planes Competing for Funding, the Super Hornet Is the One Closest to Production. In the Emerging Defense Landscape, That Is the Biggest Advantage—and Biggest Liability," *Washington Post Magazine*, April 16, 2000.

3. "CBO Sees QDR Tacair Revisions as Insufficient," *Aerospace Daily*, June 4, 1998, p. 1.

4. Vogel, p. 2.

5. Ibid.

6. The proposal to terminate the F-22 and F-18E/F and delay the JSF was first offered by Williamson Murray, *Fighter Procurement in the Next Century*, Cato Policy Analysis no. 334, February 26, 1999. That plan has been modified slightly here. Murray originally proposed developing a new low-cost, long-range navy strike aircraft to substitute for the F-18E/F until the naval JSF is built. As an interim solution, the author's plan instead adapts the air force's stealth F-117 strike aircraft for carrier operations.

7. Murray, pp. 15–16.

8. Quoted in Center for Defense Information's *America's Defense Monitor* television documentary, January 18, 1998.

9. Tim Smart of the *Washington Post* cites "industry analysts" as arguing that the new Eurofighter and the MiG-29 are the F-15's equal. Tim Smart, "Getting the F-22 Off the Ground," *Washington Post*, April 20, 1998. Bill Gregory and Glenn W. Goodman, Jr., imply the same when they cite a U.S. Defense Intelligence Agency estimate that the F-15 has a greater range than the Eurofighter, stealth characteristics equivalent to the Russian Su-27M, and more maneuverability than that Russian aircraft. DIA, however, believes that the F-15's stealth characteristics do not match those of the Eurofighter or France's new Rafale aircraft. Bill Gregory and Glenn W. Goodman, Jr., "New High-Low Mix: US Air Force Fighter Modernization Plan Rests on Two Strong Points," *Armed Forces Journal International*, September 1997, pp. 38, 40.

10. Murray, pp. 17, 40–41.

11. For more on the air-to-air balance with foreign nations, see Ivan Eland, "America Doesn't Need Three New Fighter Planes," *Long Beach Press-Telegram*, April 9, 1999.

12. Ibid., p. 16.

13. James Stevenson on *America's Defense Monitor*, "Fighter Jet Fix," Public Television Documentary, April 25, 1999.

14. For the F-22 cost, see George Wilson, "Cohen Should Halt Dial-a-Threat Games," *Air Force Times*, February 2, 1998, and Jeff Huber, "Catch F-22," *Proceedings*, September 1997, p. 38. For the F-15E cost, see *America's Defense Monitor*, "Fighter Jet Fix."

15. See Eric Planin and Bradley Graham, "Panel's Vote on Funds Imperils New Jet Fighter," *Washington Post*, July 13, 1999, p. A4. Planin and Graham place the F-22's cost even higher: $187 million per aircraft.

16. Lisa Burgess, "USAF Moves on F-22 Production Despite Criticism," *Defense News*, July 20–26, 1998, p. 42; Patrick Kelly, "Senator Raises Fresh Concerns over F-22 Fighter Costs," *Defense Week*, February 17, 1998, p. 6, and "F-22 Lacks Flight Test Data in Run-Up to Production, Senate Panel Told," *Defense Week*, March 30, 1998, pp. 1, 5; and "USAF Admits F-22 Cost Hikes, Says Program Will Meet Caps," *Defense Daily*, March 4, 1999, p. 1.

17. Eland.

18. Stan Crock, "The (Not So) Super Hornet," *Business Week*, December 13, 1999, p. 134.

19. Cited in Vogel, p. 2.

20. Sandra Erwin, "Naval Aviation's Jewel Untarnished by Critics," *National Defense*, May/June 1999, pp. 20–21.

21. Tony Capaccio, "New Navy Fighter Jet Said Ready for Full-Scale Production," *Defense Week*, March 6, 2000, p. 8.

22. General Accounting Office, *Defense Acquisitions: Progress of the F-18E/F Engineering and Manufacturing Development Program* (Washington, D.C.: GAO, June 1999), pp. 4–7.

23. Cited in Elaine M. Grossman, "Navy Test Report Shows F-18E/F Struggling to Match Older Aircraft," *Inside the Pentagon* 15, no. 6, (February 11, 1999), p. 7.

24. Classified report of the Navy testers and the Coyle report cited in Grossman, pp. 1, 6, 7. The Coyle findings were also cited in James Kitfield, "DOD Fighter Program Tries to Navigate Turbulent Skies," *National Journal's Congressional Daily AM*, May 15, 1999, p. 19.

25. Cited in Grossman, p. 7.

26. Murray, p. 13.

27. Cited in James Kitfield, p. 19.

28. Quoted in ibid.

29. Quoted in Crock, p. 134.

30. Bill Gertz, "Short Takes," *Washington Times*, January 7, 2000, p. A14.

31. Cited in ibid.

32. Ibid., pp. 12–13.

33. Murray, pp. 13–14.

34. Office of Naval Intelligence, *Worldwide Challenges to Naval Strike Warfare*, pp. 34–35, cited in O'Hanlon, *How to Be a Cheap Hawk: The 1999 and 2000 Defense Budgets* (Washington, D.C.: Brookings Institution), p. 120.

35. William S. Cohen, *Report of the Quadrennial Defense Review* (Washington, D.C.: Department of Defense, 1997), pp. 45–46.

36. John Donnelly, "Pentagon Paper Slammed Joint Strike Fighter Program: Officials Now Claim Report's Issues Resolved," *Defense Week*, April 6, 1998.

37. Lane Pierrot and Jo Ann Vines, *A Look at Tomorrow's Tactical Air Forces* (Washington, D.C.: Congressional Budget Office, 1997), pp. 39, 49.

38. Murray, pp. 18–19.

39. Tim Smart, "2001: Price Odyssey for the New Fighter: Can the JSF Be Built on a Tight Budget?" *Washington Post*, July 27, 1999, p. E1.

40. Murray, pp. 21, 34.

41. Tony Capaccio, "GAO Tells Pentagon JSF Program Fraught with Delays, Overruns," *Defense Week*, March 13, 2000, pp. 1, 15.

42. Murray, pp. 34–35.

43. National Defense Panel, *Transforming Defense: National Security in the 21st Century* (Washington, D.C.: National Defense Panel, 1997), p. 49.

44. Sophearith Moeng, *The Vital Guide to Military Aircraft* (Shrewsbury, England: Airlife, 1998), pp. 63, 66, 77.

45. James Dunnigan and Albert Nofi, *Dirty Little Secrets of the Vietnam War* (New York: St. Martin's Press, 1999), p. 292; and Arnold Meisner, *Desert Storm: Sea War* (Osceola, Wisc.: Motorbooks International, 1991), p. 34.

46. Jeffrey Record, "The C-5M: A No-Brainer's No-Brainer," *Defense Week*, July 12, 1999, p. 6.

47. Congressional Budget Office, *Reducing the Deficit: Spending and Revenue Options* (Washington, D.C.: Congressional Budget Office, 1997), p. 42.

48. Michael O'Hanlon, *Technological Change and the Future of Warfare* (Washington, D.C.: Brookings Institution, 2000), pp. 72–73.

49. O'Hanlon, *Cheap Hawk*, p. 124.

50. Lawrence Korb, "The Plane That Nobody Wanted," *New York Times*, April 11, 2000, p. A31.

51. CBO, p. 36.

52. Cohen, *Report of the Quadrennial Defense Review*, p. 46.

53. Sydney Freedberg, Jr., "It's a Bird It's a Plane," *National Journal*, March 23, 2000, p. 979.

54. Ibid.

55. Congressional Budget Office, *Reducing the Deficit*, p. 36.

56. Korb, p. A31.

57. Loren Thompson, "On Track: Comanche Still Clings to Army's Number-One Modernization Spot Despite Recent Ups and Downs," *Armed Forces Journal International*, April 1998, p. 41.

58. Christopher Hellman, "Comanche Program Contains 'Significant Risks,'" *Weekly Defense Monitor* 3, no. 36 (September 23, 1999), p. 8.

59. National Defense Panel, *Transforming Defense*, p. 49.

60. George L. Seffers, "U.S. Army's Comanche Faces Cloudy Future," *Defense News*, March 30–April 5, 1998, p. 18.

61. Craig Copetas, "Apache Copters Inspire Awe in Balkans, But They May Be Wrong Birds for Job," *Wall Street Journal*, May 20, 1999, p. A15.

62. Congressional Budget Office, *Reducing the Deficit*, pp. 53–54.

63. O'Hanlon, *Technological Change*, p. 190.

64. Eric Labs and Joann Vines, *Options for Enhancing the Department of Defense's Unmanned Aerial Vehicle Programs* (Washington, D.C.: Congressional Budget Office, September 1998), p. xvii.

65. Such analysts cited in ibid.

66. "Tank Busters" television documentary, the History Channel, September 19, 1998.

67. Bradley Graham, "Pentagon's Wish List: Based on Bygone Battles?" Washington Post, August 25, 1999, p. A3.

68. "Army Approves Next-Stage Crusader Development," *Defense Week*, March 16, 1998, p. 2.

69. National Defense Panel, *Transforming Defense*, p. 47.

70. Cited in Graham, "Pentagon's Wish List," p. A3.

71. Robert Suro, "Crusader, Growing Even as It Shrinks," *Washington Post*, April 27, 2000, p. 25.

72. Jason Sherman, "Arduous Crusade: Shelve the Briefing Charts; The Army's New Artillery System Is Now Something You Can Touch. But Is It Untouchable?" *Armed Forces International*, October 1999, p. 48.

73. Suro, p. 25.

74. Andrew Koch, "Crusader Will Aid U.S. Mobility Push," *Jane's Defence Weekly*, March 1, 2000, p. 10.

75. Ibid., p. 52.

76. Jason Sherman, "Souped Up Big Time: As the Abrams Tank Program Marks Its Greatest Technological Achievement, Its Future Has Never Been More Uncertain," *Armed Forces Journal International*, May 1998, pp. 44, 46.

77. William Owens, "Revolutionizing Warfare," in Democratic Leadership Council, *War and Peace: Are We Ready?* (Washington, D.C.: Democratic Leadership Council, Winter 2000), p. 27.

78. Graham, "Pentagon's Wish List," p. A3.

79. Ibid.

80. General Accounting Office, *Marine Corps: Improving Amphibious Capability Would Require Larger Share of Budget Than Previously Provided* (Washington, D.C., GAO, February 1996), pp. 31–32.

81. Glenn W. Goodman, Jr., "A Multidimensional Force: Marine Corps Set to Reap Long-Desired Mobility Upgrades," *Armed Forces Journal International*, January 1997, p. 30.

82. Jon R. Anderson, "A Better War Wagon: New AAAV Will Protect Landing Troops with Bigger Gun and Stronger Armor," *Navy Times*, June 24, 1996, p. 17.

83. General Accounting Office, *Marine Corps: Improving Amphibious Capability* p. 31.

84. International Institute for Strategic Studies, *The Military Balance 2000–2001* (London: Oxford University Press, 1999), pp. 59, 121.

85. Department of the Navy briefing, *Current and Future Amphibious Lift Plans*, October 13, 1992.

86. Congressional Budget Office, *Improving the Efficiency of Forward Presence by Aircraft Carriers* (Washington, D.C.: CBO, August 1996), p. 17. Figures have been converted to fiscal year 2000 dollars.

87. Richard Parker, "New Roles, Danger for Aircraft Carriers," *Philadelphia Inquirer*, August 1, 1998, p. 1.

88. John Donnelly, "Shelton: Study Urging for More Subs Isn't Last Word," *Defense Week*, February 22, 2000, p. 3.

89. Department of Defense, *Information Paper*, February 7, 2000, p. 2.

90. Sherry Sontag and Christopher Drew, *Blind Man's Bluff: The Untold Story of American Submarine Espionage* (New York: Public Affairs, 1998), pp. 232–234, 240, 241, 268.

91. Cited in Bryan Bender and Andrew Koch, "Cold War Carries on Under the Sea," *Jane's Defence Weekly*, September 6, 2000, p. 27.

92. Ibid.

93. Sontag and Drew, p. 267.

94. Office of Naval Intelligence, *Worldwide Submarine Challenges* (Washington, D.C.: 1997), p. 6.

95. Kevin Peppe, "SSNs: Supporting the Battle Group?" U.S. Naval Institute *Proceedings*, May 1997, pp. 40–41; and Kenneth Hart, "The Silent Service Must Communicate," U.S. Naval Institute *Proceedings*, February 1997, p. 76.

96. Peppe, pp. 40–41.

97. Ibid.

98. Comments of Rear Adm. Malcolm Fages, Director of the Submarine Warfare Division, U.S. Navy, at the Cato Institute's Policy Forum, "How Many Attack Submarines Does the Navy Need?" April 27, 2000.

99. Sontag and Drew, p. 265.

100. Andrea Stone, "Requests for Subs Could Spark Defense Battle," *USA Today*, March 8, 2000, p. 22A.

101. U.S. Navy, "Why We Need Submarines," www.chinfo.navy.mil/navpalib/ships/submarines/centennial/whysubs/whysubs.html.

102. Department of Defense, *Report on the Bottom-Up Review* (Washington, D.C.: DoD, 1993), pp. 56–57.

103. DoD Information Paper, p. 2.

104. Donnelly, "Shelton," p. 3.

105. Comments by Eric Labs, Principal Defense Analyst, Congressional Budget Office, at the Cato Institute's Policy Forum, "How Many Attack Submarines Does the Navy Need?" April 27, 2000.

106. Capt. Dave Burgess, program manager for the New Attack Submarine (NSSN) program, and Capt. Tom Olsen, Office of the Assistant Secretary of the Navy for Research, Development, Test, and Evaluation, briefing on the New Attack Submarine, September 18, 1996.

107. Sontag and Drew, p. 271.

108. Robert Holzer, "U.S. Works to Squelch Sub Sounds," *Defense News*, February 19–25, 1996, pp. 1, 28.

109. Office of Naval Intelligence, p. 17.

110. For a more detailed comparison of U.S. and Russian submarines, see Ivan Eland, "Subtract Unneeded Nuclear Attack Submarines from the Fleet," Cato Institute Foreign Policy Briefing no. 47, April 2, 1998, p. 5.

111. Robert Hamilton, "Support Growing for More Submarines," *New London Day*, March 7, 2000, p. 1.

112. John J. Schulz, "China as a Strategic Threat: Myths and Verities," *Strategic Review*, Winter 1998, p. 9.

113. Russell Howard, *The Chinese People's Liberation Army: "Short Arms and Slow Legs,"* (Colorado Springs, Colo.: U.S. Air Force Academy, September 1999), pp. 23–24.

114. Mark Arsenault, "Navy, EB Pin Hopes on New Sub," *Providence Journal-Bulletin*, August 29, 1999, p. 1A.

115. Ibid.

116. Ibid.

117. For a more comprehensive discussion of the advantages of consolidating the submarine industrial base, see Eland, "Subtract Unneeded Nuclear Attack Submarines," p. 16.

118. Quoted in Arsenault, p. 1A.

119. Steven M. Kosiak, Center for Strategic and Budgetary Assessments briefing,

"The FY 2000 Defense Budget Request: Prospects for Modernization," March 2, 1999, p. 7.

120. Robert Holzer, "2 Teams Form to Bid For DD-21 Program," *Defense News*, June 22–28, 1998, p. 10.

121. John Donnelly, "Navy Vets Options to Alter Destroyer Competition," *Defense Week*, February 9, 1998, p. 7.

122. Valerie Bailey Grasso, *Navy LPD-17 Amphibious Shipbuilding Program: Background and Funding Options for Congress* (Washington, D.C.: Congressional Research Service, April 17, 1996), p. CRS 1-2.

123. General Accounting Office, pp. 28–29; Kosiak, p. 7; and Department of the Navy, *Highlights of the Department of the Navy FY 1998/1999 Biennial Budget*, February 1997, p. 3-2.

124. Unless otherwise noted, information in the theater missile defense section comes from Charles Pena, "Theater Missile Defense: A Limited Capability Is Needed," Cato Policy Analysis no. 309, June 22, 1999, pp. 18–25.

125. John Donnelly, "THAAD Intercepts Were Unrealistic Top Tester Says," *Defense Week*, August 23, 1999, p. 1.

126. Quoted in editorial, "Arms Cooperation Lie," *Defense News*, October 12–18, 1998, p. 54.

127. Dan Smith, "Zeroing MEADS Means Zeroing Cooperation with Europe," *Weekly Defense Monitor* 3, no. 28, July 22, 1999, p. 4.

128. Greg Seigle, "U.S. Spending Row Puts MEADS in Jeopardy," *Jane's Defence Weekly*, p. 3.

129. Richard Roesler, "Missile Threat: Scaled-Down Versions of Star Wars in the Works to Protect U.S. and Troops Overseas, *Pacific Stars and Stripes*, August 8, 1999, p. 5.

130. Cited in John Donnelly, "Airborne Laser Found Unlikely to Meet Range Requirements," *Defense Week*, March 8, 1999, pp. 1, 15.

131. Ibid., p. 15.

132. O'Hanlon, *Technological Change*, p. 103.

7

Defense Programs That Need Increased Funding or Attention

It has been said that the U.S. defense establishment is always fighting the last war. DoD continues to procure weapon systems designed during the Cold War or their successors. In certain cases, this course of action is warranted—especially if a balancer-of-last-resort strategy is adopted that is designed to fight the "big war" against a future would-be hegemon. Focusing on overseas presence missions and making forces light enough to rapidly respond to brushfire wars at the expense of "heavier" capabilities—needed to fight any aggressive great power—would be a mistake.

Yet trends in warfare and the likelihood that a low-threat environment will hold for an extended period demand a rethinking of the American defense procurement strategy, which is based largely on inertia. For instance, submarines are powerful naval weapons against an aggressive great power that possesses submarines. But no other great power will have a credible submarine force for the foreseeable future. Thus, as noted earlier, the correct course of action is to reduce the submarine force to twenty-five, end procurement of the *Virginia*-class boats, and continue development of technologies for future submarines that might be needed if and when a new hegemon arises.

That example illustrates a broader strategy of taking advantage of the current mild threat environment by reducing procurement of weapons and instead emphasizing the research and development (R&D) of future systems. Those R&D programs are needed to modernize the force in the long term or possibly to react to some future hegemonic threat. High-cost systems procured now will be out of date if the threat increases in twenty or thirty years.

Les Aspin, President Clinton's first secretary of defense, proposed such a strategy of emphasizing R&D at the expense of procurement. After the Cold War ended, overall spending on defense declined about 35 percent from fiscal year 1985, at the height of the Reagan military buildup. In contrast, R&D funding was reduced by only about 17.5 percent. Up until recently, during the post–Cold War era, the R&D account was a relatively protected part of the budget.[1] Yet despite this strategy, spending on R&D has fallen from 15 percent of the defense budget during the Carter administration and 20 percent during the Reagan administration to 8 percent now.[2] The reason for this decline is that a larger portion of the defense budget has been taken up by the rising costs of operating and supporting (maintaining and paying) the forces. (Nevertheless, in absolute real dollars, the R&D budget will remain above the average amount spent during the Cold War.)

The budget share dedicated to R&D is likely to decline farther, because operations and support costs keep going up and Aspin's original strategy of protecting R&D at the expense of procurement is likely to be reversed. The Future Years Defense Plan (FYDP) envisions the R&D account continuing to decline by about 14 percent. The decline in the R&D budget is designed to help pay for substantial increases in the procurement account.[3] The rhetoric from Congress and the Pentagon is that the "procurement holiday"—that is, living off the large number of modern weapons systems built during the Reagan defense buildup of the 1980s—has to end or the force will become dilapidated and obsolescent. But the urgency of a boost in procurement funding is largely an illusion.

The desperate need for a hike in procurement funding arises only because U.S. forces are too large. Instead of modernizing the oldest equipment with newly built systems, aging items should be retired without replacement. That is, many new systems, in development or beginning production, can be canceled. The most modern equipment remaining in the force will eventually need to be replaced, but not for many years. Again using the example of submarines: instead of purchasing about thirty *Virginia*-class submarines to replace the oldest *Los Angeles*–class (688) boats in an attempt to maintain an excessive force of fifty-five vessels, the older 688s should be retired without replacement. A force of eighteen more modern, improved *Los Angeles*–class (688I) ships (many times quieter and more effective than the earlier 688s), three *Seawolf*-class boats, and the four *Virginia*-class vessels already under contract would not need to be replaced for years to come; the first new submarine would be needed in 2014 at the earliest.

A small amount of the savings generated from canceling unneeded new weapons in procurement can be transferred to the R&D account to finance underfunded but vital items (see table 7.1), but most of the savings can be

Table 7.1
Defense Programs That Should Be Cut Back and Those That Should Receive More Emphasis

Proposed Cutbacks		Programs That Should Instead Receive Increased Emphasis
Program	Recommendation	
F-22 fighter	Cancel	F-15 C or E
F-18 E/F fighter	Cancel	F-18 C/D and/or navalized F-117
Joint Strike Fighter	Delay (and combine air force and marine versions)	F-16 and F-18 C/D and/or navalized F-117 (until JSF is ready)
C-17 airlifter	No further procurement	Modernize C-5s or buy commercial aircraft
V-22 tiltrotor aircraft	Cancel	CH-53s or CH-60 Blackhawks
Comanche helicopter	Cancel	Kiowa warriors (if needed)
Crusader self-propelled artillery	Cancel	R&D for a lighter self-propelled howitzer
M-1 tank upgrades	Cancel	R&D for lighter tank
Antitank weapons	Reduce number of programs	No replacement needed
Advanced Amphibious Vehicle	Reduce number purchased	No replacement needed
CVN-77 aircraft carrier	Cancel	No replacement needed
Future aircraft carrier	Delay	No replacement needed
Virginia-class submarines	Buy only four submarines	R&D for a future submarine
DD-21 destroyer	Cancel	R&D on replacement for CG-47 cruiser
LPD-17 amphibious ship	Reduce number purchased	No replacement needed
MEADS	Cancel	Patriot PAC-3
THAAD	Cancel	Navy theaterwide
Airborne laser	Cancel	Navy area
		R&D for a new long-range bomber
		R&D for STOVL and VTOL technology
		Unmanned aerial vehicles
		Mine countermeasures
		Long-range precision measures
		Command, control, communications, and intelligence
		Electronic warfare
		Defense against chemical and biological weapons
		Cruise missile defense for U.S. forces

used to replace aging systems with improved versions of those systems or returned to the taxpayers in the form of reductions in the defense budget (after all, absolute real spending on R&D remains high).

A NEW LONG-RANGE BOMBER

Because the air force is buying two new tactical fighter aircraft—the F-22 and the JSF—and the C-17 transport plane, it cannot afford to define the mission requirements for a new bomber until 2013 or to begin producing the new aircraft until 2034. The ratio of dollars invested in tactical fighters versus bombers will increase from about five to one in 1999 to more than thirty to one in 2003.[4] By 2034, some B-52Hs will be over seventy years old. Yet, as noted earlier, air bases close to the front used by tactical fighters are becoming more vulnerable to attack from enemy ballistic missiles. Instead of investing so much in tactical aircraft, the air force should accelerate its schedule for fielding a reasonably priced bomber (unlike the exorbitantly expensive B-2) that would be more efficient and survivable than tactical fighters. The bomber would deliver heavy payloads from more remote, invulnerable bases in the theater of operations.

Advances in long-range, precision-guided, air-to-ground munitions, however, may render obsolete a stealthy manned penetrating bomber like the B-2. Furthermore, during the war in Kosovo, the stealthy F-117 and B-2 aircraft—advertised as stand-alone strike aircraft—received protection from aircraft that jammed enemy radar. Thus, perhaps a cheaper nonstealthy "bomb truck" would be adequate. The bomber could be accompanied by fighter escorts, might deliver precision weapons at stand-off ranges, or might be unmanned. Given the long lead time for R&D programs on modern weapon systems to bear fruit, a program for a new bomber should be started immediately.

STOVL AND VTOL AIRCRAFT TECHNOLOGY

The increasing vulnerability of air bases close to the front could be further negated by developing short-takeoff-and-vertical landing (STOVL) or vertical-takeoff-and-landing (VTOL) tactical aircraft. Instead of congregating at large air bases like conventional tactical aircraft, the STOVL and VTOL aircraft could be dispersed to less vulnerable, austere airfields.

The marines already fly the AV-8B VTOL aircraft and have its replacement—the STOVL version of the JSF—in development. Because of range and payload penalties associated with the current generation of VTOL aircraft, the marines use the AV-8B primarily for close air support (shorter-range missions involving bombing to support ground troops).[5] If more money were invested in the STOVL technology to replace the Harrier, those range and payload penalties might lessen or even evaporate. The air force might then be more enthusiastic about adopting STOVL for its version of the JSF.

In the long run, advances in STOVL or VTOL technology might allow aircraft carriers to increase their firepower or decrease their size (and vulnerability). If less runway is needed for aircraft to take off, more planes can operate from a smaller deck. As noted earlier, more advanced STOVL or VTOL technology might even allow the elimination of the aircraft carrier and dispersion of its aircraft to less vulnerable, smaller surface ships.

Lt. Dave Adams, a futurist in the Chief of Naval Operations Strategic Studies Group at the Naval War College, in Newport, Rhode Island, even foresees the DDG-51 *Arleigh Burke* destroyer with its own wing of twenty-five vertical-takeoff unmanned aerial vehicles (twenty of which would be used to strike enemy targets).[6] Such vehicles might also be launched from submarines. The U.S. Navy is already conducting trials of several VTOL unmanned aerial vehicles.[7]

UNMANNED AERIAL VEHICLES

The wars in the Persian Gulf and Kosovo showed that unmanned aerial vehicles (UAVs)—remotely piloted aircraft—could be invaluable for reconnaissance and pinpointing targets (even providing low-altitude target designation for laser-guided bombs despite the presence of clouds). Often, killing a target with precision weapons is easier than finding and identifying it in the first place.[8] The military, however, has invested much more in precision weapons than in UAVs for reconnaissance, surveillance, and targeting.

Tactical UAVs, with their on-board sensors, could provide real-time visual surveillance and targeting information to commanders. UAVs with high endurance and large payloads could gather strategic intelligence—for example, information on early warning of troop movements or missile launches.[9] UAVs could also jam an adversary's radars or communications, assess battle damage to the enemy after attacks, act as communications relay platforms, provide meteorological data, detect the use of chemical or biological weapons, and assist in search and rescue operations. Microrobotic technologies may eventually allow the production of very small UAVs.

In the future, unmanned vehicles with large payloads—unmanned combat air vehicles (UCAVs)—might be able to attack and suppress enemy air defenses, conduct deep-strike missions, or even attack mobile targets. Recent technological advances—more sophisticated computers, artificial intelligence capabilities, sensors, data-transmission capacity, and inexpensive satellite-guided bombs—make UCAVs more viable.[10] The goal of the military's UCAV advanced technology demonstration program is to field a system that is one-third the cost of the next-generation JSF aircraft—that is, an unmanned attack aircraft costing about ten million dollars per copy.[11] Removing the pilot allows the size and weight of the aircraft to be reduced and more violent maneuvers to be performed.[12] Also, the expensive training and infrastructure required to create highly skilled pilots could be reduced (the training for one pilot costs two million dollars).[13]

UCAVs are less futuristic than is commonly believed; no technological barriers exist to developing such systems.[14] Production could begin in 2004, and dozens could be in the force by 2010.[15] (Influential advocates for UCAVs want to bring them into the force sooner and in more ambitious roles.)[16] Both the navy and the air force have UCAV programs and may develop requirements for the air vehicles.[17] Already, the air force will drop bombs from its Predator UAV.[18]

Because unmanned aerial vehicles with large payloads are already available (in Israel) or will become available (in the United States), such aircraft might allow a reduction of the number of JSF aircraft produced. Replacing manned aircraft with UCAVs could ultimately save the taxpayers significant amounts of money. Alternatively, producing an unmanned version of the JSF might be possible and desirable. According to John Warner, then-chairman of the Senate Armed Services Committee, it is "reasonable that one-third of the operational deep strike aircraft could be unmanned within ten years."[19] Congress has asked the air force to analyze whether a larger UCAV could replace the B-2 bomber.

Yet despite the enormous promise of UAVs and UCAVs, the military services have skimped on R&D funding for them because they might take jobs away from pilots. Also, UAVs and UCAVs take scarce resources away from sexier weapons systems, such as three new manned tactical aircraft. But ultimately, they also have the potential to perform inexpensively the difficult missions that pose the greatest danger to the lives of pilots. DoD and Congress must force the services to devote more R&D money to unmanned systems that can eventually save money and act as powerful force multipliers.

A LIGHTER TANK

As noted earlier, the four light divisions have no heavy tanks. Those divisions can get to the battlefield quickly via airlift aircraft (that is, they have good strategic mobility) but cannot move quickly on the battlefield once they get there (that is, they have poor tactical mobility) or provide much firepower. For that reason, light divisions do not fit well into a balancer-of-last-resort strategy, which is designed to fight major wars. Thus, in the restructured force, the number of such divisions is drastically reduced.

But the heavy divisions needed to carry out the strategy have drawbacks too. Unlike light divisions, they have good tactical mobility but poor strategic mobility. In practice, only one of the heavy M-1 Abrams tanks (seventy tons) in those divisions can fit into the gargantuan C-5, the largest of the military cargo planes. Thus, heavy armored and mechanized infantry divisions must be moved by sea. The procurement of lighter tanks would improve strategic mobility by increasing the quantity of equipment that could be moved by sea in a given amount of time. Lighter tanks also require less fuel and ammunition, which also require significant lift capacity to transport. In any war that the United States gets involved in overseas, the faster the U.S. military can build up the required forces and supplies in the theater, the less vulnerable those forces will be to enemy attacks and the more effective they will be on the battlefield.

In addition, a lighter tank for the heavy divisions might make armored forces less vulnerable on the future battlefield. Many in the Israeli army believe that main battle tanks will become vulnerable to modern stand-off firepower.[20] Tanks with heavy armor may become especially vulnerable to improved antitank missiles; tank-busting systems seem to be developing an edge over tanks. In contrast, faster and more maneuverable light tanks may be able to increase their survivability by deemphasizing heavy armor and emphasizing agility, by using stealth technologies, and by engaging the enemy at long ranges with greater firepower (using powerful, high-velocity guns). The speed and mobility of lighter tanks would allow U.S. forces to surprise the enemy, thereby increasing survivability, and permit U.S. armor to mass for the attack and then disperse more quickly to reduce the window of vulnerability to enemy fire.[21] Lighter tanks can transit the narrow streets of urban areas (where future combat will occur) and unreinforced roads and bridges better and more quickly than can today's heavier models. Lower requirements for fuel and ammunition would make the logistical "tail" of heavy divisions leaner and less vulnerable to enemy missile attacks.

The National Defense Panel's recommendations on land forces were wise ones:

- Become more expeditionary: fast, shock-exploiting forces. . . .
- Reduce systems that are difficult to move and support; shift to lighter, more agile automated systems;
- Develop the twenty-first century tank to be a unique vehicle relying on speed, agility, and hyper-velocity gun technology for operational effectiveness (the Panel's view is that 30–35 tons is the appropriate weight range).[22]

Many of the world's armies are moving to lighter tanks, and so should that of the United States.[23] But each generation of tanks that the U.S. Army builds has been bigger and heavier than the previous one. The army culture seems wedded to heavy armor, as though it is still planning to fight Warsaw Pact forces in Central Europe.

The army and the Defense Advanced Research Projects Agency may be on the wrong track with the Future Combat Vehicle. They want it to replace the M1 Abrams tank, the M-2 Bradley fighting vehicle, the Avenger air-defense system, and the Paladin self-propelled howitzer. In times of budgetary constraints, it is wise to create multimission platforms (for example, Navy Aegis cruisers and destroyers), but the army's effort may be overly ambitious. More important, even if several smaller, specialized robotic vehicles (twenty tons each) are controlled from a manned mother ship, the whole system would probably weigh as much as the M-1 tank and be only incrementally more mobile, strategically.[24] Only if the firepower, tactical mobility, and survivability of the system could be made much greater than for the M1, so that fewer systems would be needed, would strategic mobility be enhanced enough to make the system more desirable. (In any case, the army should not give up on promising unmanned ground vehicles. The chairman of the Senate Armed Services Committee has suggested that within fifteen years a third of U.S. ground combat vehicles could be unmanned.)[25]

In contrast, the Marine Corps—a service less enamored with heavy systems—has an "expeditionary family of fighting vehicles" in the early stages of development. The forty-ton vehicles might have laser guns, use advanced composite materials, be able to disguise their signatures as those of benign vehicles, switch between wheel and track mode, and deploy integrated electronic defenses against attack.[26]

In the interim, before some sort of future tank can be built, General Shinseki, army chief of staff, has pushed for the development of "medium weight force" that would include a medium armored vehicle. The goal seems to be to buy a wheeled, twenty-ton armored vehicle that will fit in a C-130, the military's smallest transport aircraft. To fill out six medium-weight brigades— which are designed to be transported anywhere in the world in 96 hours— the army will buy 3,000 of the lighter vehicles with variants including infantry carriers, tank-like mobile guns, and reconnaissance and command vehicles.[27] Although wheeled vehicles are faster on the roads, tracked vehicles have greater speed over broken ground. A lighter army must remain focused on war fighting, not peacekeeping, for which the wheeled vehicle is better suited. Therefore, a new light tank should be tracked or have the capability to switch between tracks and wheels.

A serious, unified army–Marine Corps R&D effort to develop a future light tank with new gun technology is needed. If a lighter, more agile tank were developed, survivability (of both the tank and the leaner logistical tail), firepower, and both tactical and strategic mobility could be improved. In short, the firepower of heavy divisions should be retained, but the heavy divisions should be made lighter and more agile.

A LIGHTER SELF-PROPELLED ARTILLERY PIECE

A lighter self-propelled artillery piece is also needed to make the heavy divisions more agile. The modified Crusader system, with reduced size, weight, and capacity, is scheduled to be fielded by 2005 to replace the aging M109 Paladin self-propelled gun. But even the modified Crusader is too heavy (fifty tons) and does not use the most advanced technologies. The National Defense Panel implied that fewer Crusaders should be purchased.[28] Instead, the Crusader should be canceled; a lighter self-propelled gun should be developed, one that is more suited to a future agile army.

MINE COUNTERMEASURES

Sea mines, even the primitive ones used in the Korean War and Desert Storm, have wreaked havoc with amphibious assaults in the post–World War II era. If any hope exists that even limited amphibious assaults can be conducted in the future (a prospect cast into doubt also by the advent of satellite reconnaissance and precision-guided weapons), a solution must be found to the problem of mines in coastal areas.

Mines are an "asymmetric threat"—that is, they are inexpensive weapons that can be used by the weak as a potent hammer against the strong. Even poor rogue states can afford cheap, but deadly, sea mines. For example, contact mines (suspended just below the water's surface to explode on contact with a ship) can be made for as little as one or two thousand dollars each. According to the navy, more than fifty nations have mines and minelaying capabilities—an increase of 40 percent since 1986.[29]

In the Korean War, Gen. Douglas MacArthur planned an amphibious assault on Wonsan, North Korea, but was foiled when two U.S. minesweepers were lost to pre–World War I mines laid by the North Koreans with Russian help.

In Desert Storm, the Marines were prevented from making an amphibious landing on the coast of Kuwait because Iraq had sown the Persian Gulf littoral in unexpected places with World War I–era mines. Military planners estimated that as many as forty days would have been needed to clear an area of water from which to launch the amphibious assault. Two expensive U.S. ships—a sophisticated Aegis cruiser and an amphibious assault ship acting as a command post for mine-clearing operations—were hit by the mines.[30] A $1,500 mine inflicted $3.5 million worth of damage on the amphibious vessel.

After the Gulf War one analyst concluded, "Mine clearing is too slow, even in a non-threatening environment, and nearly impossible in a hostile environment. The Navy has to figure out a way to detect, identify, and clear mines for amphibious assaults, or the Marines are going to be put out of business."[31] Pentagon planners were quoted as saying that the marines would have taken terrible casualties if an amphibious assault had been attempted through the minefields during the Gulf War. A former Navy official was more direct; "One reason mine warfare is front and center is that the Marine Corps is scared to death."[32]

Slow rates of mine clearance can destroy the element of surprise, which can be so decisive in any amphibious assault. If the enemy finds out where the assault is coming, it can concentrate forces to overwhelm the landing troops. In fact, missiles on the shore can protect the minefields, to make clearing the mines prior to an assault very difficult and bloody.

Clearing sea mines in forty feet of water or more is easier than in very shallow water or in the surf zone. The navy has little capability to clear mines in those areas. In shallow water, the navy can use divers to find and neutralize the mines by hand, but that method is dangerous and slow even under ideal conditions.[33] The General Accounting Office reported that although improving mine clearing in shallow water is a high priority, many of the projects working toward this end are short of funds.[34] In the surf zone, the navy is virtually unable to clear small land mines. The service is conducting research and development on promising technologies in those areas, but mine countermeasures have never received a high priority in the navy's budget.

In fact, as this brief historical sketch showed, the navy does not seem to learn from past mistakes. Despite the role of Iraqi mines in preventing the American amphibious assault in the Gulf War, Navy and Marine Corps spending on mine countermeasures programs dropped from $600 million in fiscal year 1992 to about $300 million in fiscal year 1997.[35] This reduction came despite a rhetorical commitment by the Department of the Navy after the Gulf War to pay more attention to the problem of mines. In 1998, Lt. Gen. John Rhodes, commander of the Marine Combat Development Command, excoriated the Pentagon's lack of action and budget commitment to mine countermeasures, characterizing its efforts as "a lot of great talk." Rhodes added that the navy's investments since the Gulf War have "not produced any system ready for deployment."[36]

Clinton's secretary of defense, William Cohen, was also unhappy with the navy's progress in mine countermeasures. Cohen was a vociferous critic of the navy's neglect of such programs. In 1998 and 1999, he warned it not to dip into the mine countermeasures budget to fund other more favored programs.[37] Despite its low funding for the unglamorous mine-clearing mission (only a few hundred million dollars in a $300 billion defense budget), the navy would prefer to use some of that money to build expensive warships. Cohen doubled the budget for mine warfare, from roughly a half a billion dollars a year to twice that by 2004.[38]

The navy will need to invest more in technologies for mine countermeasures, both dedicated (mine-clearing ships and helicopters) and organic (mine-detection and neutralization capability for surface combatants and submarines). Dedicated mine clearance is done before a carrier battle group or sealift ships arrive off a foreign coast. But the time required to get dedicated forces into position to conduct surveillance and clear minefields has been characterized by Navy officials as excessive for military operations.

Thus, the navy is developing organic mine-clearing systems that can deploy with battle groups and amphibious forces. But as the navy emphasizes, no "silver bullet" solution to the problem of sea mines exists. Organic mine-clearing systems will not, by themselves, solve it.[39]

In addition to increasing funding for research and development in mine countermeasure technologies, the navy needs to invest in transportation assets for the current dedicated mine-clearing force. At the insistence of Congress, the navy has reluctantly spent billions of dollars on dedicated military sealift to transport heavy forces to foreign theaters (those vessels are not as glamorous as warships, either). Yet before the sealift ships could enter a foreign port and unload troops and heavy military equipment, mines would often need to be cleared. War plans, however, are still based on the naïve assumption that waterways early in the conflict will be safe for sealift.

Unfortunately, mine-clearing ships are small and not built to take the rigors of clearing mines immediately after a transoceanic voyage. After crossing the ocean, they would need extensive maintenance and repair, which would significantly slow the clearing of mines. Therefore, a few large oceangoing transport vessels need to be purchased to haul the mine countermeasures ships to the theater.

Yet the navy is reluctant to spend the pittance required to purchase a few Flo-Flo (flow-on flow-off) ships. The small mine-clearing ships would sail onto the Flo-Flo to be carried across the ocean and off of it on the other side to begin clearing mines immediately. To transport the mine-clearing ships to a foreign theater, the navy insists that it can contract for a heavy-lift ship to be available within two weeks of need (the ship may be transporting commercial goods somewhere else in the world). The problem with that approach is that mine clearing is one of the first things that needs to be done to prepare a theater for military operations. The two weeks (fourteen days) needed to take possession of the leased ship must be added to the time it takes to load, transport, and unload the ships in theater (at least sixty days and probably more) and then clear the mines (one hopes the navy can clear the mines a little faster than the forty days estimated during the Gulf War). Maj. Gen. Edward Hanlon, as Director of Expeditionary Warfare in the Office of the Chief of Naval Operations, admitted, "That's the biggest problem we have with mine sweepers—the time lines."[40] Yet the navy has not taken one obvious step that would significantly contract the time horizon.

The navy prefers to station or deploy a few mine-clearing ships in the Middle Eastern and East Asia theaters. But those vessels would be insufficient for a major war or could be out of position if a war broke out elsewhere in the world; in either case, a need would exist for mine countermeasures ships to be transported. In addition, the balancer-of-last-resort strategy cuts back on naval forward presence and relies on ships sent from the United States in time of crisis. For all of those reasons, Flo-Flos are needed to transport the entire mine-clearing fleet.

If the Navy purchased eight commercial Flo-Flo ships needed to transport its twenty-six mine-clearing ships, a crucial two weeks, and maybe more, could be subtracted from the time required to clear mines in the theater of operations. All 26 ships might be needed during a large regional war; twenty-six mine countermeasures ships from various nations were used during the Gulf War.[41] Buying the heavy-lift ships would probably save much more than just two weeks; eight Flo-Flo ships would probably be much harder to find in a hurry than one and would probably require more than two weeks to transit to U.S. ports from all over the world. This eight-ship heavy-lift force would cost only $400 million ($40–50 million per ship).

The United States has invested money in dedicated sealift ships (rather than relying on commercial vessels that may take longer to round up during a war). But this investment may have been wasted money if the sealift ships cannot enter quickly into a foreign port because no dedicated transports are available for mine clearing ships to get there first and begin clearing mines.

In short, some of the savings achieved by terminating the aforementioned weapon systems should be invested in developing technologies for mine clearing and in procuring the ships needed to transport the mine countermeasures force to overseas theaters of operation.

LONG-RANGE PRECISION WEAPONS

Although U.S. interventions in Kosovo and the Persian Gulf were dubious, they vividly illustrated that precision weapons now dominate warfare. Instead of dropping tens or hundreds of "dumb" iron bombs with the hope of knocking out a target, the military uses precision-guided munitions with a goal of "one target, one bomb." Of course, that ideal has not yet been achieved, but precision weapons are bringing it closer. According to the General Accounting Office, during World War II about nine thousand dumb bombs would have been needed to hit a hardened aircraft shelter. In the Vietnam War, only three hundred bombs would have been needed. During the Gulf War, only four precision weapons were needed.[42]

During the Gulf War, the effectiveness of laser-designated weapons— which have receptors that home on reflections of laser beams shone on a target by aircraft or troops on the ground—was limited by dust, smoke, rain, and clouds. During the next decade, satellite-guided missiles and bombs will overcome the need for laser designation and its environmental limitations.[43] But further improvements are needed.

As air-defense systems extend their range, precision-guided weapons also need to increase their range, so that aircraft can fire them from outside or above the dangerous air-defense envelope.[44] Those weapons will be able to hit targets currently restricted to expensive cruise missiles, at far lower cost.[45] Therefore, longer-range air-to-ground precision missiles—such as the navy's Stand-Off Land Attack Missile, Expanded Response (SLAM ER), the air force's Joint Air-to-Surface Missile (JASSM), and the Joint Stand-Off Weapon—should be purchased in large quantities (but not before they are thoroughly tested). SLAM ER, with a range of about 170 miles, can hit both ships and targets on land. JASSM has a long range (three hundred miles) and is not easily seen by radar (that is, it is stealthy).[46]

Enemy air defenses also need to be rendered inoperable. Antiradiation missiles (ARMs) are used to home in on the signals of enemy air-defense radar. Taking down those radars is one of the first critical tasks in any air campaign. Although ARMs are widely used, their performance has at times proved disappointing. Simple counters to ARMs include using decoy transmitters and switching off target radars. In addition, the small warheads of ARMs, which hit radar antennas, do not disable the sites for very long. In the future, ARMs will be faster, will seek targets with two types of sensors, and will memorize the location of the radar in order to hit it even if it shuts down. The Advanced Anti-Radar Guided Missile (AARGM), currently under development, will have a range of over a hundred miles, a dual-mode passive radar and active millimetric-wave radar seeker, and a small size that will allow it to fit in the internal bay of a stealth aircraft (for example, the F-117).[47] Because rendering enemy air defenses inoperable is such a vital mission, more funding should be allocated to developing the AARGM and other new ARMs.

Currently, the United States has only a limited capability to destroy underground bunkers and almost none to destroy safely any chemical or biological agents stored in them.[48] The U.S. regional commanders in chief have a requirement for a bomb or missile that will penetrate twenty feet into the ground. The deepest-penetrating bomb that the United States currently has in its arsenal—the GBU-28—will drive only four to six feet into the ground.[49] The GBU-28 relies on speed and weight (five thousand pounds of explosives) to penetrate several floors of subterranean structures before exploding. The air force's Advance Unitary Penetrator—a developmental bomb that has a void detector, which counts subterranean spaces and detonates at programmed destinations—will penetrate only ten feet into the ground.[50] Another approach exists that will improve U.S. bunker-busting capabilities but will not fulfill the requirement: fitting two warheads onto the air force's Conventional Air Launched Cruise Missile; the first antitank warhead blasts a hole through the concrete bunker so that the second can explode inside the bunker.[51]

More funds need to be allocated to developing a deep-penetrating weapon. Advances in drilling technology now allow deep holes to be dug rapidly and filled with concrete to create impregnable bunkers for command centers or storage sites for chemical and biological weapons.[52] One approach being discussed is using conventionally armed land-based or sea-based ballistic missiles, whose penetrating power is increased by their fall from space onto targets.

The United States should also invest in penetrating versions of the successors to the Tomahawk cruise missile and the SLAM missile—the Tactical Tomahawk and the Grand SLAM, respectively. In addition to penetrating hard targets, the Tactical Tomahawk has an inflight redirection capability, a three-hour loiter feature that allows it to hover over potential targets for faster response than when being fired from a ship, and an onboard camera for preattack surveillance or postattack battle damage assessment.[53] The Grand SLAM can hit hard targets from 200 miles away.

Another major problem is that any conventional bomb or missile that hits an underground storage bunker containing biological or chemical weapons might disperse the highly toxic materials over a wide area. Thus, a conventional incendiary warhead needs to be developed to incinerate such toxins. Research is being done on such a warhead, but more funding should be allocated to the task.

With the advent of such precision weapons and sophisticated command, control, communications, and intelligence (C3I) systems, platforms like the F-15 fighter can be upgraded rather than replaced. Even the upgraded versions would represent quantum leaps over existing capabilities. (For example, Whitten Peters, as acting secretary of the air force, predicted that the next-generation JASSM will give the current bomber force ten times more lethality than the larger bomber fleet at the end of the Cold War. The F-15 will also carry the JASSM.[54] Thus, instead of investing in three new types of fighter aircraft costing $340 million, the Defense Department should terminate two of the aircraft and invest some of the savings in new precision weapons and C3I systems. A long-overdue change in DoD's investment priorities is required to reflect then-Secretary of Defense Cohen's statement that the air operation in Yugoslavia underscored the need for more precision munitions and intelligence-gathering systems.[55]

COMMAND, CONTROL, COMMUNICATIONS, AND INTELLIGENCE SYSTEMS

The Pentagon's rhetoric about the "revolution in military affairs" implies rapid advances in command, control, communications, and intelligence (C3I) systems. Those systems, however, remain underfunded relative to weapons platforms. For the military, a system that does not destroy something is less glamorous than those that do, and therefore it receives less funding. But C3I systems are "enablers" or "force multipliers" that allow weapons to augment their combat power. For example, airborne early-warning aircraft, such as the Airborne Warning and Control System (AWACS) aircraft, detect and track incoming enemy aircraft so that American fighters can intercept and fight them more effectively and efficiently. AWACS magnifies American air-to-air combat power dramatically.

Yet despite the military's chronic complaints about the shortage of such aircraft, the investment in AWACS has fallen short of what is needed.[56] Air force units flying the AWACS have been stretched too thin by the questionable commitments around the globe. The deployments need to be scaled back, and more money needs to be invested in modernizing the AWACS aircraft, which currently contains outdated technology. (AWACS is still the best military airborne early-warning aircraft in the world, but civilian computing technology has leaped ahead of its capabilities.)

The Joint Surveillance and Target-Attack Radar System (JSTARS)—a commercial aircraft with a radar that can detect and track moving targets on the ground—is also stretched too thin. The U.S. order for the planes was cut from nineteen to thirteen aircraft; NATO was originally supposed to buy the remaining six JSTARS aircraft but canceled the order. The United States should buy those six aircraft for itself. During the questionable conflict in Kosovo, JSTARS received wide acclaim from commanders for helping aircraft strike targets on the ground. In a major conflict, JSTARS could provide a potent defensive force multiplier, using the comparative advantage of American airpower against the attacking ground forces of an aggressive power.

The Persian Gulf War demonstrated another deficiency in American C3I systems. The U.S. military had trouble targeting and destroying mobile Iraqi surface-to-surface Scud missile launchers. By the time the United States detected a Scud launch and sent U.S. aircraft to attack the site, the mobile missile had moved (using "shoot and scoot" tactics). To shorten U.S. reaction time, it would be ideal to transmit real-time, information from satellites, manned surveillance aircraft (U-2 spy planes, P-3 maritime patrol aircraft, and JSTARS), and unmanned aerial vehicles directly into the cockpits of attacking aircraft. Despite the lessons of the Gulf War, DoD has still not fielded a real-time targeting system.[57] Because future enemies probably will prefer cheaper mobile missiles to more expensive air forces, funding needs to be increased for C3I systems that can help attack missiles before they are launched. Investment in this preemptive mission will complement investments in theater missile defense by reducing the number of missiles that the defenses will face.

DoD should also invest more in advanced sensors—for example, radars that penetrate foliage or are contained in artillery rounds, microrobots, or micro air vehicles. Those sensors can collect surveillance and other information and even detect biological and chemical warfare agents.[58] The Pentagon is currently researching such cutting-edge technologies, but more funding is needed.

ELECTRONIC WARFARE

Because sensors and command, control, and communications are so important to modern warfare, the ability to jam (electronically interfere with) an enemy's systems is vital. Jamming aircraft frequently accompany U.S. bombers and attack aircraft on bombing missions. The jamming aircraft negate air-defense radars and communications so that the enemy cannot use them to shoot down American planes and pilots. (Jamming aircraft also sometimes carry antiradiation missiles that home in on the signal of enemy air-defense radars to destroy them.)

Yet, as noted earlier, systems that do not kill anything receive a lower priority in the military than those that do. Despite the vital nature of electronic warfare and chronic complaints about shortages of such aircraft, the military has not invested adequately in those systems. The air force retired its fleet of EF-111s (an electronic warfare version of the F-111 fighter-bomber). That retirement left the navy's EA-6B Prowler as the military's only jamming aircraft. During the war in Yugoslavia, U.S. aircraft had to suspend operations against Iraqi air defenses in the two no-fly zones over Iraq because the scarce Prowlers had to redeploy to Serbia and Kosovo. Expansive U.S. commitments have stretched a neglected fleet of aircraft to the breaking point. The Pentagon is now reassessing the force structure for electronic warfare.[59] DoD will fund an additional squadron of Prowler aircraft and accelerate upgrades to the EA-6B fleet.[60]

Those initiatives will help, but electronic warfare has for too long been given a low priority compared to weapon systems. The military needs to increase emphasis on, and funding for, electronic combat (both R&D and procurement). The only A-6s that have not been retired are the EA-6Bs—which shows that the electronic warfare community must make do with what it can get. The U.S. military often funds unneeded, complex, and costly weapon systems at the expense of important systems that integrate weapons or multiply combat power. This mindset has to change, and increased funding for electronic warfare is a good place to start.

INVESTING TO COMBAT BIOLOGICAL AND CHEMICAL WEAPONS

In the future, biological and chemical weapons—delivered by missiles or other means, such as sprayers—will likely be a burgeoning threat to U.S. forces on the battlefield. Biological warfare (BW) and chemical warfare (CW) especially threaten massed ground forces, tactical air forces at air bases and on aircraft carriers in coastal waters, seaports and airfields, storage facilities, and staging areas.[61] BW agents—with their delayed effect (symptoms caused by most agents will not manifest themselves for a couple of days)—are less useful on the battlefield than the immediately effective chemical weapons. But biological weapons could be used against U.S. logistics bases, ports, and airfields in rear areas. Operations at those locations would probably be suspended at the slightest hint of a lethal attack in order to assess the extent of the contamination. Biological weapons are also ideal weapons of terror against the civilian population in the U.S. homeland—although missiles would not be the ideal means of delivery.

A September 1998 report by the Senate Veterans Affairs Committee concluded: "Despite lessons learned about readiness shortfalls during the Gulf War, the U.S. Department of Defense still is not fully prepared to fight a war where the threat exists of exposure to CB weapons."[62]

In the future, offensive attacks—for example, by U.S. aircraft carrying precision-guided munitions—may be able to destroy some enemy mobile missile launchers before the missiles are launched (although no Iraqi missile launchers were destroyed in this way during the Gulf War). But a better bet is to attack storage sites for CW and BW warheads, which can be found more easily than mobile launchers. A weapon is needed that can hit deeply buried and reinforced storage sites for the warheads and vaporize the deadly agents. In addition, active defenses, such as theater missile defenses, once deployed, may also destroy missiles carrying BW and CW agents.

But offensive measures and active defenses are not enough. Improved passive defenses are also needed. For example, dispersing large ground formations can reduce their vulnerability to such unconventional attacks. In addition to the advantages mentioned earlier, lighter, more agile ground forces may have less vulnerability to BW and CW attacks. Passive defenses also include devices for detecting agents, protective clothing, equipment for decontamination, and vaccines, antibodies, and antidotes. DARPA has focused its research on three main areas: new sensors to detect BW and CW agents, sophisticated diagnostics to determine if a person has been contaminated, and advanced therapeutics and medicines.[63]

The ability to detect rapidly the use of BW and CW against U.S. forces and civilian populations at home is limited. Therefore, most of the R&D funds spent on combating BW and CW are being funneled to improve detection and warning of such attacks.[64] Progress in detecting BW agents is a couple of years behind that for CW agents. But sensors that can detect CW agents at long distances still need to be developed. Longer detection ranges will permit U.S. forces to detect BW and CW agents and take protective or evasive action before casualties occur.

Devices are needed for detection and identification of agents at specific locations and over a wider area (eventually those two functions will be integrated into one system). Some detectors will be miniaturized and automated for use in the field (by soldiers, vehicles, aircraft, and ships) as well as in the laboratory. Devices are needed that use multiple sensors (for BW agents in particular) and can detect multiple agents. Ground-based, UAV-based, and space-based sensors are possible. The Defense Science Board recommended covert ground-based sensors, UAV-based sensors, microrobotic sensors (on mini-UAVs and small wheeled vehicles), and thermal sensors to cover wide areas. All sensors will eventually be networked to move toward real-time detection, identification, and warning of biological agents. In the nearer term, the goal is to reduce the detection-identification sequence of BW and CW agents from thirty minutes to five.[65]

Money needs to be shifted in the DoD budget from other programs to BW and CW detection. Many detection systems are under development and could benefit from increased funding. Antidotes and decontamination equipment may be useless if the BW and CW agents cannot be detected and identified.

The U.S. military has masks and suits for protection against BW and CW agents, but in warm climates those suits can cause heat exhaustion and impede operations. Thus, improvements in protective wear are needed. More and better protective equipment is also needed for fire departments and paramedics, which would provide the first response to a BW or CW attack on a U.S. city. Significant breakthroughs in new lighter, selectively permeable protective fabrics are imminent. For buildings, DARPA is developing large filter systems that might screen out BW and CW agents.

Research on decontamination techniques and equipment has received less emphasis than the development of technologies for agent detection and protective clothing. But by combining hair-conditioning creams and toothpaste, government chemists have created a foam that can neutralize many BW and CW agents (bacteria such as anthrax, viruses, and nerve and mustard agents) in confined spaces (for example, buildings). In somewhat more open spaces, such as subways or airports, the foam could be used as a spray or fog.[66] Will this foam have any applications on the open battlefield? At least it might be used to decontaminate protective suits. Other substances are also being developed for decontamination.[67] DoD also needs to evaluate the effectiveness of ultraviolet radiation to deactivate microorganisms and viruses in aerosols. More funding is probably needed in those promising research areas.

Both the U.S. military and civilian authorities have insufficient supplies of the vaccines and antidotes needed to combat BW and CW attacks. Although some vaccines and antidotes may need to be stockpiled, such substances have limitations. For example, vaccines would be of little use for most BW attacks against military and civilian targets. Knowing rapidly which of the many possible BW agents was being used in an attack would be difficult, making vaccination almost impossible. In addition, no vaccines exist for some hazardous BW agents.[68] Even if a vaccine exists, BW weapons can be genetically engineered to defeat it. Nevertheless, maintaining a limited (in number and types) stockpile of vaccines and antidotes for the agents most likely to be used—for example, anthrax—would probably be prudent. In the long term, R&D should be funded on nonspecific defense—that is, ways of making the human body more resistant to any invading foreign agent.[69]

In addition, DoD needs to fund a testbed to try out new technology for combatting BW and CW agents on the battlefield and at home. Many of the technologies being developed can be used for both missions.

But according to John Roos of the *Armed Forces Journal International*,

"By even the most optimistic assessments, it will be more than a decade before US forces are trained and equipped to operate effectively on contaminated battlefields."[70] Such operations may be needed on battlefields of the future. Thus, some of the savings from terminating unneeded Cold War weapon systems (see chapter 6) should be used to increase funding for the technologies needed to combat BW and CW and the test facility needed to perfect them.

CRUISE MISSILE DEFENSE FOR U.S. FORCES AND THE U.S. HOMELAND

Overwhelmingly, the debate on missile defense—both for the American homeland and for U.S. forces fighting overseas—has focused on the threat from ballistic missiles. Yet the fact that the United States is concentrating on defending against ballistic missiles may cause potential adversaries to develop cruise missiles, to circumvent that defense. Cruise missiles are more accurate than ballistic missiles and may be less expensive and less difficult for potential enemies to acquire. Unlike ballistic missiles, which use gravity for propulsion after their engines burn out, cruise missiles are essentially unmanned aircraft that rely on their engines for most of the flight to the target. Like ballistic missiles, cruise missiles can carry nuclear, biological, and chemical weapons.

Current antiaircraft systems (for example, the Patriot) can shoot down cruise missiles, but with greater difficulty than for aircraft. Cruise missiles have much smaller radar silhouettes than aircraft. Thus, cruise missiles could be difficult to detect, track, and kill with existing active defenses.[71] Also, because cruise missiles are smaller than ballistic missiles, offensive operations against them are more difficult. The cruise missiles can be launched from a variety of platforms—aircraft, ships, submarines, or ground-based launchers—without much modification.

Although short-range antiship cruise missiles have proliferated to many countries, only a few countries currently possess long-range land-attack missiles—for example, the Tomahawk, used by the United States. Yet technological challenges would not prohibit even underdeveloped nations from developing or purchasing those systems. Cruise missile production does not require two complex technologies found in ballistic missiles: reentry vehicles or advanced inertial guidance systems. Cruise missiles can rely on GPS (Global Positioning System) signals for midcourse guidance and on radar, laser, or infrared sensors for terminal guidance.[72] According to a National Defense Industries Association report, "Commercial GPS navigation instruments, compact avionics, flight programming software and powerful, lightweight jet propulsion systems provide the tools needed for a Third World country to upgrade short-range anti-ship cruise missiles or to produce new land-attack cruise missiles (LACMs) today."[73] The success of the Tomahawk will probably lead to a proliferation of longer-range missiles.[74] Even shorter-range cruise missiles could pose a problem for U.S. forces and the United States itself; for example, ships could appear off the coast armed with cruise missiles carrying nuclear, biological, and chemical weapons.

Defending the U.S. Homeland

Thus, DoD needs to use some of the savings garnered through canceling unneeded big-ticket weapons to increase research and development funding for cruise missile defense. But that defense must be focused on improved systems to counter cruise missiles targeted at U.S. forces rather than those aimed at the American homeland. Defending the United States against a cruise missile, short or long-range, is a daunting task. Unlike the ballistic missile, which has a predictable trajectory when its engines burn out, the cruise missile is in powered flight and can approach a target from any direction.

The many possible attack paths create the need for a defense in depth using several air-defense systems, each with its own probability of killing the incoming cruise missile. The best example of this challenging task is the layered defense that U.S. aircraft carriers maintain against antiship missiles. The defense consists of several sophisticated weapon systems defending concentric circles around the carrier. The formidable defense required for even this small "point" target shows that defending the thousands of miles of U.S. coast from cruise missiles would be prohibitively expensive. Prominent defense analysts estimate that defending the United States against cruise missiles could easily cost between ten and twenty billion dollars a year.[75] The U.S. Army's draft operational concept for national missile defense (which now includes the threat from cruise missiles) concludes that point-defense systems on land—such as the Patriot and short-range air-defense systems—"will continue to be scarce and could only be used to protect limited assets. Furthermore, TAMD [Theater Air and Missile Defense] systems are likely to be deployed overseas or preparing for deployment during periods of heightened tensions."[76] Thus, they might be unavailable to defend the homeland.

According to the army's draft concept, the North American Aerospace Defense Command (NORAD), responsible for the air defense of the United States, "cites the need for a family of CMD [cruise missile defense] systems to 'detect, validate and warn of an impending cruise missile threat; and . . . take appropriate action in conjunction with supporting [commanders in chief] to negate all cruise missiles before they either reach their target or chemical/biological dispersal points.' " But the army says that fulfilling NORAD's goals will be "extremely difficult. The effort will be resource-intensive, engagement timelines will be very short, and positive identification of air-breathing threats will be challenging."[77]

According to the National Defense Industries Association, "Current technology enables fielding large numbers of low-cost land-attack cruise missiles that can overwhelm even capable defenses."[78] In the future, the challenge of defending the American homeland against cruise missiles will become even more daunting, as more sophisticated cruise missiles—able to maneuver, or stealthy—proliferate around the world. Like terrorist attacks with weapons of mass destruction (WMD), cruise missile attacks on the homeland, carrying either conventional warheads or WMD, are extremely difficult to defend against. The U.S. government should make an effort to develop defenses against threats to the homeland that are manageable— that is, ballistic missiles—but admit that some threats are intractable, rather than waste billions of dollars trying to defend against them. Adopting a policy of military restraint overseas to lower the U.S. target profile then becomes even more important to the nation's security.

Defending U.S. Forces

The difficulty in protecting large areas of the American homeland from cruise missiles should not preclude developing systems to provide at least some protection for small areas on the battlefield (high-value targets, such as headquarters, logistics bases, ports, and airfields). Limited battlefield defense against cruise missiles is a manageable problem.

Different sensors are needed to detect cruise missiles, because, unlike ballistic missiles, they do not have rocket plumes, and they fly at low altitudes. The Cruise Missile Defense Initiative is developing truck-mounted electronic systems to correlate data from army, navy, and air force radars to enhance detection of such small targets and provide the information to ships, aircraft, and missile batteries that will destroy them. Cruise-missile defenses may employ AWACS and JSTARS surveillance aircraft, but creating an integrated surveillance grid against low-flying, stealthy cruise missiles will be very difficult.[79]

Defense in depth for high-value targets on the ground can be provided by upgrades to the long-range Patriot. In addition, dispersing maneuver forces and making them lighter, to make them more agile and reduce their large logistics "footprint," would make ground operations less vulnerable to attack by cruise missiles. Similarly, relying less on tactical aircraft that require large bases close to the front would increase the survivability of air forces to cruise missile attacks. Instead, the air forces should rely more on short-takeoff-and-landing (STOVL) aircraft flying from dispersed airfields, and on heavy bombers that can operate from bases farther from the front. As noted earlier, the navy has developed expensive concentric defenses for its carrier battle groups. Naval defenses might be improved by using stealth technology for ships and improving advanced STOVL aircraft to reduce the size of the carrier or eliminate it altogether.

CONCLUSION

The previous discussion showed that many big-ticket weapon systems could be terminated or delayed. Most of the savings should be given back to taxpayers, but some should be redirected to neglected areas of the defense budget. Because of the current "threat hiatus," much of that redirection of resources would transfer money from Cold War weapons to R&D in underfunded areas of great promise. Of the neglected programs mentioned in this chapter, the ones deserving the greatest attention are a new bomber, unmanned aerial vehicles, short-takeoff-and-vertical-landing technology (STOVL), and technologies to help U.S. forces and the American people combat biological and chemical weapons. The first three are high priorities because tactical fighters and their bases are increasingly vulnerable to enemy attack. The last effort is important because hostile states or terrorists that are "outgunned" by the United States may believe that its Achilles' heel is its vulnerability to attack using biological or chemical weapons.

The increased funding for *selected* R&D programs to ameliorate U.S. vulnerabilities, however, should be coupled with the adoption of a balancer-of-last-resort strategy, which relies on a policy of military restraint overseas. Avoiding unnecessary wars would dramatically reduce the susceptibility of U.S. forces to destruction and would lower the chances of a retaliatory attack on U.S. soil by hostile states or terrorists. Eschewing interventions in foreign conflicts that do not involve vital interests would also allow the United States to reduce its defense budget.

NOTES

1. Steven Kosiak, Center for Strategic and Budgetary Assessments briefing, "The FY2001 Defense Budget Request," February 2000, p. 11.

2. David Mulholland, "U.S. Research Funding Decline Raises Ire of Lawmakers," *Defense News*, August 23, 1999, p. 4.

3. Ibid.

4. Williamson Murray, *The United States Should Begin Work on a New Bomber Now*, Cato Institute Policy Analysis no. 368, March 16, 2000, p. 13.

5. Sophearith Moeng, *The Vital Guide to Military Aircraft* (Shrewsbury, England: Airlife, 1998), pp. 82–83.

6. Cited in Sharon Denny, "UAV Fleets Could Double Firepower of U.S. Carriers," *Defense News*, June 8–14, 1998, p. 26.

7. Sharon Denny, "U.S. Tests Could Lift Vertical Takeoff UAV Sales Globally," *Defense News*, June 8–14, 1998, p. 42.

8. David Mulholland, "As Budgets Fall, Tactical UAV Market Grows," *Defense News*, September 14–20, 1998, p. 12.

9. David Eshel, "High Flying Surveillance: Israel Leads the World in the Military Employment of Unmanned Aerial Vehicles," *Armed Forces Journal International*, June 1998, p. 30.

10. Paul Richter, "Pilotless Plane Pushes Envelope for U.S. Defense," *Los Angeles Times*, May 14, 2000, p. A1.

11. John Roos, "Expanding the Envelope: U.S. Unmanned Aerial Vehicle Programs Now Range from Lightweight Reconnaissance Aircraft to Heavyweight Attack Platforms," *Armed Forces Journal International*, June 1998, p. 26.

12. Douglas Barrie, "British Air Chief Skeptical about Feasibility of UCAV," *Defense News*, November 30–December 6, 1998, p. 6.

13. Richter, p. A1.

14. David Mulholland, "U.S. Studies UCAVs for Risky Combat Missions," *Defense News*, September 14–20, 1998, p. 18.

15. Jeff Cole, "Unmanned Jets May Someday Fly as Bombers," *Wall Street Journal*, May 10, 1999, p. B1.

16. Richter, p. A1.

17. Nick Cook, "The Revolutionary UCAV," *Jane's Defence Weekly*, July 12, 2000, p. 28.

18. "Air Force Plans Demonstration of Predator's Ability to Drop Bombs," *Inside the Air Force*, May 26, 2000, p. 1.

19. "Warner: Speed Development of Unmanned Combat Systems," *Defense Daily*, February 9, 2000, p. 1.

20. "Israel's Future Defense Forces," *Jane's Defence Weekly*, August 25, 1999, p. 21.

21. Warner, pp. 52–53.

22. National Defense Panel, *Transforming Defense: National Security in the 21st Century* (Arlington, Va.: National Defense Panel, 1997), p. 47.

23. Jack Hoschouer and George I. Seffers, "Main Battle Tanks' Days May Be Numbered," *Defense News*, August 31–September 6, 1998, p. 14.

24. Sean Naylor, "U.S. Army Sees Future of Armor in FCV," *Defense News*, September 20, 1999, p. 66.

25. Warner, "Speed Development of Unmanned Combat Systems," p. 1.

26. Jason Sherman, "Fanciful Flight: How the Marine Corps Plans to Make the Abrams Tank Look Like a Model-T Ford," *Armed Forces Journal International*, November 1999, pp. 46–48.

27. Thomas Ricks and Roberto Suro, "The Wheels Turn in Army Strategy," *Washington Post*, November 16, 2000, p. A1.

28. National Defense Panel, p. 49.

29. P. J. Skibitski, "Gansler Wants Beach Zone Plan Next Year," *Inside the Pentagon*, May 25, 2000, p. 4.

30. H. Dwight Lyons, Jr., Eleanor A. Baker, Sabrina R. Edlow, and David A. Perin, *The Mine Threat: Show Stoppers or Speed Bumps?* (Alexandria, Va.: Center for Naval Analyses, July 1993), pp. 1, 6–7.

31. Quoted in Stephen C. LeSueur, "New Study of Navy's Mine Countermeasures Says 'Bold Approaches' Needed But Finds No Silver Bullet for MCM," *Inside the Pentagon*, October 22, 1992, p. 1.

32. Quoted in ibid., p. 6.

33. Lyons, Baker, Edlow, and Perin, p. 18.

34. General Accounting Office, *Navy Mine Warfare: Budget Realignment Can Help Improve Countermine Capabilities* (Washington, D.C.: GAO, March 1996), p. 35.

35. Colin Clark, "Marine Calls Pentagon Mine Policy 'A Lot of Great Talk,' " *Defense Week*, April 13, 1998, p. 1.

36. Quoted in ibid.

37. "Secretary 'Fences' MCM Spending: Dissatisfied Cohen Steers New Course for Navy on Mine Warfare," *Inside the Navy*, April 20, 1998, p. 1; "Navy Resists the Lesson That in the Future, Enemies May Not Fight on Our Terms," *St. Louis Post-Dispatch*, p. B7; and "Cohen Delivered Both Increases, Imperative for Navy Mine Warfare," *Inside the Navy*, February 15, 1999, p. 7.

38. Michael O'Hanlon, *Technological Change and the Future of War* (Washington, D.C.: Brookings Institution, 2000), p. 179.

39. Skibitski, p. 4.

40. Quoted in Clark, p. 8.

41. Scott Truver, "Exploding the Mine Warfare Myth," *Proceedings*, U.S. Naval Institute, October 1994, p. 38.

42. Cited in Tim Smart, "Newest 'Smart' Weapons Would Redefine Air Campaign," *Washington Post*, February 1, 1998, p. A6.

43. David Ruppe, "U.S. Has Few New Munitions to Hit Iraq, Study Says," *Defense Week*, March 9, 1998, p. 14.

44. William Matthews, "Post-Gulf War Advances Make Smart Bombs Better," *Defense News*, September 7–13, 1998, p. 72; and John Donnelly, "Lockheed Martin's JASSM Win May Give Pentagon More Flexibility," *Defense News*, April 13, 1998, p. 2.

45. Jeffery Barnett, "Funding Two Armies: Why Paying for the Army's Transformation Could Spark an Interservice Brawl," *Armed Forces Journal International*, May 2000, p. 14.

46. Duncan Lennox, "On Target?" *Jane's Defence Weekly*, September 9, 1998, pp. 73, 86.

47. Ibid., pp. 75, 86.

48. Smart, p. A6.

49. Nick Cook, "The Big Question: Can Saddam Be Beaten by Bombing Alone?" *Jane's Defence Weekly*, February 25, 1998, p. 21.

50. "ACTD: A Near-Term Solution," *Jane's Defence Weekly Defence Industry Report*, May 1999, p. 6.

51. Lisa Burgess, "Warhead Turns Standoff Missiles into Bunker Busters," *Defense News*, July 6–12, 1998, p. 6.

52. O'Hanlon, *Technological Change*, p. 90.

53. Joris Janssen, "UK Awaits US Decision on Future of Tomahawk," *Jane's Defence Weekly*, April 22, 1998, p. 6; and Bryan Bender, "USN Penetrating Tomahawk May Take Off by 2005," *Jane's Defence Weekly*, September 9, 1998, p. 14.

54. Bryan Bender, "Lockheed Martin Takes the JASSM Prize," *Jane's Defence Weekly*, April 22, 1998, p. 8.

55. Cited in Bradley Graham, "Up in Arms: War Review Extended a Month," *Washington Post*, September 15, 1999, p. A23.

56. Carl Conetta and Charles Knight, "Bigger Budgets Will Not Cure the Pentagon's Ills," *Boston Globe*, October 8, 2000.

57. Barbara Starr, "USA's Rapid Targeting Reaches New Heights," *Jane's Defence Weekly*, March 4, 1998, p. 22; and Bryan Bender, "Allies Still Lack Real-Time Targeting," *Jane's Defence Weekly*, April 7, 1999, p. 4.

58. Walter Pincus, "From Tiny Aircraft to Robots and Radars, Pentagon Pursues New Tools," *Washington Post*, March 29, 1998, p. A2; and John Roos, "Unmasking the Enemy: Foliage-Penetrating Radar System Ready for Tests; Idea Dates Back to Vietnam Conflict," *Armed Forces Journal International*, April 1998, p. 51.

59. John Hamre, deputy secretary of defense, comments before the Lexington Institute's Air Power Conference, Dirksen Senate Office Building, September 9, 1999.

60. "Pentagon to Create Additional EA-6B Prowler Unit to Meet Demands," *Inside the Navy*, August 30, 1999, p. 1.

61. Robert W. Chandler, *The New Face of War: Weapons of Mass Destruction and the Revitalization of America's Transoceanic Military Strategy* (McLean, Va.: Amcoda Press, 1998), pp. 397–405.

62. Quoted in Greg Seigle, "Experts Highlight CBW Stockpiles in Yugoslavia," *Jane's Defence Weekly*, April 7, 1999, p. 5.

63. Christian Lowe, "Pentagon Official Outlines R&D Priorities," *Defense Week*, March 6, 2000.

64. John Roos, "Prescription for Survival: Hefty Cash Infusions Spur Progress in US Chemical And Biological Defense Programs," *Armed Forces Journal International*, October 1999, p. 72.

65. Ibid., p. 74.

66. Malcolm Browne, "Chemists Create Foam to Fight Nerve Gases," *New York Times*, March 16, 1999, p. F2.

67. Roos, "Prescription," p. 78.

68. Kenneth Alibek, Testimony before the Permanent Select Committee on Intelligence, U.S. House of Representatives, March 3, 1999, p. 6.

69. Ibid.

70. Roos, "Prescription," p. 79.

71. Bill Kaczor, "Air-Attack Fears Keep General Awake at Night," *Miami Herald*, January 31, 2000, p. 1.

72. O'Hanlon, *Technological Change*, p. 102.

73. Quoted in Daniel Dupont, "Cruise Missile Defense Attaining a Higher Profile within the Pentagon," *Inside the Pentagon*, March 23, 2000, p. 1.

74. U.S. Department of Defense, *Proliferation: Threat and Response* (Washington D.C.: DoD, 1996).

75. John Deutch, Harold Brown, and John P. White, "National Missile Defense: Is There Another Way?" *Foreign Policy*, Summer 2000, p. 96.

76. Dupont, p. 1.

77. U.S. Army's draft operational concept for national missile defense, quoted in Dupont, p. 1.

78. National Defense Industries Association report, quoted in Dupont, p. 1.

79. O'Hanlon, *Technological Change*, p. 102.

8

An Appropriate Defense Budget for the Balancer-of-Last-Resort Strategy

The costs of the force structure (elaborated in chapter 5) needed to carry out the "balancer-of-last-resort" strategy need to be estimated. Equally important, this preferable alternative defense budget needs to be estimated from the ground up. Many alternative defense budgets proposed by outside authors use the Pentagon's current budget as a starting point. Those authors subtract or add forces and their operations and support (O&S) costs from the existing defense program and budget. Those O&S costs for military units include direct expenses (for example, fuel and spare parts, and pay for personnel) and indirect costs (for example, training and medical costs) expenses but not a slice of the approximately 40 percent of O&S expenses that are fixed (for example, funds to support military bases or repair real property).[1] Those fixed costs should be allocated to those military units.

But according to economists, in the long run, all costs are variable—that is, all O&S costs should ultimately depend on the size of the forces. Because the time horizon for this study is long (force levels would be cut until an ideal force structure is reached in 2010), the assumption that excess fixed infrastructure—for example, unneeded bases and facilities—would be eliminated is a reasonable one.

In addition, the annualized cost for a military unit to acquire new weapons must also be included. That cost is simply the sum of all the expenses incurred to acquire new equipment for the unit, divided by the number of years the equipment is expected to last (the equipment's service life).

So the total cost of the force will be the sum of the annualized acquisition and O&S expenses (including a slice of the fixed costs for infrastructure) for each military unit in the revised force structure. Specifying the elements of the force structure that are truly needed to carry out a national strategy, costing out each one, and adding them up for a total is a real "Bottom-Up Review" (unlike the misnomer that the Clinton administration gave to a defense review in 1993, which was nothing more than an incremental version of the Bush administration's Base Force). Estimating the costs of the needed forces from the ground up eliminates the excess expense for residual infrastructure that is inherent in any analyses that use DoD's budget as a starting point for force reductions. The department's budget is a "black box" full of costly, hidden inefficiencies. Such inefficiencies should not be tolerated and can be minimized using bottom-up costing. If DoD is given only the funds needed to defend vital American interests, the department will be quickly forced to remove those inefficiencies from its budget.

A MUCH SMALLER DEFENSE BUDGET ACHIEVED THROUGH BOTTOM-UP COSTING WILL NOT HARM U.S. SECURITY

During the Clinton administration, the military was strained by increasing U.S. commitments overseas and declining real defense outlays. Outlays for national defense (budget account 050) dropped almost 9 percent, from about $333 billion (all figures are in fiscal year 2002 dollars) in fiscal 1994—the Clinton administration's first budget—to approximately $303 billion in fiscal year 2001. On the other hand, the Republican Congress was equally inconsistent, preferring to hike military spending above Clinton budget requests but desiring a substantial reduction in U.S. involvement in brushfire wars (for example, in Haiti, Somalia, Bosnia, and Kosovo).

The proposed budget for the balancer-of-last-resort strategy is more consistent than the approaches taken by either the Clinton administration or Congress. Spending on national defense would be reduced substantially (the United States now spends more than the next seven nations combined), but U.S. commitments overseas would be cut back even more. Under the proposal, defense spending would fall almost 40 percent (about $120 billion), from the current $303 billion in outlays to about $184 billion. Yet the United States would avoid getting involved in brushfire conflicts and would go even farther by withdrawing from its military alliances (with Japan, South Korea, the Philippines, Thailand, Australia, New Zealand, the nations of NATO, and the South American signatories to the Rio Pact). Those alliances are relics of the Cold War and reduce U.S. flexibility and security in a much-altered post–Cold War security environment.

Enjoying a very favorable geostrategic position, the United States could probably spend even less than $184 billion on national defense per year and remain one of the most secure nations on earth. In fact, with such geostrategic advantages, the United States could probably spend less

Table 8.1

Spending on National Defense: The Top Eight Nations (billions of 1999 dollars)

Country	Amount Spent in 1999 [a]	Rank
U.S. Defense Budget	275.5	1
Proposed Alternative [b]	171.5	1
Russia [c]	56.0	2
Japan	40.8	3
China [cd]	39.5	4
France	37.1	5
United Kingdom	36.9	6
Germany	31.1	7
Italy	22.0	8

Notes:

a. NATO's definition of defense spending was used for all nations. The year 1999 is the latest for which the calculation is available.

b. $183.9 billion (FY 2002 dollars) proposed budget deflated to 1999 dollars.

c. The figure has been adjusted for purchasing power parity

d. Official Chinese defense spending is roughly $12.6 billion dollars. If off-budget expenditures are included, total Chinese defense spending is $39.5 billion.

Source: International Institute for Strategic Studies, The Military Balance: 2000-2001 (London: Oxford Univ. Press, 2000) pp. 25, 58, 61, 66, 80, 120, 194, and 200.

on defense than other great powers and still remain very secure. An attempt has been made here, however, to make greater reductions in U.S. commitments than cuts in the defense budget, so that military lives would not be endangered by a force that is stretched too thin. A $184 billion-per-year budget for national defense would still lead the world (by far) and is more than enough to carry out the much more limited balancer-of-last-resort strategy (see table 8.1 and figure 8.1).

Even with the deep cuts, totaling about $120 billion, the proposed alternative U.S. defense budget is still more than three times that of the nearest great-power competitor, Russia. (The budget number for Russia grossly overstates the threat posed by a decrepit military that rarely gets all the money that it is promised.) Furthermore, the alternative U.S. defense budget is still more than half again as great as those of all the potential threat states combined (see table 8.2 and figure 8.2). The alternative remains more than twelve times as great as the defense budgets of all of the rogue states (Iran, Syria, North Korea, Libya, Iraq, and Cuba) combined.

Figure 8.1
Spending on National Defense: The Top Eight Nations

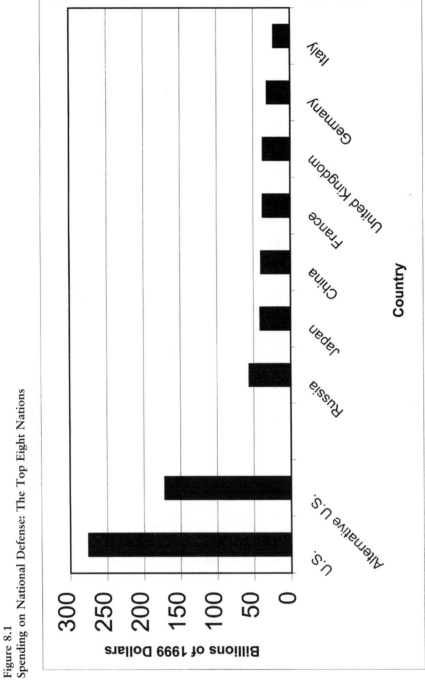

Source: International Institute for Strategic Studies, Military Balance 2000-2001.

Table 8.2
Spending on National Defense in Potential Threat States (billions of 1999 dollars)

Country	Amount Spent on Defense in 1999[a]
Russia [c]	56.0
China [cd]	39.5
Iran	5.7
North Korea	2.1
Syria	1.9
Libya [e]	1.5
Iraq	1.4
Cuba	.8
Sudan	.4
Total	109.3

Proposed Alternative U.S. Budget   171.5 [b]

Notes:

a. NATO's definition of defense spending was used for all nations. The year 1999 is the latest for which the calculation is available.

b. The $183.9 budget in FY 2002 dollars deflated to 1999 dollars.

c. The figure has been adjusted for purchasing power parity

d. Official Chinese defense spending is roughly $12.6 billion dollars. If off-budget expenditures are included, total Chinese defense spending is $39.5 billion.

e. A 1998 expenditure figure converted to 1999 dollars.

Source: International Institute for Strategic Studies, The Military Balance: 2000-2001 (London: Oxford Univ. Press, 2000), pp. 120, 139, 140, 146, 153, 194, 202, 236, and 283.

Detailed Costs of the Reduced Force

Table 8.3 summarizes the reduced force structure and its itemized cost.

Army

As noted earlier, the balancer-of-last-resort strategy involves *helping* regional powers, in either Europe or East Asia, to repel an aggressive nation that is seeking to alter permanently the balance of power and establish hegemony over an entire region. To assist regional actors, the United States would use primarily its advantage in airpower. Under the strategy, the

Figure 8.2
Defense Spending in Potential Threat States (billions of 1999 dollars)

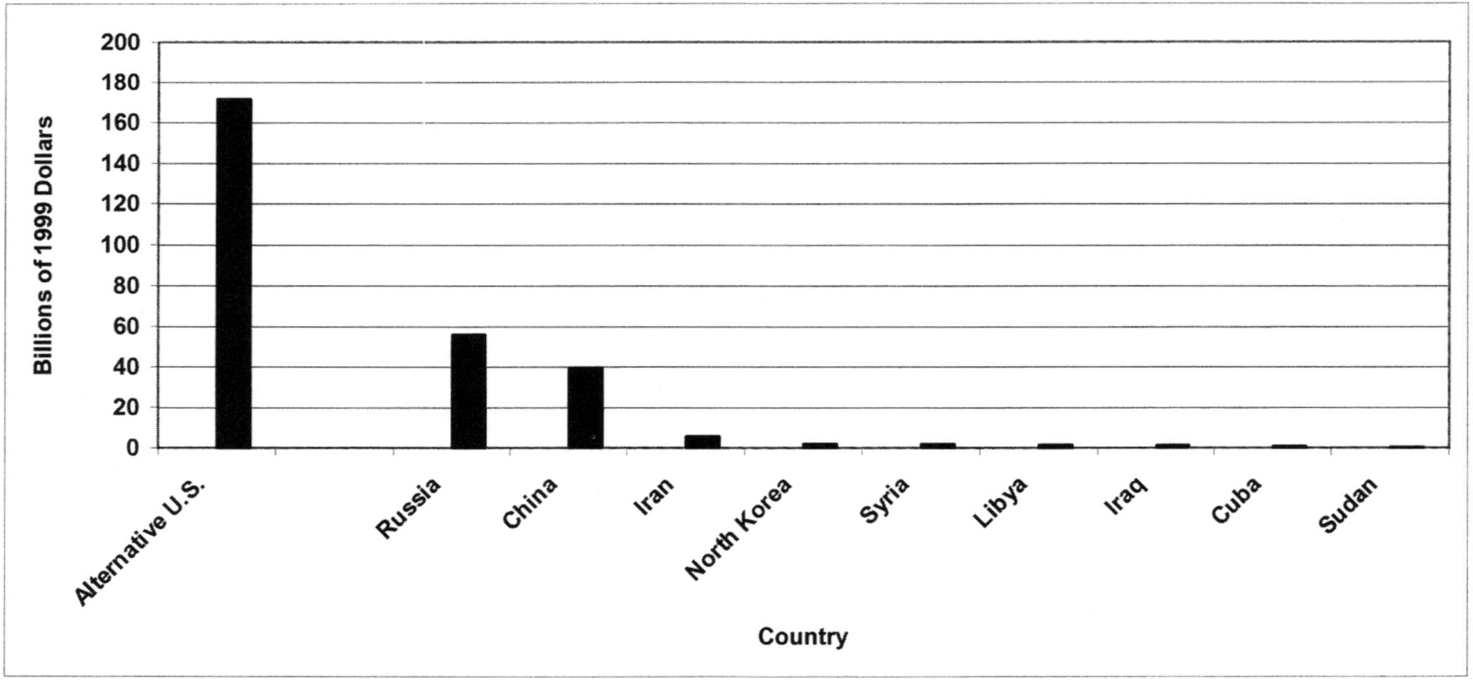

Source: International Institute for Strategic Studies, Military Balance 2000–2001.

United States would only send U.S. Army units into the fight in a desperate situation—that is, in which the army of the aggressive power was threatening to overrun the ground forces of the regional powers.

Thus, active army forces could be cut from six heavy and four light divisions to four heavy divisions and one light division. Two of the heavy divisions would be armored (at a cost of about $4.9 billion apiece annually), and two would be mechanized infantry (costing about $3.9 billion each per year). (The costs for various units in the table may appear high, but they include the annual acquisition costs for replacement equipment and full operations and support costs, including defense infrastructure.) The one remaining light division would be a hybrid airborne (landing by parachute) and air assault (transported by helicopter) unit that costs an estimated $3.4 billion annually. The estimate was derived from averaging the costs of a full airborne division and a full air assault division.

As is evident from the numbers, retaining active divisions is costly and of questionable need in a lower post–Cold War threat environment. The restructured force saves substantial sums of money by cutting five active divisions and relying more on National Guard forces. The five remaining active ground divisions should be enough to fight one war (the BUR and QDR thought so), especially given the new U.S. strategy of relying mainly on airpower to help friendly regional states halt a hegemonic aggressor. If the situation in the conflict deteriorated for friendly forces or a large U.S. force was needed to launch a counterattack to reclaim lost territory, the United States could use all five active divisions and even call up some or all of the thirty-nine combat brigades of the National Guard.

National Guard forces are a hedge against uncertainty and would probably be needed only under dire circumstances. But at a cost of only about $1.3 billion per division-equivalent per year, Guard forces provide a hedge much more cheaply than would retaining expensive active divisions (costing $3.4 billion to $4.9 billion per division). The army originally planned to convert twelve of forty-two National Guard combat brigades to support brigades, leaving thirty combat brigades. But the plan was suspended after only three brigades had been partially converted, leaving thirty-nine combat brigades. The army plan should be terminated and thirty-nine combat brigades retained as a hedge. Although the sixteen billion dollars in absolute costs seems high, the thirteen division-equivalents of firepower provided for that price is a bargain.

Marine Corps

Similarly, the reserve marine division (at a cost of $210 million annually) is about one-tenth as expensive to retain as an active marine division (costing about $2.2 billion per year). The BUR noted that four to five marine expeditionary brigades would be needed to fight each major theater war. Cutting two active divisions and retaining one active and one reserve division should cover this requirement.

Table 8.3
An Appropriate Defense Budget for a Balancer-of-Last-Resort Strategy (billions of 2002 dollars)

Force Element	Quantity	Total Annual Cost
Army		
Armored divisions	2	9.84
Mechanized infantry divisions	2	7.89
Hybrid airborne/air assault division	1	3.43
Special operations groups (active/reserve)	1/3	6.04
National Guard brigades	39	16.35
Marine Corps		
Divisions (active/reserve)	1/1	2.40
Air wings (active/reserve)	0/0	0.00
Navy		
Carrier battle groups (active/reserve) [a][b]	4/2	18.43
Other combat ships and missiles		
Cruisers [a]	3	0.36
Guided missile destroyers [a]	57	5.95
Attack submarines [b]	13	1.38
Ballistic missile submarines and		
D-5 ballistic missiles	10/240	5.84
Amphibious lift (MEBs) [c]	1.25	2.29
Other logistics and auxiliary ships	9	0.93
Mine countermeasures ships	27	1.23
Antisubmarine warfare	1 ocean capability	7.89
Sealift ships	144	4.94

Air Force		
Tactical fighter wings equivalents (active/reserve)	5/9	12.46
Heavy bombers	187	12.69
Surveillance aircraft	74	4.68
Support aircraft	503	1.26
Training aircraft	493	1.49
Intertheater airlift	278	10.75
Intratheater airlift (active/reserve)	150/275	2.08
Miscellaneous Forces		
Intercontinental ballistic missiles	0	0.00
National missile defense (100 interceptors)	Only Expanded Capability 1	2.53
Theater missile defense	Only 3 systems	.98
Electronic warfare/command, control, and communications		5.03
National intelligence and communication		21.00
Department of Energy nuclear weapons program		13.74
Total for National Defense (Budget Account 050)		183.88

Notes:

a. 24 additional cruisers were included as escort ships for the six carrier battle groups. Those cruisers, however, are interchangeable with the three other cruisers and fifty-seven DDG-51 guided missile destroyers allocated here for operations independent of the battle groups.

b. For accounting purposes only, twelve additional submarines were assigned to the six carrier battle groups (two per battle group). Submarines rarely operate with battle groups, and the submarines assigned to the reserve battle groups are active forces.

c. Marine expeditionary brigades

Source: Author's estimate using data from the Congressional Budget Office and John D. Steinbruner and William W. Kaufman, "International Security Reconsidered," in Settling National Priorities: Budget Choices for the Next Century, ed. Robert D. Reischauer (Washington, D.C.: Brookings Institution, 1996), pp. 155–196.

As noted earlier, because satellite reconnaissance, precision-guided weapons, and mines help the defense, no large-scale amphibious assault has been attempted since the Inchon landing during the Korean War. During the Cold War and post–Cold War eras, the marines have been used for peacekeeping, evacuations of U.S. civilians overseas, and as infantry for brushfire wars. The balancer-of-last-resort strategy would limit the marines' peacetime activities to small raids in retaliation for terrorist attacks and to evacuation of embassies under threat. One active division ready for a rapid response would be more than enough to carry out such missions.

In the rare event that a larger assault was needed during a war, the active division could be supplemented with the mobilized reserve division. As in the case of the army, the longer warning time likely to be associated with any major war in the post–Cold War world means that keeping large active forces in high states of readiness is unnecessary. Ample time would most likely be available to mobilize much less expensive marine reserve or army National Guard forces well in advance of any potential conflict.

Savings were also reaped by eliminating the fixed-wing air forces of the Marine Corps. During the Cold War, the marines and navy might have been operating in different places on the globe—thus requiring separate marine airpower to support the marines on the ground. With the end of the Cold War, the navy and Marine Corps will most likely be operating in the same places. Thus, marine fixed-wing air forces can be eliminated, and close air support can be provided mainly by navy aircraft flying from carriers. Navy aviators would, however, operate from amphibious ships when supporting the marines with any VSTOL or STOVL aircraft (what is now the marine STOVL version of the Joint Strike Fighter would be purchased with navy funds, as it would have been anyway, but would now be flown by navy personnel). The marines would continue to operate attack and transport helicopters from those ships.

Navy

Carrier battle groups are very expensive ($3.9 billion per battle group per year) for the limited amount of firepower that they provide. Even with the current expansive national strategy of global engagement, operating twelve carriers is a questionable use of public funds. Even the alleged advantages of maintaining a nearly continuous forward maritime presence with aircraft carriers in the Pacific, the Mediterranean, and the Arabian Sea—deterrence of conflict, the reassurance of allies, and the intimidation of potential aggressors—are difficult to document empirically.

But the major purpose for the military under balancer-of-last-resort strategy is to deter—and if that fails, to fight—a major war. Under that strategy, forward naval presence is drastically reduced, making a twelve-carrier fleet even more questionable. As noted in a previous chapter, land-based airpower is much more efficient in an all-out war than is carrier-based aviation. In the vast majority of major conflicts, friendly nations in the region would gladly provide land bases. Furthermore, since the land-based air forces of regional nations have been augmented, the carrier's combat potential is no longer what it was. Finally, the carrier is a large and inviting target for antiship missiles launched from land and sea.

Six carriers are retained to help control the sea lanes if they are threatened and to provide sea-based airpower in the rare major war in which no land bases are available. But because the strategy dramatically curtails forward-presence missions, two of the six carriers and their battle groups could be put in reserve, for mobilization in the event of a major war. The other four carriers would be rapidly available to deter or stop any nation or group of pirates from attacking U.S. shipping on the high seas or to handle any rare shows of force that needed to be undertaken. To perform those activities, the carriers would most likely be "surged" from U.S. ports rather than kept deployed overseas.

Retaining four active battle groups would cost about $15.6 billion per year in total costs (for both replacement equipment, and operation and support costs). Much can be saved by converting two of the battle groups to reserve status. Reserve battle groups cost about $1.4 billion each per year, a $2.8 billion per year for two of them. Thus, the total cost for four active and two reserve carriers and their supporting combat and logistics ships is $18.4 billion.

The United States is a maritime power and needs the strongest navy on earth. A two-hundred-ship American navy built around six carrier battle groups would not be the biggest navy in the world but would be, by far, the most capable. As noted earlier, six large carriers would dominate the world's seas, because there are very few large or medium-sized carriers on the planet that can accommodate aircraft that can take off and land conventionally. The United States would also retain six medium-sized amphibious carriers, which have aircraft that can take off and land vertically.

Although the navy has complained about a dwindling force, it has ships that are far more capable than their predecessors. Those new ships would be retained in the two-hundred-ship fleet; older and less capable ships would be decommissioned. For fighting major wars, fewer and more expensive multimission ships are better than many less-capable single-mission vessels. Using scarce funds to build numerous single-mission ships merely to satisfy requirements for overseas presence or land attack does not enhance security.

All twenty-seven of the advanced CG-47 *Ticonderoga*-class cruisers (with the Aegis air defense system) would be retained: twenty-four to guard the six battle groups and three to operate independently. Also fifty-seven of the planned fifty-eight DDG-51 *Arleigh Burke*–class destroyers would be built for independent operations. In reality, those eighty-four ships would be very powerful, flexible, and largely interchangeable—capable of providing air defense for a carrier battle group or a group of ships without a carrier, or of independent operations. The two types of ships are well-rounded, multimission ships that can also perform land attack and antisurface and antisubmarine warfare (the *Ticonderoga* class is better at antisurface missions, the *Arleigh Burke* class slightly better for antisubmarine).[2] Other navies in the world have nothing to compare to such ships.

Building and operating all the ships in the *Arleigh Burke* class is expensive (almost six billion dollars), but most of them have already been purchased. Most of the costs of the *Ticonderoga*-class ships are included in the costs of the carrier battle groups. (Although the two types of ships are virtually interchangeable, that rule was adopted for accounting purposes.)

As noted earlier, the two attack submarines assigned to protect each carrier battle group are of questionable value. Nevertheless, for accounting purposes, twelve submarines are included in the costs of the six battle groups. The costs of the other thirteen attack submarines are estimated separately ($1.4 billion per year for thirteen submarines). In reality, the twenty-five attack submarines would probably operate more or less independently from the battle groups. During peacetime, the smaller submarine force would conduct intelligence missions; during wartime, it would protect sea lanes from enemy submarines (if the opponent has any), land special forces ashore, and covertly attack land targets with Tomahawk missiles. Extrapolating, a force of twenty-five submarines would cost about $2.7 billion per year.

The United States would also retain a force of ten Trident ballistic missile submarines. Each of those submarines would be armed with twenty-four nuclear ballistic missiles, with five warheads each. This force would give the United States 1,200 invulnerable, sea-based nuclear warheads. (Another three hundred warheads would be carried on B-2 bombers, to give the United States a total of 1,500 nuclear warheads. All land-based intercontinental ballistic missiles would be scrapped.) The cost of that Trident force and the nuclear infrastructure needed to support it would be $5.8 billion per year.

As noted earlier, the Marine Corps would be cut in half, from the current four divisions (three active and one reserve) to two divisions (one active and one reserve). Under the current scheme, the navy provides enough amphibious ships to lift 2.5 marine expeditionary brigades. The restructured force cuts both the number of marine divisions and the amount of navy lift by 50 percent. So the navy would retain enough amphibious ships to lift 1.25 MEBs, at an annual cost of $2.3 billion.

The navy always pledges to improve MCM capabilities, but it would rather spend money on more glamorous combat aircraft and warships than on clearing paths to the beach for the marines. Therefore, even though the restructured force cuts the navy by over a third, from more than three hundred ships to two hundred, the twenty-six mine-clearing ships and one mine countermeasures command ship remain untouched. A force of that size was needed to clear mines in the Persian Gulf War and would probably meet the needs of a future regional war. This fleet is relatively cheap, at a cost of $1.2 billion annually.

Similarly, in its quest to funnel all money into combat ships and aircraft, the navy has also neglected sealift, which is used primarily to transport the army's equipment to foreign theaters. The ships that Congress ordered to be built are now coming into the sealift fleet.

The restructured force reduces army forces from those required to fight two wars "nearly simultaneously" (ten divisions) to those needed to fight one war (five divisions), but it leaves sealift largely unchanged (about 140 ships). (Eight Flo-Flo ships were added to transport the mine clearing fleet to foreign theaters.) The BUR originally required U.S. armed forces to be able to fight two wars only "nearly simultaneously" rather than "simultaneously." One of the major reasons for this subtle difference was that the United States has insufficient lift to transport the forces for two wars at the same time. The BUR assumed that lift assets would transport forces to one theater and then move other forces to the second theater. In other words, the United States currently has a one-war sealift capacity. So the restructured force cuts active army forces by 50 percent but does not cut sealift capacity. The army should be able to transport five active divisions with the existing sealift.

Although much commercial shipping was hired to transport military equipment in Desert Shield/Desert Storm, those ships require more time to travel to the loading ports and be readied to transport military cargo. Military sealift ships can be available much faster. The smaller, restructured force is designed to operate from the United States rather than from overseas bases and therefore needs to be able to travel from U.S. ports to a foreign theater quickly. Thus, a one-war capacity of dedicated military sealift is retained so that the entire restructured active army force can be transported quickly if needed. Some commercial sealift, however, may still be needed to augment the dedicated military fleet, especially if some or all of the National Guard combat forces (thirty-nine brigades) has to be mobilized. But the time required by the Guard units to mobilize and get to embarkation ports could be used to obtain commercial sealift for their transport.

The dedicated military sealift for one war costs about $4.9 billion annually to retain. (That total includes the eight Flo-Flo ships added to transport the mine-clearing fleet to open foreign ports for army units aboard sealift ships.) The expensive investment in sophisticated ground forces may be for naught if they cannot get to the battle quickly; the investment in sealift and Flo-Flo ships is relatively small and worthwhile.

Air Force

The restructured force cuts the number of air wings from twenty (12.5 active and 7.5 reserve) to fourteen (five active and nine reserve). In other words, six active air wings are eliminated, and 1.5 are converted into reserve wings. Retaining fourteen wings more than meets the BUR requirement of ten wings to fight one war. In an age in which airpower is dominating warfare, that larger force hedges against uncertainty. But in the current low-threat environment, more wings should be in the reserves than in the active forces. Longer warning times are available for the emergence of an aggressive great-power rival, and reserve forces cost less than active ones. An active air wing costs $1.09 billion per year, while a reserve wing costs $.78 billion per year. So five active wings and nine reserve wings would cost $12.5 billion per year.

Because land bases near the battlefield are becoming more vulnerable to enemy attack by ballistic and cruise missiles, 187 long-range heavy bombers (B-2s, B-1s, and B-52s) are retained. Unlike more vulnerable land-based tactical fighter aircraft, long-range bombers can efficiently carry large loads of munitions from remote and survivable bases in the theater of operations, or even from the United States (as they did during the war against Serbia).

Retaining 187 bombers will cost $12.7 billion per year. A long-range bomber fleet is expensive but one that is particularly good at stopping armored invasions. Desert Storm and the war against Serbia clearly showed that airpower now dominates warfare. The United States has always enjoyed a comparative advantage in this realm.

Land-based tactical fighter aircraft may now be vulnerable to enemy attack. Sea-based tactical aircraft are inefficient in the amount of ordnance that they can deliver. They also face an erosion of their already limited range by the greater vulnerability of the aircraft carrier to mines, diesel submarines, and antiship cruise missiles in littoral waters, pushing it and them further out to sea.

If ever needed, bombers flying from the United States could provide a rapid response that even land and sea-based tactical aircraft could not equal unless there just happened to be an air base or aircraft carrier very near the trouble spot. (Adopting the balancer-of-last-resort strategy, drastically reducing U.S. military presence overseas, would greatly reduce the chances that such tactical aircraft would be nearby.) Thus, the best investment in airpower is in heavy bombers. As expensive as bombers may seem, they cost about the same as maintaining fourteen wings (five active and nine reserve) of tactical aircraft, at $12.5 billion per year; they are much cheaper than six carrier battle groups (four active and two reserve), at $18.4 billion per year.

As noted, the United States does have sufficient intertheater airlift to fight one war. (The balancer-of-last-resort strategy will not divert airlift capacity for brushfire wars or peacekeeping.) Thus, the restructured force reduces military forces substantially but retains the substantial intertheater (120 C-17s, 104 C-5s, and 54 KC-10s) and shorter-range intratheater (150 active and 275 reserve C-130s) airlift capacity. Airlift in the air force (like sealift in the navy) is unglamorous but critical, especially since the balancer-of-last-resort strategy will rely on the projection of forces from the United States rather than on an extensive U.S. presence overseas. Maintaining a substantial intertheater capacity would cost $10.8 billion per year and retaining a robust intratheater capacity would cost $2.1 billion annually.

Intercontinental Ballistic Missiles and Miscellaneous Forces

No funds are allocated for land-based ICBMs, because they would be eliminated from U.S. nuclear forces; the United States would rely on a dyad of heavy bombers (B-2s) and ballistic missiles submarines. Reducing the number of total U.S. warheads to 1,500 would allow Russia to reduce and dismantle a substantial portion of its arsenal of decaying and dangerous nuclear weapons. In addition, deep cuts in the U.S. arsenal would lessen the vulnerability of the Russian weapons that are still functional and thus the need for the Russians to launch on warning of an impending attack. That launch posture is very dangerous, especially when the decrepit Russian early-warning system is prone to error. Finally, reducing the threat to the Russian nuclear arsenal might make Russia more amenable to renegotiating the ABM Treaty to allow the deployment of a limited U.S. national missile defense.

With the U.S. warhead total reduced to 1,500, most of the U.S. arsenal (1,200 warheads) should be under the sea and therefore invulnerable to attack. A lesser number of warheads (three hundred) should be retained on bombers. Unlike ICBMs, bombers can be recalled without launching their weapons if a crisis dissipates. ICBMs are somewhat redundant to sea-launched ballistic missiles and much more vulnerable to attack. In the long term, keeping the five hundred Minuteman III ICBMs (one warhead apiece) would require replacement of their guidance and propulsion systems—an expensive undertaking.[3]

The United States should renegotiate the Anti-Ballistic Missile Treaty with the Russians so it is allowed to build a *limited* land-based national missile defense (if the technology is proven through thorough development and testing) that could destroy a few warheads from a rogue state. The United States should build only what the Clinton administration called "Expanded Capability 1." That system would entail building a new X-band radar and a hundred interceptors in Alaska and upgrading early-warning radars in other locations. (It would not involve the Space-Based Infrared System–low satellite network.) Expanded Capability 1 would defend the entire United States from an attack of 20 to 30 ICBMs that use simple decoys. Expanded Capabilities 2 and 3 are more costly and would defend against missiles with more sophisticated decoys. Expanded Capabilities 2 and 3 are unneeded against attack from rogue states, which would likely use only simple decoys, and they would needlessly alarm the Russians. The Expanded Capability 1 system would cost about $2.5 billion a year (includes potential cost growth).[4]

For theater missile defense, the United States should build on three existing air defense systems and cancel three others. The army's THAAD, the air force's Airborne Laser, and the army's Medium Extended Air Defense System (MEADS) should all be canceled. THAAD is primarily a system for defending wealthy allies and has had developmental problems. The Airborne Laser is technologically risky and depends on secure airspace and forward air bases, which may not be available. MEADS is mobile and provides 360-degree coverage for maneuver forces but provides the same function as the transportable and more directional Patriot PAC-3, for a much higher cost (an estimated $12.3 billion versus $6.9 billion). PAC-3 also has a much longer range than MEADS (twenty-five to thirty miles versus five to six miles).

The United States should buy the Area Defense ($6.9 billion), Theater-Wide Defense ($5.6 billion), and Patriot PAC-3 ($6.9 billion) systems. All of these build on existing air-defense systems, which makes them more economical; the total acquisition cost is $19.4 billion. Assuming that theater missile defense systems have a service life of twenty years, the cost per year becomes roughly a billion dollars.[5] (No additional costs for operation and support would be incurred, because systems already being operated by the army and navy would be modified to perform the theater missile defense mission.)

The current intelligence budget is about thirty billion dollars annually.[6] Although good intelligence is important, the Cold War is over. Cuts already made in the intelligence budget have never fully reflected that good fortune. A nation that is no longer intervening all over the world could trim its intelligence budget farther and still have the best capability in the world. There are some areas of the world (for example, Africa and Southeast Asia) in which the United States has little geostrategic or economic interest. Intelligence resources devoted to those areas should be reduced. In addition, some resources should be shifted from technical collection methods—for example, satellites—to human intelligence operations, which are less expensive. Human intelligence is better for tracking new threats—such as terrorism and the proliferation of weapons of mass destruction—than are satellites. Thus, the intelligence budget could be cut to 21 billion dollars per year without compromising security.

Trim the Nuclear Labs

According to official U.S. government projections, by 2005, the Department of Energy (DoE) will spend about $14 billion (in 2002 dollars) on nuclear weapons.[7] This sum is included in the budget for national defense (account 050). DoE has developed the Stockpile Stewardship program to sustain the long-term safety and reliability of the stockpile of nuclear warheads in the absence of explosive nuclear testing. The stewardship program would develop simulations of nuclear explosions and conduct other non-explosive nuclear research, to obviate the need for explosive testing. The program originally assumed that the Senate would approve the Comprehensive Test Ban Treaty. The Senate, however, correctly rejected the treaty. Until the new technology is proved, the United States must retain the option to test nuclear weapons to ensure their safety and reliability.

Nuclear weapons are too important to the nation's security to be unsafe or unreliable. They are the ultimate deterrent to threats by other nations to the security of the American homeland or to truly vital U.S. interests. In a post–Cold War world, however, the number of warheads in the U.S. stockpile can be drastically reduced—but not to zero. With a smaller stockpile, the reliability of the warheads becomes even more vital. Today's nuclear warheads do not have much tolerance for degradation of key components.[8] Nuclear weapons age in unpredictable ways and could fail to work when needed. Although renouncing the U.S. informal unilateral moratorium on nuclear testing is unnecessary now, the option to test aging weapons or to test new types of warheads in the future must be retained (in the present benign threat environment, no new warheads need to be designed).

With that caveat, the Stockpile Stewardship program should be retained. A fairly robust modeling and research program to maintain the vital U.S. nuclear deterrent is probably a good idea. If simulation and research are eventually demonstrated as viable substitutes for explosive testing (this may be difficult for some components in a warhead), the CTBT might eventually be ratified with no ill effects to U.S. security. Unfortunately, some possibility also exists that the Senate will reconsider and pass the CTBT before the new technology is proved. The Stockpile Stewardship program would be at least a hedge against that contingency.

In addition, DoE will conduct "zero yield" subcritical (nonexplosive) tests at the Nevada test site to maintain the capability to resume explosive tests if needed. The president has ordered DoE to retain that capability. If the test site were closed and a new threat developed or a major problem arose with the stockpile that only testing could rectify, a resumption of testing could be delayed. Thus, keeping the test site open is necessary.

Although the Stockpile Stewardship program should be retained, it could be trimmed slightly without adversely affecting U.S. security. Currently, DoE retains three nuclear laboratories: the Los Alamos and Lawrence Livermore labs, which design nuclear weapons, and the Sandia lab, which engineers the nonnuclear components of nuclear weapons. In a post–Cold War world in which the nuclear stockpile should and will shrink substantially, Los Alamos and Lawrence Livermore represent redundant and excess design capacity. According to an option developed and analyzed by David Mosher of the Congressional Budget Office, most of the design function might be consolidated at Los Alamos, where most of the warheads that will probably remain in the reduced stockpile were originally designed. Under the option, savings would result from laying off two-thousand employees. A small cadre of scientists would remain at Lawrence Livermore to independently review the work of Los Alamos. Lawrence Livermore would also retain large computation facilities for modeling nuclear explosions and other facilities. Mosher's estimate of the savings from this option is about $300 million per year in 2005 (in 2002 dollars).[9] However, he assumes the closing of the Nevada test site. Keeping that site open costs roughly $100 million per year.[10] Thus, trimming the labs would provide net savings of about $200 million a year.

A saving of about $200 million a year on the nuclear labs seems scant compared to the savings that the alternative budget reaps in other categories of forces. But the nuclear forces are the ultimate guarantor of U.S. security. It is vital to ensure the safety and reliability of the nuclear stockpile through testing or simulation (especially when the inventory of warheads is growing smaller). Also, it is important to retain the capability to design and possibly test new weapons if the United States must again improve or build up its nuclear arsenal. Therefore, the alternative budget retains $13.7 billion of $13.9 billion planned spending for DoE nuclear activities.

CONCLUSION

Cutting about 40 percent (about $120 billion) from the budget for national defense would be compatible with the balancer-of-last-resort strategy. A $184 billion defense budget would still allow the United States to have by far the best military in the world, while taking advantage of the nation's relatively secure geostrategic position. The budget for national defense can be reduced without harming U.S. security because the balancer-of-last-resort strategy reduces U.S. commitments overseas without sacrificing American vital interests. Despite substantial reductions, the defense budget would be reduced less than U.S. commitments, so that military forces would not be stretched too thin.

NOTES

1. For an excellent primer on O&S costs, see Lane Pierrot, *Operations and Support Costs for the Department of Defense* (Washington, D.C.: CBO, July 1988), p. 14.

2. James Dunnigan, *How to Make War: A Comprehensive Guide to Modern Warfare for the Post–Cold War Era*, 3rd ed. (New York: William Morrow, 1993), p. 232.

3. William Perry and Ashton Carter, *Preventative Defense: A New Security Strategy for America* (Washington, D.C.: Brookings Institution, 1999), p. 90.

4. Author's estimate, derived from Geoffrey Forden and Raymond Hall, *Budgetary and Technical Implications of the Administration's Plan for National Missile Defense* (Washington, D.C.: Congressional Budget Office, 2000), pp. 6–15. The author assumes that the system would have a twenty-year life.

5. Charles Pena, "Theater Missile Defense: A Limited Capability Is Needed," Cato Institute Policy Analysis no. 309, June 22, 1998, pp. 14–25. Figures in chapter 6 have been adjusted to 2002 dollars.

6. Dan Smith, "The Belgrade Bombing Gaffe," *Weekly Defense Monitor* 3, No. 19 (May 13, 1999), p. 5. Figure adjusted to 2002 dollars.

7. Steven Kosiak, *Analysis of the FY2001 Defense Budget Request* (Washington, D.C.: Center for Strategic and Budgetary Assessments, 2000), p. 25. The total, originally in FY2005 dollars, was converted to FY2002 dollars.

8. O'Hanlon, *Cheap Hawk*, p. 88.

9. David Mosher, "Reduce the Scope of DOE's Stockpile Stewardship Program," in Congressional Budget Office, *Budget Options for National Defense* (Washington, D.C.: CBO, 2000), pp. 33–34.

10. O'Hanlon, *Cheap Hawk*, p. 90.

9

Conclusion

U.S. security policy is currently illogical and does not fit the U.S. geostrategic situation. In fact, the policy actually harms the nation's security.

Even in a more interdependent world—a phrase that usually means a world with better communication and transportation, which in turn leads to greater trade, investment, and immigration between nations—the United States is extremely secure from conventional invasion. An air attack against the United States would encounter the enormous difficulty of being sustainable over vast distances. America's robust nuclear arsenal—the most potent on the planet—would render any kind of an attack by a potential adversary suicidal. In fact, bordering two vast oceans and two weak neighbors, and being a half a world away from most major conflicts and potential enemies, the United States may have the most secure geostrategic position of any great power in history.

Yet U.S. foreign and defense policy fails to reflect that secure situation. The Cold War battle against Soviet-backed communism spurred the United States to undertake profligate interventions around the world—many of which were questionable even then (for example, the Vietnam War). Even if justified in the abstract, wealthy allies in the affected regions should have undertaken them.

Today, although the threats to U.S. security have dramatically lessened, U.S. foreign policy remains on autopilot. The United States continues to intervene regularly in remote regions that have nothing to do with U.S. security—for example, Panama, Iraq, Somalia, Bosnia, Haiti, and Kosovo. Such an extended defense perimeter can actually reduce U.S. security, by aggravating one of the few real threats to U.S. security—the proliferation of weapons of mass destruction to rogue states and terrorist groups.

To deter U.S. intervention in their countries or regions or to retaliate with an attack on U.S. soil if the United States does intervene, rogue states will be encouraged to obtain weapons of mass destruction and the means to deliver them. Terrorist groups might also strike the United States with such weapons in revenge for U.S. military action overseas. Moreover, if U.S. interventions continue to alarm China and Russia, their governments may sell weapons of mass destruction, or the technology to make them, to rogue states or terrorist groups. Or the Russian government could simply stop cooperating with U.S. efforts to make Russia's weapons more secure.

Profligate U.S. intervention is already causing closer ties between Russia and China in an effort to balance U.S. assertiveness. For example, the two nations began to develop closer relations after the U.S.-led NATO intervention in Kosovo. Why needlessly aggravate relations with the only two non-allied nations that can strike U.S. territory with long-range nuclear missiles, in order to achieve amorphous gains in stability in regions unimportant to core U.S. security interests? Russia and China are not now threats to U.S. security, so why turn them into hostile nations?

If the United States adopted a balancer-of-last-resort strategy, the threat of proliferation and use on U.S. soil of weapons of mass destruction could be reduced, and relations with the two most important countries in the world would be more cordial. Under the strategy, the United States would intervene only to *help* friendly nations, when truly vital U.S. interests were at stake—that is, if Europe or East Asia were threatened with being overrun by an aggressive great power. (The United States also needs to protect U.S. trade on the high seas from unfriendly nations or modern-day pirates, and to ensure the nation's freedom to use space for military and commercial purposes.)

In addition to lowering the exposure of the United States to attacks by weapons of mass destruction, a balancer-of-last resort strategy would have several other advantages. Intervening in fewer conflicts overseas would lower the risk that the United States could get bogged down in quagmires that would waste U.S. resources and lives. In addition, such a strategy would spur wealthy allies to enhance their own military capabilities and to create regional arrangements that would be primary lines of deterrence and defense against a potential hegemon (should one arise). Now, free-riding allies and clients around the world manipulate the United States into coming to their rescue—even if the crisis of the day has only a remote effect on U.S. vital interests.

Adopting a more restrained strategy for military intervention fits well with U.S. tradition. The United States pursued such a strategy for most of its history, until World War II and the Cold War caused it to slide into the aberration of interventionism. Such rampant military action has needlessly aggravated U.S. relations with important nations around the world and endangered the American homeland by making retaliatory strikes with weapons of mass destruction more likely. However, the policy's worst effect may be the undermining of U.S. constitutional government. Ever since the Korean War, American presidents have taken the nation into major armed conflicts without constitutionally mandated congressional declarations of war or authorizations. The founders of the nation would liken this behavior to that of European kings who made their populations suffer through wars for their own aggrandizement. To guard against such behavior from U.S. presidents, the founders gave the power to declare war to the Congress. The *perceived* need for rapid military action during the conflicts of the Cold War led to the unconstitutional consolidation of the war-making power in the executive branch. Long after the Cold War is over, however, presidents still make the constitutionally dubious claim that they can go to war without a congressional declaration. Congress has failed to rein in the president and defend the Constitution. For example, the House of Representatives refused to approve the Clinton administration's air war in Kosovo but funded it anyway.

Without providing the military additional resources, some on the Left argue for the frequent use of U.S. military power to defend international norms of human rights and to undertake peacemaking and peacekeeping missions. That disconnect unfairly stretches the military and endangers the lives of military personnel. On the other hand, some on the Right advocate cutting back on overseas commitments significantly but increasing the defense budget substantially. That posture is simply a waste of the taxpayer's money and leads to pressure to use the massive armed forces (abroad and at home) that have been purchased. By adopting the much more restrained balancer-of-last-resort strategy—that is, requiring the military to do much less overseas—military forces and the defense budget can be cut substantially without undermining U.S. security. In fact, national security will be enhanced, because the United States will have fewer enemies overseas.

If the balancer-of-last-resort strategy is adopted, the budget for national defense (account 050) could be reduced from about $303 billion to about $184 billion, a savings of almost 40 percent. That reduced budget would still allow the United States to be the dominant military power on the planet.

The lower budget would still give the United States what the Pentagon would call the capability to fight "one-plus" major theater wars. The ground forces—the army and marines—would be cut the most, the air force the least, and the navy somewhere in the middle. In any effort to help friendly nations fight off an aggressive great power, those nations would be responsible for providing the ground forces. The United States would provide airpower, which dominates the modern battlefield. Providing airpower allows the United States to use its comparative advantage on the battlefield and reduces American casualties in defense of other nations. Friendly ground forces (and some U.S. ground forces, if needed) could hold or channel enemy ground forces so that U.S. airpower could destroy them. If the threat on the ground became so severe that large U.S. ground forces were needed, the army National Guard could be mobilized.

As a maritime nation, the United States needs a strong navy. A reduced fleet of six carrier battle groups and six amphibious ready groups would remain dominant on the world's seas. The smaller navy would also provide power projection to supplement the air force in most wars and be the dominant player in rare wars in which no land bases were available.

The reduced budget would still allow the United States to continue to develop and possibly build a limited, land-based national missile defense to counter missile attacks by rogue states. That deployment could cause alarm in Moscow, even though the few warheads that the system could destroy would not threaten the large, but deteriorating, Russian arsenal of nuclear weapons. Thus, the United States should drastically reduce its own arsenal to a dyad (bombers and submarine-based ballistic missiles) of 1,500 warheads, most of which would be at sea and invulnerable to enemy attack.

Critics will point out that the United States, with smaller conventional and nuclear forces, might be vulnerable to the rapid military buildup of a great power—like Adolf Hitler's buildup in the 1930s. But times have changed. In the 1930s, the United States had to catch up to Germany and Japan; also, time needed to develop and build a weapon system was short. Today, the U.S. military has a vast technological lead over all other militaries on the globe, and long periods are required to develop and produce complex weapon systems. Therefore, the United States will have plenty of warning time for any emerging peer competitor. The smaller, high-tech force that $184 billion per year would buy would be the most potent military on the planet today and would be the kernel around which any future U.S. military expansion could occur.

Some would ask whether such a significant cut in the defense budget would undermine the status of the U.S. as a superpower. The answer is a resounding "no." In the past, excessive defense spending in peacetime or wartime caused great empires to collapse—the Soviet Union and British empire are examples. If the United States does not reduce its overseas commitments and stay out of expensive foreign conflicts, it may experience the same decline as those nations. Reducing the bloated U.S. defense budget— which allows the political leaders to conduct crusades overseas—will strengthen the U.S. economy and ensure that the United States will be a superpower well into the new century. A strong economy is the root of any nation's power in the international system. War-induced inflation would corrode that economic strength (for example, stagflation in the U.S. economy in the 1970s resulted, in part, from the effects of the Vietnam War).

In short, an extended defense perimeter is costly and may actually undermine U.S. security. In other words, by adopting a more restrained balancer-of-last-resort strategy, which advocates using military force only when U.S. vital interests are threatened, the United States could achieve greater long-term security for a smaller expenditure of public funds.

Selected Bibliography

Aspin, Les. "An Approach to Sizing American Conventional Forces for the Post-Soviet Era." Armed Services Committee, U.S. House of Representatives. Washington, D.C., January 24, 1992.

Bahgat, Gawat. "Oil Security in the New Millennium: Geo-Economy vs. Geo-Strategy." *Strategic Review* 26, no. 4 (Fall 1998).

Bandow, Doug. *Tripwire: Korea and U.S. Foreign Policy in a Changed World.* Washington, D.C.: Cato Institute, 1996.

Barnet, Jeffrey. "Funding Two Armies: Why Paying for the Army's Transformation Could Spark an Interservice Brawl." *Arms Force Journal International*, May 2000.

Black, Jeremy. *War and the World: Military Power and the Fate of Continents, 1450–2000.* New Haven, Conn.: Yale Univ. Press, 1998.

Blasko, Dennis. "Evaluating Chinese Military Procurement from Russia." *Joint Forces Quarterly*, no. 14. Autumn–Winter 1997–98.

Buchanan, Patrick. *A Republic Not an Empire: Reclaiming America's Destiny.* Washington, D.C.: Regnery, 1999.

Carpenter, Ted Galen. "Kosovo as an Omen: The Perils of the 'New NATO,' " in Ted Galen Carpenter, *NATO's Empty Victory: A Postmortem on the Balkan War.* Washington, D.C.: Cato Institute, 2000.

———. *A Search for Enemies: America's Alliances after the Cold War.* Washington, D.C.: Cato Institute, 1992.

Center for Defense Information. *1999 CDI Military Almanac.* Washington, D.C.: *America's Alliance After the Cold War.* CDI, 1999.

Chandler, Robert W. *New Face of War: Weapons of Mass Destruction and the Revitalization of America's Transoceanic Military Strategy.* McLean, Va.: Amcoda Press, 1998.

Cohen, William. *Annual Report to the President and the Congress*. Washington, D.C.: Department of Defense, 1999.

———. *Report of the Quadrennial Defense Review*. Washington, D.C.: Department of Defense, 1997.

Committee on Governmental Affairs, U.S. Senate. *Proliferation Primer: A Majority Report of the Subcommittee on International Security, Proliferation, and Federal Services*. January 1998.

Conetta, Carl, and Charles Knight. "Inventing Threats," *Bulletin of Atomic Scientists*, March–April 1998.

Congressional Budget Office. *Budgeting for Defense: Maintaining Today's Forces*. Washington, D.C.: CBO, September 2000.

———. *Reducing the Deficit: Spending and Revenue Options*. Washington, D.C.: CBO, 1997.

———. *Improving the Efficiency of Forward Presence by Aircraft Carriers*. Washington, D.C.: CBO, August 1996.

———. *The Costs of Expanding the NATO Alliance*. Washington, D.C.: CBO, March 1996.

Conry, Barbara. "U.S. Security Strategy," in *Cato Handbook for Congress*. Washington, D.C.: Cato Institute, 1999.

Defense Science Board, *Report of the Task Force on Information Warfare-Defense*. Washington, D.C.: Department of Defense, November 1996.

Department of the Navy. *Highlights of the Department of the Navy FY 1998/1999 Biennial Budget*, February 1997.

Deutch, John, Harold Brown, and John P. White. "National Missile Defense: Is There Another Way?" *Foreign Policy*, Summer 2000.

Dunnigan, James. *How to Make War: A Comprehensive Guide to Modern Warfare for the Post–Cold War Era*, 3rd ed. New York: William Morrow, 1993.

Dunnigan, James, and Albert Nofi. *Dirty Little Secrets of the Vietnam War*. New York: St. Martin's Press, 1999.

Easterbrook, Gregg. "Apocryphal Now: The Myth of the Hollow Military," *New Republic*, September 11, 2000.

Eland, Ivan. "Let's Make National Missile Defense Truly 'National.' " Cato Foreign Policy Briefing no. 58, June 27, 2000.

———. "America Doesn't Need Three New Fighter Planes." *Long Beach Press-Telegram*, April 9, 1999.

———. "Tilting at Windmills: Post–Cold War Military Threats to U.S. Security." Cato Policy Analysis no. 332, February 8, 1999.

———. "Does U.S. Intervention Overseas Breed Terrorism? The Historical Record." Cato Institute Foreign Policy Briefing no. 50, December 17, 1998.

———. "Subtract Unneeded Nuclear Attack Submarines from the Fleet." Cato Institute Foreign Policy Briefing no. 47, April 2, 1998.

Erwin, Sandra. "Naval Aviation's Jewel Untarnished by Critics." *National Defense*, May–June 1999.

Eshel, David. "High Flying Surveillance: Israel Leads the World in the Military Employment of Unmanned Aerial Vehicles." *Armed Forces Journal International*, June 1998.

Freedberg, Sydney, Jr. "It's a Bird It's a Plane." *National Journal*, March 23, 2000.

Forden, Geoffrey, and Raymond Hall. *Budgetary and Technical Implications of the*

Administration's Plan for National Missile Defense. Washington, D.C.: CBO, 2000.

General Accounting Office. *Navy Mine Warfare: Budget Realignment Can Help Improve Countermine Capabilities.* Washington, D.C.: GAO, March 1996.

———. *Marine Corps: Improving Amphibious Capability Would Require Larger Share of Budget Than Previously Provided.* Washington, D.C.: GAO, February 1996.

———. *National Security: Impact of China's Military Modernization on the Pacific Region.* Washington, D.C.: Government Printing Office, 1995.

George, James L. "Is Readiness Overrated? Implications for a Tiered Readiness Force Structure." Cato Policy Analysis no. 342, April 29, 1999.

Gill, Bates. "Modernization of the People's Liberation Army." *Joint Forces Quarterly*, no. 14, Autumn–Winter 1997–98.

Goodman, Glenn W., Jr. "A Multidimensional Force: Marine Corps Set to Reap Long-Desired Mobility Upgrades." *Armed Forces Journal International*, January 1997.

Gouré, Daniel, and Jeffrey M. Ranney. *Averting the Defense Train Wreck in the New Millennium.* Washington, D.C.: Center for Strategic and International Studies, 1999.

Grant, Rebecca. "Origins of the Deep Attack Weapons Mix." Washington, D.C.: IRIS Independent Research, 1997.

Grasso, Valerie Bailey. *Navy LPD-17 Amphibious Shipbuilding Program: Background and Funding Options for Congress.* Washington, D.C.: Congressional Research Service, April 17, 1996.

Gregory, Bill, and Glenn W. Goodman, Jr. "New High-Low Mix: US Air Force Fighter Modernization Plan Rests on Two Strong Points." *Armed Forces Journal International*, September 1997.

Hart, Kenneth. "The Silent Service Must Communicate." U.S. Naval Institute *Proceedings*, February 1997.

Hellman, Christopher. "Comanche Program Contains 'Significant Risks.' " *Weekly Defense Monitor* 3, no. 36 (September 23), 1999.

Henderson, David R. "The Myth of Saddam's Oil Stranglehold," in *America Entangled: The Persian Gulf Crisis and Its Consequences*, ed. Ted Galen Carpenter. Washington, D.C.: Cato Institute, 1991.

Hendrickson, Ryan. "Clinton's Legal Dominion: War Powers in the Second Term," *National Security Studies* 5, no. 1 (Winter 1999).

Heritage Foundation. *Defending America: Ending America's Vulnerability to Ballistic Missiles.* Washington, D.C.: Heritage Foundation, 1996.

Hiro, Dilip. *The Longest War: The Iran-Iraq Military Conflict.* New York: Routledge, 1991.

Hoffman, Stanley. *World Disorders: Troubled Peace in the Post–Cold War Era.* Lanham, Md.: Rowan and Littlefield, 1998.

International Institute of Strategic Studies. *The Military Balance 2000–2001.* London: Oxford Univ. Press, 2000.

Isenberg, David. "The Quadrennial Defense Review: Reiterating the Tired Status Quo." Cato Institute Policy Analysis no. 317, September 17, 1998.

————. "The Misleading Military 'Readiness Crisis.'" Cato Institute Foreign Policy Briefing no. 35, July 25, 1995.

Ji, You. *The Armed Forces of China.* Australia: Allen and Unwin, 1999.

Keaney, Thomas, and Eliot Cohen. *Gulf War Air Power Survey, Summary Report.* Washington, D.C.: Government Printing Office, 1993.

Kennedy, Paul. *The Rise and Fall of Great Powers.* New York: Random House, 1987.

Kober, Stanley. "Reclaiming the War Power," in *Cato Handbook for Congress, 106th Congress.* Washington, D.C.: Cato Institute, 1999.

Korb, Larry. "Force Is the Issue: The United States Needs to Decide Just What Kind of Military Force It Wants in the Coming Years." *Government Executive,* January 2000.

Kosiak, Steven. *Analysis of the FY2001 Defense Budget Request.* Washington, D.C.: Center for Strategic and Budgetary Assessments, 2000.

Labs, Eric, and Joann Vines. *Options for Enhancing the Department of Defense's Unmanned Aerial Vehicle Programs.* Washington, D.C.: CBO, September 1998.

Lyons, H. Dwight, Jr., Eleanor A. Baker, Sabrina R. Edlow, and David A. Perin. *The Mine Threat: Show Stoppers or Speed Bumps?* Alexandria, Va: Center for Naval Analyses, July 1993.

Maynes, Charles. "Relearning Intervention." *Foreign Policy,* no. 98 (Spring 1995).

McCain, John. "Ready Tomorrow: Defending American Interests in the 21st Century," March 1996.

McCutcheon, Chuck. "Computer-Reliant U.S. Society Faces Growing Risk of 'Information War.'" *Congressional Quarterly,* March 14, 1998.

Meisner, Arnold. *Desert Storm: Sea War.* Osceola, Wis.: Motorbooks International, 1991.

Moeng, Sophearith. *The Vital Guide to Military Aircraft.* Shrewsbury, England: Airlife, 1998.

Mosher, David. "Reduce the Scope of DOE's Stockpile Stewardship Program," in Congressional Budget Office, *Budget Options for National Defense.* Washington, D.C.: CBO, 2000.

Murray, Williamson. "The United States Should Begin Work on a New Bomber Now." Cato Institute Policy Analysis no. 368, March 16, 2000.

————. "Fighter Procurement in the Next Century." Cato Institute Policy Analysis no. 334, February 26, 1999.

National Commission on Terrorism. *Countering the Threat of International Terrorism: Report of the National Commission on Terrorism.* Washington, D.C.: Government Printing Office, 2000.

National Defense Panel. *Transforming Defense: National Security in the 21st Century.* Arlington, Va.: NDP, December 1997.

National Defense University. *1998 Strategic Assessment: Engaging Power for Peace.* Washington, D.C.: NDU, 1998.

————. *1997 Strategic Assessment: Flashpoints and Force Structure.* Washington, D.C.: NDU, 1997.

Nordlinger, Eric. *Isolationism Reconfigured: American Foreign Policy for a New Century.* Princeton, N.J.: Princeton Univ. Press, 1995.

O'Hanlon, Michael. *Technological Change and the Future of Warfare*. Washington, D.C.: Brookings Institution, 2000.

———. *How to Be a Cheap Hawk: The 1999 and 2000 Defense Budgets*. Washington, D.C.: Brookings Institution, 1998.

Office of the Secretary of Defense. *Proliferation: Threat and Response*. Washington, D.C.: Government Printing Office, November 1997.

Owens, William. "Revolutionizing Warfare," in Democratic Leadership Council, *War and Peace: Are We Ready?* Washington, D.C.: Democratic Leadership Council, Winter 2000.

Pena, Charles. "From the Sea: National Missile Defense Is Neither Cheap Nor Easy." Cato Foreign Policy Briefing no. 60, September 6, 2000.

———. "Arms Control and Missile Defense: Not Mutually Exclusive." Cato Institute Policy Analysis no. 376, July 26, 2000.

———. "Theater Missile Defense: A Limited Capability Is Needed." Cato Institute Policy Analysis no. 309, June 22, 1999.

Pena, Charles, and Barbara Conry. "National Missile Defense: Examining the Options." Cato Institute Policy Analysis no. 337, March 16, 1999.

Peppe, Kevin. "SSNs: Supporting the Battle Group?" U.S. Naval Institute *Proceedings*, May 1997.

Perry, William, and Ashton Carter. *Preventative Defense: A New Security Strategy for America*. Washington, D.C.: Brookings Institution, 1999.

Pierrot, Lane. *Operations and Support Costs for the Department of Defense*. Washington, D.C.: CBO, July 1988.

Richardson, James D., ed. *A Compilation of the Messages and Papers of the Presidents, 1789–1897*, vol. 1. Washington, D.C.: Government Printing Office, 1898.

Roos, John. "The Cutting Edge: A Beijing-Taipei Showdown Would Pit Quantity vs. Quality." *Armed Forces Journal International*, May 2000.

———. "Prescription for Survival: Hefty Cash Infusions Spur Progress in US Chemical and Biological Defense Programs." *Armed Forces Journal International*, October 1999.

———. "Expanding the Envelope: U.S. Unmanned Aerial Vehicle Programs Now Range from Lightweight Reconnaissance Aircraft to Heavyweight Attack Platforms." *Armed Forces Journal International*, June 1998.

———. "Unmasking the Enemy: Foliage-Penetrating Radar System Ready for Tests: Idea Dates Back to Vietnam Conflict." *Armed Forces Journal International*, April 1998.

Sadowski, Yahya. *The Myth of Global Chaos*. Washington, D.C.: Brookings Institution, 1998.

Sandler, Todd, and Keith Hartley. *The Political Economy of NATO*. Cambridge: Cambridge Univ. Press, 1999.

Schlesinger, James. "Raise the Anchor or Lower the Ship: Defense Budgeting and Planning." *National Interest*, Fall 1998.

Schmidt, Rachel. *Moving U.S. Forces: Options for Strategic Mobility*. Washington, D.C.: CBO, 1997.

Selden, Zachary. *Biological Weapons: Defense Improves, but the Threat Remains*. Washington, D.C.: Business Executives for National Security, December 1997.

Shambaugh, David. "China's Military Views the World: Ambivalent Security." *International Security* 24, no. 3 (Winter 1999–2000).

Sherman, Jason. "Arduous Crusade: Shelve the Briefing Charts. The Army's New Artillery System Is Now Something You Can Touch. But Is It Untouchable?" *Armed Forces International*, October 1999.

———. "Souped Up Big Time: As the Abrams Tank Program Marks Its Greatest Technological Achievement, Its Future Has Never Been More Uncertain." *Armed Forces Journal International*, May 1998.

———. "Fanciful Flight: How the Marine Corps Plans to Make the Abrams Tank Look Like a Model-T Ford." *Armed Forces Journal International*, November 1999.

Shulz, John. "China as a Strategic Threat: Myths and Verities." *Strategic Review* 26, no. 1 (Winter 1998).

Smith, Dan. "Running Out of a 'Few Good Men and Women.' " *Weekly Defense Monitor*, February 25, 1999.

Sontag, Sherry, and Christopher Drew. *Blind Man's Bluff: The Untold Story of American Submarine Espionage*. New York: Public Affairs, 1998.

Spencer, Jack, and Joe Dougherty. "The Quickest Way to Global Missile Defense: First from the Sea." *Heritage Foundation Backgrounder* no. 1384, July 13, 2000.

Staar, Richard. "Russia's New Blueprint for National Security." *Strategic Review* 27, no. 2 (Spring 1998).

Stohl, Rachel. "U.S. Leads World as Top Arms Exporter." *Weekly Defense Monitor*, June 18, 1998.

Taylor, Jerry. "Oil: Not Worth the Fight." *Journal of Commerce*, September 1, 1998.

Thompson, Loren. "On Track: Comanche Still Clings to Army's Number-One Modernization Spot Despite Recent Ups and Downs." *Armed Forces Journal International*, April 1998.

Towell, Pat. "Pentagon's Chief of Testing Reinforces Bipartisan Movements to Postpone Anti-Missile System." *Congressional Quarterly*, February 19, 2000.

———. "Military's 'Can-Do' Budget Stance Heightens Hawks' Frustrations." *Congressional Quarterly*, March 14, 1998.

"War Powers Act," Public Law 93–148, 93rd Congress, House Joint Resolution 542, November 7, 1973.

Warner, Volney. "Technology Favors Future Land Forces." *Strategic Review* 26, no. 3 (Summer 1998).

Watson, Bruce, Bruce George, Peter Tsouras, and B. L. Cyr. *Military Lessons of the Gulf War*. London: Green Hills Books, 1991.

The White House. *A National Security Strategy for a Global Age*. Washington, D.C.: White House, 2000.

Wilson, George C. "Why Is the Pentagon Ignoring the Defense Science Board?" *National Journal*, February 7, 2000.

Index

About the Author

IVAN ELAND is Director of Defense Policy Studies at the Cato Institute. He has had nineteen years experience in national security policy. Dr. Eland has written about U.S. defense policy, terrorism, military threats to the United States, naval weapons and deployments, weapons of mass destruction, NATO, economic sanctions, and international trade. He has appeared on major television programs such as CNN's Crossfire and ABC news. Prior to working with Cato, he was principal defense analyst at the Congressional Budget Office and a national security policy analyst at the U.S. General Accounting Office.